BLUES EMPRESS
IN BLACK CHATTANOOGA

BLUES EMPRESS

IN BLACK CHATTANOOGA

Bessie Smith and the Emerging Urban South

MICHELLE R. SCOTT

UNIVERSITY OF ILLINOIS PRESS
Urbana and Chicago

Library of Congress Cataloging-in-Publication Data
Scott, Michelle R.
Blues empress in black Chattanooga : Bessie Smith
and the emerging urban South / Michelle R. Scott.
p.   cm.
Includes bibliographical references (p.   ) and index.
ISBN-13: 978-0-252-03338-4 (cloth : alk. paper)
ISBN-10: 0-252-03338-8 (cloth : alk paper)
ISBN-13: 978-0-252-07545-2 (pbk. : alk. paper)
ISBN-10: 0-252-07545-5 (pbk. : alk. paper)
1. Smith, Bessie, 1894–1937. 2. Singers—United States—
Biography. 3. Blues (Music)—Tennessee—Chattanooga—
History and criticism. 4. African Americans—Tennessee—
Chattanooga—History. 5. Chattanooga (Tenn.)—History.
I. Title.
ML420.S667S36   2008
782.421643092—dc22 [B]   2007052615

For my grandmothers,
Ruth Leach and Marion Nixon Vincent,
and
My parents,
Edgar and Caryl Scott

CONTENTS

PREFACE

"What do *you* know about the blues?" and "Why are you interested in Bessie Smith?" are questions I was repeatedly asked as I embarked upon my study of Bessie Smith and Chattanooga several years ago. As a child of the 1970s and 1980s and a native of the West Coast, my passion for the story of a southern woman who sang the blues in the 1920s apparently seemed out of place in a time when America's popular music genres included hip-hop and "neo-soul" music.

I first learned of Bessie Smith as a high-school student, when I listened to the scratchy albums my mother had purchased when she studied blues music in college. I was intrigued by the sketch on the cover of a voluptuous black woman lounging on a chaise in a beaded gown with feathers in her hair and was even more amused by the titles of the songs that spoke of pigfeet, bottles of beer, and a "kitchen man." Yet I cannot say that I knew anything about the blues until I really listened to the Bessie Smith tune, "Lost Your Head Blues," when I was in my own undergraduate jazz history courses. Aside from some B. B. King songs and a parody performance of a wizened old bluesman on the 1990s television variety show "In Living Color," my blues consciousness had been nearly nonexistent. Yet as I heard the words, "I was with you baby when you didn't have a dime / Once ain't for always and two ain't but twice," powerfully belted out without the aid of modern amplification, I realized that the blues was not so far removed from the rhythm-and-blues and popular songs being played on the radio at the time. I felt what Bessie was saying, and her strong vocal delivery stayed in my consciousness. Bessie Smith did not have a "pretty" voice like Ella Fitzgerald or Sarah Vaughan, but her emotional delivery ensured that a listener would grasp her feelings vividly when she said she "was going to leave you baby, ain't going to say goodbye," or when she implored America's wealthy to "open up your heart and mind" in "Poor Man's Blues."

In later years, when I read that Smith began her career singing the blues on the street corners of Chattanooga, I became fascinated with her early history and the larger function of the music she sang. What was the connection between her commercial image and the community she sang for? How does someone evolve from a near-orphan to "Empress of the Blues" without seeming to lose a connection to the place from where she came? As my project progressed, I began to take notice of youth street performances in the places I traveled, wondering how they might mirror the experiences of an adolescent Smith. What was the larger significance of the young boy performing go-go music on buckets on the Mall in Washington, D.C., or the family of singers in the subway in New York City, or the accordion-playing adolescent near La Fontana de Trevi in Rome? The transition from amateur street performer to internationally famous musician is rarely completed successfully. Yet Bessie Smith made this journey in an era where her race, gender, and class status should have made that success nearly impossible in the segregated United States. The world remembers her voice, appearance, and legendary antics, but the story of how blues music spoke to the humanity of working-class black Americans may not be equally remembered. There was much more to the Empress's realm than even "Backwater Blues," "Empty Bed Blues," or "I Need a Little Sugar in My Bowl" can convey, and to get a glimpse of the early environment of one of the world's greatest blues singers, downtown Chattanooga at the dawn of the twentieth century is the place to begin.

ACKNOWLEDGMENTS

This work began as a seminar paper for a Cornell University class in African American women's history in Spring 1997 and eventually evolved into my doctoral dissertation and finally the completed manuscript. I was fortunate to have a group of dedicated advisors who helped me shape this work from the initial research stages to the final written drafts, including Robert L. Harris, Margaret Washington, Steven Pond, and Jacqueline Goldsby. I am especially grateful to the chair of my committee, Robert L. Harris, for the steadfast guidance he has offered since he met me as an undergraduate participant in the Minority Summer Research Exchange Program in 1994.

I thank Joan Catapano, Rebecca Crist, and Matthew Mitchell at the University of Illinois Press for editing the text and answering my many queries as the manuscript moved through each publication stage. Kay Peterson at the Archives Center of the Smithsonian Institution and the Photoduplication Services at Library of Congress were also essential in helping me acquire the images for the book.

I completed the present book during my time as a faculty member at the University of Maryland, Baltimore County. I appreciate the support of all my colleagues in the history department, especially Kriste Lindenmeyer, who read and critiqued portions of the manuscript; John Jeffries, who supported my search for outside funding; and Terry Bouton, Amy Froide, and Anne Sarah Rubin, who offered their encouragement and friendship. The dedicated students of History 713 in fall 2004 offered weekly insightful and lively discussions of the history of black music performance that greatly aided in the revisions of this text. I also appreciate the members of an informal writing group at UMBC in 2003–4 who helped me stay on task with my writing goals and deadlines.

I could not have completed the research and writing of this study without the financial resources of several institutions, including the Mellon Mays Completion Fellowship, UMBC Summer Faculty Fellowship, and the Henry C. Welcome Fellowship from the Maryland Higher Education Commission. I completed final revisions during my postdoctoral fellowship leave, made possible through the Career Enhancement Fellowship Program, which is administered by the Woodrow Wilson National Fellowship Foundation and funded by the Andrew W. Mellon Foundation. The initial stages of this project were funded with the help of the Ford Foundation Dissertation Fellowship, the Social Science Research Council/Mellon Mays Undergraduate Fellowship Predoctoral Grants, the Smithsonian Institution Predoctoral Fellowship, and travel and research grants from Cornell University.

I am indebted to the archives and libraries that extended their resources to me and made this project possible. I am particularly grateful for the hospitality and insight of the staff members of the Chattanooga African American Museum, particularly Vilma S. Fields, Paul Moss, and Leroy Henderson. Much of my primary research was made possible by former and current curators and archivists at Smithsonian Institution National Museum of American History, including John Hasse, Charles McGovern, Reuben Jackson, Wendy Shay, and Deborra Richardson. I also appreciate the efforts of reference librarians at the Newspaper, Manuscripts, Performing Arts, and Geography and Maps Reading Rooms in the Library of Congress, as well as the aid of staff members at the University of Maryland's McKeldin and Clarice Smith Performing Arts Libraries in helping me track down crucial sources. Finally, the reference librarians, interlibrary loan staff, and the rare books staff at Cornell University's Olin, John Henrik Clarke, and Kroch Libraries, as well as the Sidney Cox Library of Music and Dance, were extremely helpful from the very onset of my study.

As this study progressed, I presented excerpts at several different forums and I was fortunate to obtain positive critical feedback. I thank the commentators, fellow panelists, and audience members at meetings of the ASA, ASALH, Berkshires Conference for Women's History, the Blues Tradition Conference at Penn State, the IASPM International Meeting, the Society for the History of Children and Youth, and the Career Enhancement Fellowship Fall Retreat for their constructive critiques. I am sincerely indebted to my Wilson Fellows cohort, Thomas Hennessey, Tera Hunter, David "Honeyboy" Edwards, Mary Sies, Jacqueline Stewart, Kathleen Thompson, and Clyde A.

Woods. Their queries and encouragement helped to delve deeper into Bessie's musical past. I am extremely grateful for the mentorship of Daphne Duval Harrison, who read and critiqued the manuscript in its entirety.

I am blessed to have the support of both family and friends who greatly enriched my life throughout this process. I thank my parents, Edgar T. Scott and Caryl R. Scott, my sisters, Akelah (Lisa) Scott and Kelli Scott, and my niece and nephew, Ifetayo and Diallo, all whose love and guidance is steadfast and constant. I also appreciate the unwavering support of my grandmother, Marion Nixon Vincent, who has instilled in me an appreciation for the African American past and prayed for me all along the way. I would like to thank all of my extended family, who offered me much-needed support and well wishes throughout this entire process.

I am greatly indebted to the lifelong friends I have made during my educational career. The presence of Anitra L. Hankins, Shelley Hawkins-McCray, Jessica Brewster Johnson (who all met me when Oakland was my only home); and Leslie M. Alexander, Nicole Guidotti Hernandez, Jean Kim, Laura McGough, Angel David Nieves, Susie Lee Pak, Christopher Roberson, Gabriela Sandoval, Jennifer M. Wilks, Jolanda Williams, and Thabiti Willis has greatly enriched my life and allowed me to complete my degree and this manuscript without losing my sanity, sense of purpose, spirituality, or sense of humor. All the conclusions reached in this study can be attributed to the author solely.

BLUES EMPRESS
IN BLACK CHATTANOOGA

INTRODUCTION
UNCOVERING THE LIFE OF A BLUES WOMAN

Down in Chattanooga, there's hospitality.
The finest bunch of people in the state of Tennessee.
Tired, tired of roaming this way.
Got the blues for Chattanooga, I'm going back to stay
    someday.

—IDA COX, "Chattanooga Blues"

In Chattanooga, Tennessee, in the early 1900s, African Americans were not a downtrodden minority but a vibrant 40 percent or more of the population.[1] Only thirty years removed from the abolition of slavery and four years after the Supreme Court legalized racial segregation, black Chattanoogans struggled with but were not entirely eclipsed by racial discrimination and intolerance. If one traveled along Chattanooga's downtown streets in the 1900s, one would encounter drug stores, restaurants, grocery shops, and barbershops patronized, managed, and even owned by African Americans. Visitors to the city would see black consumers purchasing household items from the James and Allen Drug Company on East Ninth Street or observe a crowd of young black men joking, laughing, and sharing the latest anecdotes outside one of the area's many barbershops. Moving along Ninth Street, a traveler would notice several theaters marked by large marquees advertising the latest vaudeville or variety shows, many of them featuring African American musicians, dancers, and actors. The clatter of streetcars and the cries of vendors hawking everything from newspapers to soft drinks composed a cacophony of street sounds, and in the midst of this noise from the typical workday, the husky voice of a street performer singing a blues tune in exchange for a spare penny or nickel might also be heard. To the surprise of some observers, this husky voice did not stem from a weary man hunched over an old banjo but from a ten-year-old locally born African American girl performing to supplement her family's meager income.[2]

By November 1925, at the Orpheum Theater in Newark, New Jersey, the ten-year-old girl had matured into a young woman, and a crowd of "chocolate brown" people, similar to a gathering at an African American "camp meeting," congregated to hear her perform the familiar and comforting sounds of blues music. As the lights lowered and "the saxophone began to moan," the woman, adorned in a sequined dress, finally appeared and belted out her story of the "Sobbin' Hearted Blues." The crowd of primarily working-class African Americans, some newly transplanted from the South, responded to the lyrics with cries of "amen" and "that's right," for they understood the woman's story. To the right of the mesmerizing singer, a placard in the corner of the stage read, "BESSIE SMITH."[3]

Bessie Smith (1892–1937) is a prominent figure in American popular culture and African American history.[4] She was among the first African American vocalists to be recorded, and her voice and stage presence furthered a blues-music craze that began in 1920, reached new heights with Smith's first recordings in 1923, and lasted until the 1930s. As a leader of this new craze, Smith helped transform the blues from a regional African American music into a national art form whose popularity is evidenced in the development of "race records."[5] Between 1924 and 1929, Smith sold over four million records nationwide and was known as Columbia Records' "Empress of the Blues."[6] She wrote several of her own songs, performed on Broadway, had her own traveling revue that included dancers, singers, and comedians, acted in the 1929 short film *St. Louis Blues,* and became an international emblem of the classic blues woman in her dress, style, and vocal ability—all in an age in which many female performers did not have control over their careers and when women who performed in genres other than sacred or classical music challenged the boundaries of "respectable" womanhood. Bessie Smith's life and legacy are the subject of stage and screenplays and commercial products from t-shirts to greeting cards. In Chattanooga, the place of her birth, Smith is honored with her own museum and performance space, the Bessie Smith Hall. The theater is a featured attraction in many guide books on Tennessee travel and a draw for visitors who want to pay respect to Chattanooga's own Empress and the streets where she held court.[7]

Bessie Smith. Library of Congress, Prints and Photographs Division, Carl Van Vechten Collection, LOT 12735, no. 1044, LC-USZ62-94955.

The depictions of Smith in a sequined dress belting out the blues is a familiar image of the musical artist known for her renditions of "St. Louis Blues" and "'T Ain't Nobody's Business If I Do." Nevertheless, the image of Smith as a young performer in the streets of Chattanooga, Tennessee, is equally intriguing. The representation of a traditional blues performer as a wandering, guitar-playing adult male is more common in the public memory than that of a young adolescent girl. Why was a young *girl* on the street—the center of the public sphere and an almost exclusively male domain? As an adolescent street performer, Smith was not an anomaly but one among many. What role did these street entertainers and their music serve in the

Chattanooga black community and in sustaining and preserving African American culture more broadly? These issues are at the center of this study, which examines Bessie Smith's early life and environment, focusing on the influence of Chattanooga's black community on her career until she relocated to Philadelphia and made her first Columbia recording in 1923.

Bessie Smith has been the subject of several popular books, including Paul Oliver's *Bessie Smith* (1959), Carman Moore's *Somebody's Angel Child* (1969), Elaine Feinstein's *Bessie Smith* (1985), and perhaps the most referenced biography, Chris Albertson's *Bessie* (1972; reissued in 2003). Although these works often illuminate Smith's blunt, independent attitude, sexually explicit behavior, love for alcohol, and the transformative effects of her recordings in American music, most discuss her as a musical legend rather than as a southern African American woman. Additionally, few works attempt to fully capture details of the Chattanooga social landscape that shaped Smith as a youth—details that I offer as a complement to the biographical studies of her adult career as a popular blues star.

This study probes the connections between Bessie Smith, the young street performer, and the southern urban environment that greatly influenced her lifestyle and her musical career. I move beyond an examination of Smith as a cultural icon and explore what she and blues culture meant to African American working-class communities in the early twentieth-century South. I use "blues culture" to refer to the various forms of communication and the creation of community that developed in African American recreational environments such as saloons, vaudeville houses, tent shows, juke joints, house parties, and street corners.

In the past two decades, several scholars of African American history have examined the role of blueswomen in expressing, transmitting, and sustaining African American culture. These scholars include Michele Russell, Hazel Carby, Daphne Duval Harrison, Patricia Hill Collins, and Angela Davis.[8] Although these authors discuss a variety of topics, including the blatant sexuality in blueswomen's lyrics and women's roles in the development and popularization of blues music, all espouse the theory that the recordings and life histories of blueswomen can illuminate a vast array of experiences of African American working-class women that are often excluded from the traditional canon of American history. Through examining Bessie Smith in the context of her working-class and largely female-dominated environment, I seek to build upon the work of these feminist blues scholars.

The more recent literature concerning blueswomen also examines the sociopolitical functions of the blues environment. In *Race Rebels* and *To*

Joy My Freedom, the historians Robin D. G. Kelley and Tera Hunter, respectively, contend that black recreational spaces can serve as alternative sites of protest. Although typical protest measures like boycotts and demonstrations were infrequent in the Jim Crow South of the early twentieth century, this does not mean that African Americans suffered through racial oppression and discrimination in silence. Kelley argues that if historians "looked deeper beyond the veil [into the black recreational environment], beyond the public transcript of accommodation and traditional protest, they would find more clamor than silence."[9] Hunter delves into the "clamor" that Kelley refers to when she explores the significance of juke joints and dance halls in black Atlanta. She maintains that "the blues inspired active movement rather than passive reception, and dance provided the mechanism for the audience to engage the performer in a ritual communal ceremony."[10] Kelley's and Hunter's studies suggest that some historians have overlooked the subtle political functions of black recreational spaces in the late nineteenth and early twentieth centuries. I address this concern with my investigation of Smith and blues culture in black Chattanooga and maintain that African Americans' ability to gather and socialize as a community can be viewed as a form of resistance in a society dominated by whites who saw them primarily as subservient laborers and inferior beings.

Although working-class black recreational environments were often thought to be "evils that menace the integrity of the home" by conservative African Americans and mainstream society, these environments were essential in preserving the humanity of working-class African Americans.[11] Patrons listened to music, danced, and laughed, but they were also able to share their true feelings about economic hardships, relationships, and racism in a social space away from the gaze of an oppressive white population. For a brief moment, working-class blacks were able to shed the symbolic veil or mask of the subservient laborer that they were forced to wear in American society. In the saloon or juke joint, blues music became more than entertainment but a music of self-definition and personal liberation. Smith matured as a young woman and a musical artist in this environment of black self-definition.[12]

This book is not strictly a biographical study of Bessie Smith but rather an attempt to contextualize the community and conditions within which entertainers like Smith developed. Smith's life is explored through the issues of industrialization, southern rural-to-urban migration, black community development in the postemancipation era, and black working-class gender conventions in the early twentieth century. By the 1880s, many African Americans, tired of agricultural work and eager to explore the freedom of mobility officially granted to them with emancipation, flocked to the South's growing urban centers, where they formed sizable black communities. Ultimately, the rise of blues culture and the success of women in the formerly male-dominated genre of blues music were intrinsically connected to the rapid migration and industrialization that occurred in the late nineteenth and early twentieth centuries and the new spaces for black women created in the midst of this significant period of migration. Exploring Chattanooga, the city of Smith's birth where she honed her craft, is the key to understanding this important trend.

As a large industrial and transportation center, Chattanooga played a pivotal role in southern African American migration movements between 1880 and the early 1900s. It typified the urbanized southern environments that African American migrants sought out long before they made their moves to northern or western cities. Although several studies have examined African American migration to northern cities such as Chicago and New York, only recently have studies analyzed earlier migrations to southern cities like Chattanooga.[13] While general narratives of black migration processes abound, black Chattanoogans played a role in reshaping the early twentieth-century South, and their stories provide greater definition to the narrative of Smith's musical origins.

The following chapters are organized thematically and chronologically. Chapter 1 chronicles the growth and development of the African American community in Chattanooga immediately after the period of Union-army occupation to the onset of migration in 1880. By December 1865, over six thousand African Americans had sought refuge on the outskirts and in the streets of Chattanooga.[14] This sizable population became the basis of the urban black working-class community of which Smith and her family became a part. This chapter explores the class divisions that emerged when "contraband," captured or escaped slaves, joined together with free blacks on the outskirts of war-torn Chattanooga. African American newspaper articles and Chattanooga slave recollections illustrate the extent to which boundaries were blurred between "free" and "freed" blacks in the immediate aftermath of the war and when and how these boundaries have been repositioned over time. These issues are examined to offer insights into the development of the black working class, the group that was instrumental in creating black blues culture. The musical environment of these early black Chattanoogans is then analyzed to determine the precursors of the Chattanooga blues culture. Chapter 1 also details how the black population participated in building Chattanooga into an industrial and trade center in the upper South.

Chapter 2 investigates how the black community was transformed as a result of the wave of migration from 1880 to 1900. Between 1880 and 1890 alone, the city's African American population more than doubled, from 5,062 to 12,563.[15] This influx of people from lower southern states like Georgia and Alabama and from outlying rural areas in Tennessee dramatically altered employment experiences, housing options, intra-racial class dynamics, and the recreational landscape. Within this section, the discussion of community development begun in the first chapter continues and highlights class conflicts within the African American community that were a result of the merging of rural and urban black populations. Exploring changing class dynamics will prove significant in the later discussion of how Smith rearticulated definitions of *working-class* womanhood through her participation in Chattanooga blues culture.

An examination of the transformations that resulted from massive migration also leads me to explore race relations in Chattanooga as a whole. The black community of Chattanooga did not exist in a vacuum apart from what was occurring in the rest of the South. Chapter 2 discusses the interactions between white and black residents that occurred once blacks Chattanoogans grew to over one-third of the city's population and had to face increasing discriminatory and exclusionary policies in public accommodations and local politics as a result of Jim Crow segregation.

Chapter 3 opens with a discussion of the Smith family's migration to Chattanooga from Alabama in the 1880s, followed by an analysis of the societal forces Bessie Smith encountered growing up on the streets of Chattanooga. Through city directories and census materials, I reveal what types of educational opportunities and jobs were open to African Americans. I particularly focus on women's distinctive labor tasks, to learn what Smith would have been surrounded and influenced by as a child in a household primarily composed of working women.

Within this chapter I also discuss the inner dynamics of Smith's family life from the 1890s through the early 1900s. This discussion is important in the exploration of the female-centered environment of her youth (Smith was raised by her sisters after the premature death of their parents), which directly influenced her music, her independent and often overbearing personality, and her personal relationships. I also explore how central spirituality was to the Smith family, arguing that although Bessie Smith broke away from the established church as a blues artist, she held on to and redefined her personal spirituality through her music. The almost camp meeting–like atmosphere

that she created in her performances suggests that she conveyed her reformulated spirituality to her audiences.

Chapter 4 examines the recreational life of black Chattanoogans from
1900 through 1910, the decade that most influenced Smith's early musical
consciousness. I establish what type of music was listened to, where it was
performed, how it was advertised, and how central it was to African Americans. I probe Smith's early musical influences and flesh out the contours of
the blues and musical scene that she was intent on joining in her later adolescent years.

In a portion of this chapter, I also uncover how migration and urbanization
created a window of opportunity for women to enter blues culture. Rapid
migration and the resulting increased population necessitated that women
challenge the notion that the streets and public space in general were a male
domain. African American women often took jobs that led them away from
the home as market vendors, hairdressers, or managers of eating establishments. Some women may have also sought refuge in the musical and theatrical
entertainment of the streets as an outlet from their jobs as live-in domestics
and washerwomen. All of these factors paved the way for a young woman
like Bessie Smith to develop her craft in a typically male-dominated realm.

Chapter 4 also focuses on the resistance that was leveled at blues and
working-class recreational environments from religious and racial uplift organizations, specifically the criticism female patrons and performers would have
encountered. As the daughter of a Baptist preacher, Bessie Smith would have
faced some difficulties as she strove to perform the "devil's music"; uncover-
ing religious and class criticisms of black social spaces helps illuminate these
difficulties. Chapter 4 concludes with a portrait of the rise of blues culture in
the context of increased segregation measures and argues that the existence
of recreational sites was an implicit form of black activism and alternative
resistance.

Chapter 5 delves into Smith's early years (1909–23) on the vaudeville circuit before she became a national success. I explore her relationship with Ma
Rainey, the "Mother of Blues" and one of the first female blues singers in the
nation. I challenge the argument that Smith patterned her entire style and
repertoire after Rainey but acknowledge that they did have a mentor-protegée
relationship. Other blues performers' interactions with Smith (particularly
those of Wayne Burton, Buster Bailey, Lillie Glover, W. C. Handy, and Sidney
Bechet) are also briefly examined to gain insight into Smith's personality.

Although Smith formally left Chattanooga after 1910, her relationship
with its black community did not end. She continued to financially sup-

port her family through her musical career and made regular visits to the city until she permanently relocated her siblings to Philadelphia in the mid 1920s. Additionally, the national headquarters of the Theater Owners Booking Association (TOBA) was located in Chattanooga, and Smith was one of its most popular headliners. Hence, she continued to perform in the Chattanooga blues scene at one of the organization's premier venues, the Liberty Theater. The remainder of the chapter explores how this ongoing tie to an urban southern community influenced Smith's life and career, especially in terms of her race-consciousness.

At the conclusion, this study weaves the text back to where it began: with Bessie emerging from the footlights ready to embody her role and legacy as a blues empress and how that legacy is currently remembered on the streets of Chattanooga, the Empress's original stage.

1

BEYOND THE CONTRABAND CAMPS
BLACK CHATTANOOGA FROM
THE CIVIL WAR TO 1880

When Israel was in Egypt's land,
O let my people go!
Oppressed so hard they could not stand,
O let my people go!
Go down, Moses,
Way down in Egypt's land,
And tell King Pharaoh
To let my people go!

—"A SONG OF THE 'CONTRABANDS'"

In the late fall of 1863, Chattanooga, Tennessee, was a southern city that had experienced tremendous change in its physical and demographic landscape. The battles of the Civil War had marred the early industrial city, leveling churches, office buildings, and homes, twisting railroad lines, and overturning cobbled streets. The war had also ripped many families in half, particularly when Chattanooga citizens were forced to choose between their pro-Union sentiments and the reality that Tennessee had seceded and become a Confederate state in June 1861. Confederate soldiers lined the streets and controlled the city until the devastating and bloody battles of Chickamauga, Lookout Mountain, and Missionary Ridge prompted the soldiers in gray to flee the area and leave Chattanooga to the Union troops.

The aftermath of the Union occupation serves as a backdrop for further analysis of how the city's unique system of slavery influenced the subsequent class and gender stratifications within the black community in the immediate postwar years. As emancipation approached, former slaves and free blacks such as Mollie Eaton, William Lewis, Anna Irwin, and George Sewell formed fundamental black Chattanooga institutions with the labor, church services, educational training, and leisure activities they conducted in antebellum Chattanooga and within the confines of the contraband settlement.

As the Union troops flooded into town in September 1863, so too did escaped slaves with the hopes of finding "safety, sustenance, and freedom."[1] These newly freed people crowded into a settlement of tents known as Camp Contraband. The contraband settlement lay across the river only yards from downtown Chattanooga, and by November 26, 1864, over 3,893 refugees from Chattanooga and the surrounding areas lived there, while hundreds more poured in each day.[2] The freedmen lived in squalid conditions in makeshift huts that barely protected them from the elements. They survived with little food and clothing and struggled with a poor sanitation system that left them susceptible to fatal diseases. Nevertheless, Camp Contraband afforded formerly enslaved blacks with something they had never known as plantation workers or city laborers: the opportunity to congregate with a modicum of physical freedom. It also marked the beginnings of the black working-class community and recreational culture that young Bessie Smith would encounter in the late 1890s.

Blacks in Antebellum East Tennessee

The story of the development and growth of the black Chattanooga community is older than the city itself. As early as 1820, enslaved and free blacks were noted on the census rolls of Ross's Landing, the territory that preceded the city of Chattanooga.[3] Some scholars maintain that African descendants were present even prior to the formation of Ross's Landing, when runaway slaves from neighboring colonies sought refuge with tribes of the Cherokee nation, the original inhabitants of eastern Tennessee.[4] While small in number, black people played a decisive role in transforming Ross's Landing into the town and later the gateway transportation city of Chattanooga through their labor. Although there were fewer than two hundred blacks in Hamilton County during Chattanooga's founding years, when the territory gained town status in 1839, the black population had surpassed its original size to a total of 584 slaves and ninety-three free blacks out of a total population of 8,175 in Hamilton County.[5] Despite this growth, the size of the black community was miniscule in comparison to those in middle and western Tennessee. The small number of blacks in the town and the county can be attributed to the unique place Chattanooga and eastern Tennessee held in the southern economy.

While large cotton and tobacco plantations could be found throughout much of western and middle Tennessee, the mountainous terrain and rocky soil of Chattanooga did not lend itself to the efficient production of cotton and tobacco. Farming was a part of the area's economy, but farmers primarily raised staple or subsistence crops that did not require a large labor force. Hence, the nature of slavery was unique in the city and in Hamilton County at large, and this would have a sustained effect on race relations and social dynamics within the post–Civil War black community.

The dynamics of the slave communities in eastern Tennessee are difficult to discern and are often absent from texts that discuss slavery in Tennessee generally. Examining the region's economic development suggests some of the various activities in which slaves in the Chattanooga area may have been engaged. Agricultural production was not the main source of Chattanooga's income, although farming did take place in rural Hamilton County, as it did in much of the antebellum South. Small landowners produced relatively large amounts of buckwheat, butter, cheese, hay, grass seed, flax, flaxseed, maple sugar, sorghum, beeswax, honey, wine, and orchard products.[6] Most of these goods were produced for consumers in the immediate region, but

Chattanooga and Missionary Ridge from Cameron Hill. Library of Congress, Prints and Photographs Division, Detroit Publishing, LC D4 10637 LC.

others were packaged and shipped from Chattanooga's docks on the Tennessee River to the lower South. Enslaved Africans who lived on the outskirts of Chattanooga were instrumental in the planting, harvesting, and sale of all of these products; they worked on small farms run by yeoman farmers.[7]

While slaves had various individual daily experiences, rural black laborers generally toiled on farms with fewer than two or three other slaves, who were often their biological family members. On average, Hamilton County and Chattanooga slaveholders only owned between one and five slaves.[8] Consequently, enslaved African Americans would work side by side with their white masters. A Tennessee farmer, Peter Donell, remarked that he worked with the "darkes [owned by his father], plowed, howed, mowed, cut wheat oats, split rales, done anything the darkes done."[9] In some rare instances, this close contact with a master and his family fostered opportunities that did not exist on large plantations elsewhere in Tennessee. The former Hamilton County slave Louis Watkins remarked that he and his family were allowed to attend church, were taught to read and write, did not fear separation due to sale, and "his overseer never whipped him."[10] Such treatment, especially access to literacy, would bolster the success of Watkins and others who shared similar experiences in developing the post–Civil War Chattanooga black community.[11]

Aside from Watkins and his family's experiences, closer proximity to a master's family and fewer slaves on a farm meant a greater amount of tasks for the slaves to perform. There was no differentiation between "house" and "field" slaves or partial and whole hands. Tasks were often divided by gender, but that did not mean that male labor was confined to tasks outside the home; nor were women's tasks solely within the home. Every laborer performed whatever task was necessary to maintain the small farm. The recollections of the former slave Mary Emily "Mollie" Tate Eaton provide an excellent example of the activities that many rural slaves completed regularly. Even at the age of five, Tate recalls that she, her sisters, and her mother, Nancy Eaton, were responsible for all the laundry, cooking, gathering and toting water, growing small amounts of cotton, picking, seeding, carding, spinning, and weaving it into cloth, and gathering herbs to dye the cloth. Mollie's father, Issac Eaton, and her brothers built their shelter, operated the sugar-cane mill and the whiskey still, and barreled the alcohol for sale throughout the region.[12]

Such tedious and labor-intensive activities left enslaved African Americans with little time to socialize. Hence, enslaved African Americans creatively fused recreation and musical activity into many of their day-to-day activities. Enslaved and free Africans had incorporated music into their leisure and labor practices since they arrived in the North American continent in 1619. In the colonial period prior to 1800, observers noted that Africans performed music, drumming, and movement during the funerals of loved ones. Sung in celebration that the deceased would no longer have to endure the trials of earthly existence and to help in the family's grieving process, ritual funeral practices often confused white spectators, who expected funerals to be somber and solemn and instead witnessed a "song that grew animated and cheerful," accompanied by "dancing and merriment."[13] During that same period, music could also be heard echoing from slave festivals and holidays like Pinkster (the holiday for black laborers that accompanied the Dutch festival of the day of Pentecost), Election Day, or Christmas, specifically in northern colonies.[14] Aside from ritual practices or infrequent breaks from work, the workplace was a more prevalent site of black musical activity in the colonial era and after. Slaves who were adept musicians were called upon to be perform at their white masters' country dances, balls, or dancing schools in addition to their other tasks.[15] The slave fiddler was a particularly revered figure in plantation culture, and black string-band music was a staple at white and black rural celebrations.[16] Black laborers also used song in their various work tasks, including the harvest of cash crops like cotton and tobacco, weaving cloth, cutting sugar cane, shucking corn, preparing food, or washing laundry.[17]

In antebellum Hamilton County, blacks were allowed select periods of leisure time with other enslaved workers whenever seasonal labor required more than the immediate workers on an individual farm. Thus, when white masters gathered at quiltings, hog killings, log rollings, corn shuckings, and barn raisings, they often brought their slaves along to share in the activities and aid with the work.[18] The phrase "leisure time" does not entirely describe the purpose of these recreational moments, for much of the free time granted to enslaved laborers was used by masters to quell thoughts of rebellion among the slaves or, as the scholar Saidya Hartman argues, "to secure submission of the enslaved by the successful harnessing of the body."[19] Nonetheless, music, food, and fellowship were often part of these activities, and the sense of community African Americans were able to create at these times served as the foundation for what would later be southern black blues culture. The former Tennessee slave John McCline provides a good example of how music, recreation, and work intertwined during farm activities in his discussion of a corn husking:

> The greatest event on . . . a place and the one most enjoyed by the colored people was the corn huskings bees which were in vogue on beautiful nights. . . . On the night when the shucking is to begin, fifty men, or more women,

and many visitors from neighboring places would join in. Someone would start a song familiar to all present, and the good work would go on until twelve o'clock. . . . [T]hen supper was eaten with a relish and the merriment wound up, as a rule, with a dance engaged in and enjoyed by all. Vann played the fiddle with dexterity and enthusiasm, and was assisted by Abe, with the banjo.[20]

McCline's experiences were shared by many slaves in rural East Tennessee and the greater South. Although opportunities for fellowship were not plentiful, when enslaved laborers were able to gather together they fostered a communal culture that was centered around labor activities but also included an opportunity to momentarily escape from all the rigors of the workday. Workers met and socialized with people who would not generally be found on their home farm. At these seasonal events, music was used to move the pace of the work along (corn shucking, barn raising, log splitting, etc.) and also as a celebratory release when the labor tasks were completed.[21] The communal labor experience was one of the few times that black laborers in rural Hamilton County were able to meet and share moments with others who understood the trials and tribulations of their existence as an enslaved people and as racial and cultural minorities.

The experiences of slaves who lived in urban Chattanooga varied from those in rural Hamilton County. Chattanooga had begun to grow rapidly after its incorporation as a town, and by the mid 1850s, a visitor to the area would remark that "Chattanooga is a very flourishing town of nearly five thousand inhabitants, and rapidly increasing in population. . . . [T]he town [is] beautifully situated on the Tennessee River, which threads its serpentine course below, forming in front the Moccasin Bend."[22]

In the immediate years following this observation, a population of 192 free blacks and over 1,400 enslaved blacks lived in Chattanooga and Hamilton County.[23] The numbers of the enslaved population in town often ebbed and flowed due to the existence of a slave yard and trading center operated by A. H. Johnston and Company.[24] Johnston's office was located on Market Street and Ninth Street, opposite the growing Union railroad depot, and it hosted slave auctions up until a month before the Union occupation of Chattanooga in fall 1863.[25] If slaves were not bought at auction, they were purchased through private sales, which were advertised in the local classifieds. Ultimately, the majority of the town slave population was composed of hired slaves whom rural Hamilton slaveholders lent out to employers in the town limits.

Hiring out slaves was a common practice among Tennessee slaveholders; it benefited the hirer with cheap labor and profited the owner "by having his slaves employed in a certain remunerative capacity when they were not needed at home."[26] While some slaves were only hired out to other farms to help with seasonal crops, many masters in Hamilton County hired out their enslaved blacks to work on the expanding industries in Chattanooga. With its prime location on the Tennessee River, Chattanooga was a water-transportation gateway to the South, particularly between 1830 and 1840. Hired slaves who worked along the river loaded flatboats and steamboats with iron, coal, cotton, corn, hogs, and cattle from the surrounding regions.[27] Later, with the completion of the Western and Atlantic railway line in 1845 and the subsequent six lines that were built by the end of the nineteenth century, more enslaved and, later, freed laborers were brought into Chattanooga to build the railways and serve as workers in the railyard.[28] Hence, black workers labored to make Chattanooga a transportation gateway between the upper and the lower South.

Chattanooga was not only a transportation hub in the antebellum era but a fledgling manufacturing center as well. Some of the city's primary manufactured goods included boots, shoes, carriages, flour, meal, leather, lumber, steel and iron machinery, coal, and butchered meats, particularly pork and beef.[29] Like other enslaved laborers in more urban or industrial areas such as Atlanta, New Orleans, Philadelphia, or New York, Chattanooga slaves performed a variety of the tasks involved in producing manufactured goods. Enslaved laborers could be found grinding meal in the grain mills, tanning cow hide in the tanneries, and working with molten metals in the iron foundries. Other male town slaves worked as blacksmiths or day laborers for city industries such as the Bluff Furnace, the Vulcan Iron Works, or the A. Bell Flour Mill.[30] Whites employed black female slaves as washerwomen and domestics in the prominent homes, boarding houses, and hotels in the downtown district, such as the Crutchfield House.[31]

Being a slave within the confines of Chattanooga city limits at times held slight advantages over being a rural enslaved laborer. Owners of hired slaves generally did not work alongside their slaves and thus could be seen as "absentee" slaveholders. Having an absentee owner allowed a slave some degree of mobility and control over his or her life. Hired slaves generally lived in housing provided by their employer, often in the basement of a home or shop, if a slave labored in the downtown area. The experiences of the Chattanooga slave Benjamin Holmes reveal the degree of autonomy a hired slave could possess. Holmes was a South Carolina slave who was sold at auction in Charleston and later bought by a local Chattanooga merchant named Kaylor. Mr. Kaylor hired Holmes out as a day laborer in a hotel and eventually entrusted his entire business to Holmes when the Civil War commenced.[32]

At times, the limited autonomy granted to town slaves permitted them the opportunity to keep and save a portion of their wages and subsequently buy their freedom. Although self-emancipation was not common, two noted black Chattanooga residents, William Lewis and E. Washington, purchased their freedom with their earnings as blacksmiths and wagonmakers and eventually purchased the freedom of their immediate family.[33] These self-emancipated slaves were one primary component of the free black community in Chattanooga.

Formerly enslaved black laborers who did not buy their own emancipation were occasionally, prior to 1831, emancipated by their masters, often because they were the product of a union between white male slaveholders and black female slaves.[34]

Evidence that East Tennessee slaveholders infrequently freed their mixed-race children and that free blacks occasionally had relationships and conceived children with local whites is suggested in the 1860 Hamilton County census, in which it was noted that out of the 192 free persons of color, over 70 percent (or 135 people) were "mulatto" (having at least one white or other nonblack parent), while only forty-five people were designated as "black."[35] Hence, although small, there was a distinct class of "free persons of color" in antebellum Chattanooga. The small number of free blacks performed many of the same tasks as town slaves, but they also worked as draymen, barbers, tailors, seamstresses, and street vendors.[36] Although the free black Chattanoogans in no way held the same socially powerful place as did the free Creole population of New Orleans, for example, their existence and the financial success they achieved prior to the war caused some class divisions within the black community once emancipation and Reconstruction arrived.

Urban Hamilton County blacks gathered to socialize whenever the opportunity arose. Public recreation was often limited through conduct laws, which prohibited slaves and free blacks from gathering and restricted public congregation except for religious worship.[37] However, urban black residents developed a recreational culture alongside their labor-related activities, much like their counterparts did on the rural outskirts of Chattanooga. Again music, particularly vocal music, was at the center of this recreational and work culture.

Black laborers throughout the southern states often sang worksongs as they completed the various tasks of the urban workplace, and the streets became one of the sites of black culture. Urban worksongs functioned in the same way as the music that accompanied rural labor tasks: as a method of alleviating the monotony of manual labor and a way of setting the pace for an individual task. Workers in industrial manufacturing like cloth or commercial tobacco production might incorporate music on the shopfloor by having a leader chant the beginning of a song with the remainder of the laborers joining in on the refrain.[38] In Chattanooga, railroad workers chanted to speed the pace of laying track. Additionally, street vendors used musical refrains to advertise their products and created chants about such goods as corn, onions, twine, or tin. Workers on the docks of Ross's Landing sang songs as they loaded and unloaded flatboats for travel down the Tennessee River. These waterfront songs were lyrical tunes that described the rigors and adventures of a boatman's life.[39] Boatmen and other urban slaves were able to communicate with each other through song and forge an expressive culture as they sang "Poor Rosy, Poor Gal," or "Sold Off to Georgy."[40] More importantly, boatmen, as the noted musicologist Eileen Southern suggests, were among the first African American itinerant musicians who were responsible for the geographic transmission of black folksongs, as their songs were passed up and down the riverfronts of Memphis, Mobile, and New Orleans.[41]

An equally significant site of the creation of antebellum urban black culture was the black church or place of spiritual worship. Unlike many plantation workers, urban slaves in Chattanooga were at times allowed to conduct their religious ceremonies in the town's white churches. Robert Mallard, a traveler to Chattanooga, observed one such ceremony:

> I was much interested and yet at the same time shocked, by a spectacle which I witnessed two nights ago. Hearing singing in the neighborhood of the hotel, I went to the church from which it proceeded. It belongs to the white congregation of a Cumberland Presbyterian church. I stood at the door and looked in—and such confusion of sights and sounds! The Negroes were holding a revival meeting. Some were standing, others moving from one seat to another, several exhorting along the aisles. The whole congregation kept up one loud monotonous strain, interrupted by various sounds: groans and screams and clapping of hands. One woman specially under the influence of the excitement went across he church in a quick succession of leaps. . . . I was astonished that such proceedings were countenanced in even a Cumberland church.
>
> One of the women servants at this hotel, I understand, kept up her shouting after she returned from the meeting the entire night and was not quieted until the next day at nine o'clock. . . . [During the next night of the prayer meeting] the leader knelt near the pulpit . . . and offered up a well-composed prayer in very good language. . . . Beneath his distinct utterance I could hear a deep bass tone and a really musical treble, interrupted by an occasional shout

of "Amen" and a keen shriek. What religion is there in this? And yet I could scarcely doubt the sincerity and even piety of some who offered prayer.[42]

The odd spectacle that "shocked" Mallard was a typical African American religious celebration that provided the enslaved African Americans of Chattanooga, like other southern slaves, an opportunity for fellowship and offered a temporary but purposeful escape from the labors of the day. Through the revival, black Chattanoogans experienced an emotional and spiritual release and for a moment had the freedom to worship as they wished. This communal celebration also reflected elements of a shared African culture that would have seemed bizarre and even unholy to a western observer such as Mallard. Nonetheless, the dancing movements, possession by the Holy Spirit, praying, and singing derive from African methods of worshipping deities and the ancestors, cherished deceased family members. As the music scholar Samuel Floyd notes, the revival scene was "a syncretized product, born of the synthesis of African religion and Christianity."[43] On a more pragmatic level, religious worship was one of the few opportunities where a large number of Chattanooga blacks could legally gather outside of the workplace.[44] Hence, religious gatherings provided another opportunity for the enslaved to meet with each other and perhaps share news of family members and friends who worked on regional farms or information on upcoming alternative opportunities for employment. Ultimately, black spirituality served as a key element in the formation of black recreational and blues culture that emerged in the post-Reconstruction period, just as it had sustained and strengthened communal bonds during the antebellum era.

Black Life during the Civil War and the Contraband Period, 1861–65

The Civil War had a tremendous effect on the composition, size, and dynamics of all southern communities, and Chattanooga was no exception. With the mobilization for war came a dramatic shift in southern social relations and an increase in the possibilities for black geographic mobility. Consequently, the foundations for the sizable African American working-class community that the young Bessie Smith and her family joined in the 1880s can be traced to the period of Confederate and Union military occupation during the Civil War.

Chattanooga and East Tennessee as a whole did not readily support secession or the war itself. The region's lack of complete dependence on black slave labor made many East Tennesseans wary of supporting a war that appeared to be based on the preservation of the institution of slavery. Most East Tennesseans did not have a moral objection to slavery, as evidenced by the small existing slave population. However, many believed that the war should be fought by those who owned and profited the most from slavery—the plantation owners and not the small yeoman farmers or fledgling industrialists. Tennessee was the last state to secede from the Union, and when the initial vote was made in February 1861, Hamilton County voted 1,260 to 854 not to separate.[45] Pro-Union sentiment remained strong in the region for much of the war; nevertheless, Tennessee became a Confederate state in June 1861. There was no refuge for loyal Unionists, and several prominent Unionist citizens, including Tom Crutchfield, the owner of the Crutchfield House Inn and employer of several free blacks and hired slaves, were forced to flee the city.[46]

The composition of the Chattanooga population began to shift with the Confederate occupation. The white population multiplied in number when injured and convalescent soldiers from throughout the army flooded into Chattanooga as it became a way station for Confederate military forces. Additionally, the African American population in the region increased during this period. As masters and overseers enlisted in the Confederate army at the start of the war, hundreds of slaves fled their plantations and farms in pursuit of freedom behind Union lines. Unfortunately, many fugitive slaves were captured and held in Chattanooga by the Confederate forces. Although most local Chattanooga citizens worked to support the incoming soldiers by offering shelter, food, and supplies, rebel soldiers also pressed local slaves and fugitives into military service to build up fortifications. African Americans converted commandeered buildings into makeshift hospitals, aided with food preparation, and collected supplies for the new Confederate refugees.[47]

The populace of Chattanooga continued to swell during Union occupation of the city. After a series of significant battles in 1863, the Confederate forces could no longer hold off the Union army. Led by Gen. William S. Rosecrans, the Union officially wrested Chattanooga from Confederate rule in September 1863 after the devastating battle of Chickamauga in which 1,657 Union and 2,312 Confederate soldiers were killed and over twenty-four thousand wounded.[48] The city soon became a haven for Union soldiers, camp followers, white refugees, and escaped and abandoned slaves. The latter of these new settlers crowded into a village of makeshift huts and shanties across the river from downtown Chattanooga known as "Camp Contraband."[49] Nearly four thousand people made the camp their temporary home within a year of Union occupation. By December 1865, over six thousand African Americans sought refuge in the contraband settlement, which had expanded between the banks of the Tennessee River and the railroad tracks.[50]

By the winter of 1863, Chattanooga began to be transformed completely by the ravages of the Civil War. In his journal, a prominent white citizen, Rev. T. H. McCallie, offered an observation of the city at the time:

> "There were no stores open, no markets of any kind, no carriages on the streets, no civil officers, no taxes, nor tax collectors, fortunately. Strangers filled our streets, our highways, and our houses. The rattle of spurs of officers and the tramp of the soldiers was constantly falling on the ear. The town was white with tents. Tents, tents, everywhere, soldiers' tents, sutlers' tents with precious little in them, tents for negroes, 'contraband' as they were called then, sometimes, 'freedmen.'"[51]

Although McCallie describes his impression of the city as a whole, he only hints at the conditions of the contraband settlement, which fared far worse than the rest of Chattanooga. The region, devastated by the ravages of war, had few resources to support its indigenous population, let alone the large numbers of black refugees. Consequently, former slaves (and some white camp followers) in the contraband settlement lived in squalid conditions, with no means of sanitation, little heat, and few sources of food. A shortage of lumber forced many blacks to build huts of grass and mud. The more fortunate refugees piled into wooden shanties, often existing in a space no larger than twelve square feet.[52]

The basic living conditions in Chattanooga's Camp Contraband were often poor, but they must be examined in the context of the horrific conditions faced in the Tennessee contraband camp system as a whole. While black laborers worked for the Union troops in Chattanooga, many were still civilians and were not entirely controlled by military authority.[53] However, the army of the Cumberland controlled the other Tennessee camps, and the refugees at these sites suffered miserably. For example, when freedmen were rounded up and placed in the Nashville camp, they experienced such overcrowding, inadequate shelter, and poor sanitation that over eight hundred refugees died between September 1862 and November 1863.[54]

The bleakness of the contraband situation is evidenced in the words of former Tennessee slaves. Andrew Moss remembered how his "grandmother went to the smoke house and scraped up the dirt where the meat had dropped" to use as part of a meal.[55] Another freedman, Nat Black, recounted how he had to sleep on a dirt-floored hut with three blankets as his only protection from the winter elements.[56]

Civil War camp scene. Library of Congress, Prints and Photographs Division, Civil War Photographs, LC-USZ62-82883.

Moss's and Black's memories of the contraband system are underscored by documents in the Union army military archives. The Union forces did little to improve the contraband system partly because of lack of resources but also because of their apparent disdain for the thousands of freedmen they encountered. This disdain and general frustration over the entire situation is captured in the words of the Nashville district commander, General Lovell H. Rousseau:

> The Negro population is giving much trouble to the Military as well as to the *people*. Slavery is virtually dead in Tennessee, although the State is excepted from the Emancipation Proclamation. Negroes leave their homes and stroll over the country *uncontrolled*. Hundreds of them are supported by the Government, who neither work nor are able to work. Many straggling negroes have arms obtained from soldiers and their insolence and threats greatly alarm and intimidate white families who are not allowed to keep arms or who would generally be afraid to use if they had them. The Military cannot look after these things and there are no civil authorities to do so. In many cases negroes leave their homes to *work for themselves* boarding and lodging with their Masters defiantly asserting their right to do so.[57]

Rousseau's comments suggest that African Americans did not fare much better under Union military forces than they had under Confederate forces. Although slavery was nearly at its end, much of the Union forces did not recognize blacks as a people entitled to control their own movements and actions but rather saw them as a menace to the government and to good "white families," a problem to be solved. This negative view of the former slaves led Union troops in Tennessee to initially refuse to have anything "to do with the negro" in June 1862. By the end of 1862, when Union forces could no longer ignore the large African American presence, they herded blacks into inadequate housing to toil long hours under armed guards as a military labor force.[58] With the exception of the promise of wages, laboring in many Tennessee camps was not much better than plantation slavery. Lieut. Col. Joseph R. Putnam, an officer stationed in Chattanooga, wrote that conditions in Nashville were so inhumane that "sometimes thirty per day die and are carried out by wagon loads, without coffins, & thrown promiscuously, like brutes into a trench."[59]

If they were fortunate enough to flee to and remain in the Chattanooga Camp Contraband settlement, many freedpersons escaped much of the worst detriments of the formal contraband camp system. Chattanooga served as a way station for many black refugees until they could be funneled out to formal Tennessee contraband camps in Nashville, Knoxville, Pulaski, or Murfreesboro. By 1863, some freedmen enlisted in the Union army and were shipped anywhere extra laborers were needed. The army organized many of these early black enlistees into regiments, which aided in the siege of Knoxville.[60] Those black refugees who remained in Chattanooga aided the city's war efforts as it became a "major supply base for operations in the rest of the Deep South."[61]

By late 1863, young Chattanooga industries began to produce many of the supplies needed for Union regiments throughout the nation. The Union forces attracted black laborers from the Camp Contraband settlement through financial incentive or even physical coercion. When a shortage of labor occurred because of the enlistment of black soldiers, the army offered to pay men and women as much as thirty dollars a month for their various services.[62] Labor in the Contraband settlement was one of the first instances in which black Chattanoogans were able to experience some measure of freedom and act as wage workers on a large scale.

The transition from slave to wage laborer was not smooth for African Americans during the contraband period. It took some time for the army to negotiate who should be paid for the services of African Americans: the former masters, some intermediary person on behalf of the former slaves, or the former slaves themselves. Tennessee was exempt from the Emancipation Proclamation, but as evidenced in Rosseau's letter, black people often took freedom into their own hands—or, rather, their feet—and simply fled from their farm, plantation, or other place of work.[63] Because labor was greatly needed in the southern regions, the military finally resolved to pay wages to African Americans in July 1862.[64] However, the Union army did not pay black laborers in a timely fashion, and the military archives are replete with documents from freedpersons who suffered "for want of money from six to twelve months since [they had completed their assigned task]."[65] Many freedpersons, such as Anna Irwin and Joseph and Hustin Abernathy, actually took it upon themselves to petition the army for back wages at the end of the war for services previously rendered.[66] This was one of the first instances in which formerly enslaved African Americans used legal channels to combat the unjust treatment they faced as wage laborers.

Despite the difficulties in obtaining promised wages, labor tasks performed and the wage-work process during the contraband period often prepared freed persons for the occupations they would undertake after the war. Tasks were generally divided along gender lines, and Camp Contraband drew rural, urban, male, and female black laborers together in one physical location. All workers built on the skills they had acquired in the antebellum era. Male laborers continued to excel as blacksmiths, sawmill laborers, and gristmill workers. Black men also planted and harvested a modicum of subsistence crops, particularly corn, vegetables, and cotton.[67] In the immediate aftermath of several local battles that physically decimated much of the city, black male laborers took on the task of foraging for food and often went to abandoned regional farms and plantations to hunt for any residual harvested crops, livestock, or material resources.[68] The army of the Cumberland also commissioned men for pay to work as teamsters, woodcutters, company cooks, officers' servants, and general laborers in the military engineering department.[69] When the railroad tracks incurred damage because of continual Confederate attacks, black male laborers aided in the reconstruction of tracks and the reconfiguration of the rail depot. Black Union army carpenters and brick masons also took on the task of reconfiguring former hotels on Lookout Mountain into infirmaries and constructing new hospitals to accommodate the thousands of wounded.[70]

The Union army hired black women "with great caution, in any case when it might lead to immorality."[71] Evidently, commanding officers feared that large groups of soldiers, to whom female laborers reported, might abuse their power and sexually molest female civilians.[72] Nonetheless, where conditions seemed favorable, the army did hire black women as cooks, nurses, and hospital attendants; women also aided with subsistence farming, transporting water, and mending clothing. The primary occupations women had performed throughout the antebellum era—laundry and other domestic duties—were also undertaken during the contraband period. One noted washerwoman, Anna Irwin, reported that she worked at military hospitals throughout the Alabama, Georgia, and Tennessee areas. With her family members and companions Laura Irwin, Rhoda Willis, and Millie Humphries, Irwin moved through the Georgia cities of Marietta, Vining, and Atlanta before settling down in Chattanooga in the latter months of 1864.[73]

While thousands of African American men and women in the Chattanooga settlement acted as military employees, the fact that Chattanooga was a transportation and communication hub to the rest of the Deep South created many opportunities for independent entrepreneurs.[74] The makeshift commercial center that arose around the contraband settlement is evidenced by the observations of a black Union soldier, John McCline, who was stationed in Chattanooga in 1863: "During the day I had walked about and saw much of the busy little city and its buildings. Walking down as far as the river, I saw many steamboats, the first I had ever seen. None of them were in motion, all seemed to be tied up. Several I noticed were loaded with cotton, others were loaded with various kinds of freight. Many peddlers were stationed along the bank, selling fruit, etc."[75]

The crowd of "peddlers," as McCline notes, was composed largely of African American and some white refugees who gathered what few goods they could find and sold them to a wanting public. The desire for goods was high at this time, for soldiers, residents, and the newly employed black military workers were eager to spend their meager wages to supplement their basic subsistence rations. Known as "sutlers," these merchants often sold small items like candy, cloth, coffee, fruit, and tobacco.[76] Other African American entrepreneurs of the contraband period obtained wagons and horses and ran their own transportation services or found washtubs to run their own laundry services.[77]

Despite the opportunities for employment and financial gain, the sheer numbers of people who entered Chattanooga and the Contraband settlement near the end of the war created organizational difficulties and a scarcity of resources for the city's occupants. Eventually, the Bureau of Freedmen, Refugees, and Abandoned Lands (commonly known as the Freedmen's Bureau) and the Western Freedmen's Aid Society of the American Missionary Association (AMA) established branches in the city in an attempt to provide the refugees and freedmen with "clothing to keep them from freezing" and food to "keep them from starving."[78] The Freedmen's Bureau did not offer any significant aid to the Contraband residents until the close of the war, but the AMA sent workers into the southern states as early as 1862 to offer relief, protection, and education. AMA workers based their aid attempts on the belief that "emancipation and liberty are but empty and mocking words if they do not convey the idea and rights of citizenship; and we protest against excluding men from the rights of citizenship, civil, or political, on account of their color."[79] These two institutions, one federal and one private, would prove vital in helping former slaves make the transition from the contraband period to emancipation and helping them establish communal institutions that would carry on during the postwar period.[80]

As the freedpersons of Chattanooga labored and generally endeavored to survive in the Contraband settlement, they simultaneously continued to build a sense of community through their recreational activities and expressive cultural practices. Contraband-period recreational activities were centered around the practices of daily living, just as they had been in the antebellum era. However, these activities all reflected the changes in society prompted by the Civil War and the hope for impending freedom. For example, freedpersons still used worksongs to accompany their labors in the camp, yet the body of songs grew more expansive as an exchange of different regional cultural practices began within the transient environment of the camp. A song such as "Poor Rosy," which was originally a boatman song during the antebellum era, might become a railyard worksong in the contraband settlement.[81] Additionally, camp musical and recreational events reflected the constant presence of the military and the desire for emancipation and an end to the war. Once again, the black Union soldier James McCline observed how the worksong could be transferred to military maneuvers when he witnessed "a calvary troop, having a splendid brass band."[82] The black brass band drew freedpersons together as they watched members of their own race in uniform rallying for yet another battle that might bring African Americans closer to true emancipation. McCline commented that it "was a great curiosity to me [and probably to the rest of the crowd] to see the members of the band sitting astride their horses and playing such beautiful tunes at the same time."[83] Black soldiers and camp residents sang as well as played the patriotic calvary tunes McCline mentioned; "Let My People Go: A Song of the Contrabands" and "John Brown's Body" in particular pulled the community together and raised their spirits.[84] Eileen Southern comments that freedpersons would often change the words to "John Brown" to fit their immediate circumstances:

John Brown's body lies a mouldering in the grave,
John Brown's body lies a mouldering in the grave,
John Brown's body lies a mouldering in the grave,
But his soul goes marching on.

was often transformed by freedpersons into:

We are done with hoeing cotton, we are done with hoeing corn,
We are colored Yankee soldiers, as sure as you born;
When Massa hears us shouting, he will think 'tis Gabriel's horn
As we go marching on.[85]

The new lyrics celebrate the right to abandon forced manual labor as a manifestation of one's free status. The lyrics also reveal the pride many African Americans had in being military personnel and suggest the sense of accomplishment freedpersons must have felt as they united and became "Gabriel's horn," agents in the destruction of the institution of slavery.

Spiritual and religious activities were as important as recreational events in sustaining and expressing the emotions of the camp community. Prayer or camp meetings continued during the war years and were especially important in the atmosphere of confusion, violence, and social upheaval. Miss Frankie Goole, a former slave who lived in East Tennessee during the contraband period, recalls the atmosphere of the camp meetings: "Lord have mercy did we have a time at them meetings, preaching, singing, and shouting. And over somewhere near they would be cooking mutton and different good things to eat. Some of them would shout until their throats would be sore. . . . [T]hey didn't care if they got home to work or not."[86] These revivals allowed Contraband residents to worship in their own personal way, apart from the gaze and authority of the white residents and soldiers in Chattanooga. Many African Americans in this period expressed the desire to solidify private forms of worship into an independent, formal black church "without white supervision" and without the restrictions of a curfew.[87] The settlement revivals were the first attempts by many Chattanooga blacks at public (outside the confines of a white church dwelling) religious independence. They were equally important as gatherings that drew together family members who had been previously separated because of sale. Black people from throughout the South in search of spouses, parents, or children could make a camp event the first location at which to reconnect familial bonds.[88] Ultimately, the "singing, shouting, and eating" that took place in the free atmosphere of the camp meeting served as one of the precursors to the secular blues-culture environment that formed as the nineteenth century came to a close.

The Initial Post–Civil War Years

As the Civil War came to an end with the surrender of the Confederate forces in mid 1865, African Americans throughout the South began the transition from slavery to freedom. One of the many challenges they negotiated in this transition was the legislative process of emancipation. In Tennessee, the legal status of African Americans had shifted prior to the federal abolition of slavery. As early as the fall of 1864, the Tennessee state government granted "negroes, mulattoes, mestizoes, and their descendants" with the status of "persons of color" who were permitted the same rights held by free blacks during the antebellum period.[89] However, "free person of color" status still came with restrictions: antebellum free blacks were not citizens, did not have suffrage, could only testify in court in nonwhite cases, and suffered a host of other restrictions on civil and property rights.[90] Nonetheless, by April 5, 1865, the Tennessee state legislature ratified the Thirteenth Amendment, which abolished the institution of slavery and granted formal emancipation to African Americans.[91] Furthermore, black residents of Chattanooga continued to reap benefits from the Tennessee Reconstruction government with the state passage of the Civil Rights Bill in April 1866, which was intended "to establish equality in the enjoyment of civil rights for all citizens of the country and to make citizens of all persons, except Indians not taxed, born in this country and subject to no foreign jurisdiction."[92] Black males in the city were granted limited suffrage in local elections in 1866 and had these rights protected for a time when Tennessee became the first Confederate state to pass the Fourteenth Amendment and reenter the Union.[93]

Despite these beneficial changes in their legal status, blacks in Chattanooga faced the hostility of white East Tennesseans, many of whom desired the removal of black people from the state. Many impoverished whites supported the "colonization of the Freedman," believing that "such a course of policy would be for the best interest of both the white and the black man."[94] This belief was more often expressed in blatantly racist terms, and observers of the Reconstruction process reported that "East Tennesseans, though opposed to slavery and succession, do not like niggers."[95] Couching their fears of economic competition from freedpersons in racist vitriol, many poor white East Tennesseans reportedly felt that "if you take away the military from Tennessee, the buzzards can't eat up the niggers as fast as we'll kill 'em."[96] Although military occupation and the existence of the Freedmen's Bureau prevented these sentiments from being realized during the initial years of emancipation, racism would offer great social and political obstacles to a peaceful transition to freedom in the greater East Tennessee region.

Postbellum social conditions in Chattanooga were not as contentious as they were in East Tennessee at large. The sociologist Robert McKenzie contends that freedpersons enjoyed freedom of geographic mobility for at least fifteen years after the end of the war.[97] McKenzie's assertions are supported by the accounts of Tennessee former slaves. Robert Falls recounts that he "remembered so well . . . how roads was full of folks walking and walking along when the Negroes were freed. Didn't know where they was going. Just going to see about something else somewhere else. Meet a body in the road and they ask 'Where you going?' 'Don't know.' 'What you going to do?' 'Don't know.'"[98] Many of the newly freed blacks who "didn't know" where they were going found their way to Chattanooga's Market or East Ninth Streets, centers of the fledgling black community.

The Civil War had brought hundreds of African Americans to Hamilton County. The new industries that grew around Civil War fortifications encouraged many of these newcomers to remain and more freedpersons to join them. Census reports note that Chattanooga's black population grew five times from 457 in 1860 to over 2,221 in 1870.[99] The influx of people helped strengthen black community institutions, which were created through the community-development efforts in the contraband settlement. The Tennessee historian Lester Lamon maintains that although the contraband camps "were themselves transitional, they served as an important, urbanizing force among black Tennesseans."[100] The array of religious, educational, and business institutions that freedpersons developed on the site of the contraband settlement and into Chattanooga's downtown region are a testament to Lamon's argument.

Churches were among the first institutions that freedpersons created in the aftermath of the Civil War. The Western Freedmen's Aid Society of the AMA was instrumental in helping freedpersons construct church buildings, and AMA missionaries were active in the formalization of African American religious activities. However, the first black religious institution was not a result of the efforts of the AMA but of the endeavors of black Chattanoogans themselves. Organized in 1866, the first black church in Chattanooga was the Rock Baptist church, alternatively known as Shiloh Baptist church and later renamed the First Baptist church in 1885. First Baptist (known as Shiloh at the time) was located on East Eighth Street and was pastored by Rev. Allan Nickerson throughout its first twenty years of existence. Founded immediately after the war, Chattanooga's first black church was "deeply imbued with the spirit of freedom" and was instrumental in aiding former slaves with their transition to freedom.[101]

Within the next decade after the war, freedpersons created several other prominent Chattanooga churches, including the First Congregational church

(1867), Union church (1871), and Tompkins Chapel AME Zion (1876).[102] The first two of these were established through the direct efforts of the AMA, while the last was more of a Chattanooga communal effort.[103] The founding of all these churches was a result of the desire for religious independence that contraband-settlement dwellers expressed during the war. Black parishioners could finally hold services in their own facilities. Nevertheless, freedpersons were not completely free from white authoritative figures in their religious institutions. First Congregational and Union were especially open to this type of authority, for the aid of the AMA came at times with heavy-handed guidance from the white ministers of AMA who were not only concerned with freedmen's sense of religious duty but with their morality. Consequently, the leading AMA Chattanooga missionary Rev. Ewing O. Tade often commented on the activities of his black parishioners as if they were small children, mentioning, "thus far our church members have all behaved well."[104] This paternalism was evident in other black Chattanooga churches as well. The religious historian Thomas Fuller comments that "Negro Baptist work in Tennessee was born almost in the lap of white Baptists, and was tenderly nursed and nurtured by them."[105]

Despite the paternalism present in the founding of black Chattanooga churches, their very existence served as a foundation of the postbellum black Chattanooga community. Churches in the urban South did more than harbor spiritual and religious activities but aided blacks with housing, education, employment, entertainment, and social services.[106] Black city residents built their homes around the churches as a testament to their central role in the community. In Chattanooga, African Americans congregated in a large neighborhood composed of boarding houses, private homes, and a commercial center developed around First Baptist church on East Eighth Street and First Congregational church on East Ninth and Lindsay Streets. The neighborhood was later referred to as "Darktown" by nonblacks.[107] Ultimately, Chattanooga churches were instrumental in providing financial aid, clothing, food, and other material goods as freedpersons strove to establish their communities.[108]

The Howard Free School was one of the next institutions Chattanooga freedpersons developed in the postbellum era. Conceived and organized in 1865 and physically built in 1870, with aid from the AMA and Rev. Ewing O. Tade, Howard School was first established as a private school for freedmen and became the first public school in the Chattanooga city school district in 1877.[109] Due to his efforts in developing Howard, Tade was appointed as Hamilton County's first superintendent of schools in 1875, and Howard later became one of the largest secondary schools for blacks in the state of Tennessee.[110] The initial faculty at Howard included Reverend Tade, Mrs. A. L. Tade, Mollie Tade, E. E. Palmer, L. C. Palmer, K. S. Mattison, A. M. Bowen, and Sophia Garland.[111] These men and women worked diligently to teach literacy to the freedmen and eventually instructed a number of black men and women who went on to become teachers at other institutions throughout the South. Tade reported that the "colored teachers" at Howard "have done well" overall, and he "organized a normal [or teacher-training] class" early in Howard's years.[112] By 1880, two black primary schools were erected and staffed by teachers who perhaps received their training at the normal classes of the Howard School.[113]

New businesses and industries were another vital element of the post–Civil War black community. Only a few years after the war, local residents reported that "business was now looking up and a brighter day seemed near at hand."[114] Male and female laborers hoped to expand their meager but hard-earned wages by investing in Chattanooga's branch of the Freedmen's Savings Bank, which opened in 1869 and initially did well.[115] Men and women continued in many of the same occupations as in the antebellum era, yet the limits on what was a designated "colored" job lessened in the postbellum period. The city directories of the 1870s reveal that black people held a vast array of jobs as general laborers, masons, draymen, shoemakers, porters, carpenters, waiters, servants, painters, deckhands, bricksmiths, milners, musicians, cooks, washerwomen, and domestics.[116] The city's black population performed a bulk of the labor tasks that allowed Chattanooga industries to function and helped make the city one of the most successful industrial areas of the South.[117] Chattanooga women such as Ann Alexander, Lavina Ford, and Amelia Thomas generally were confined to the occupations of domestic, cook, washerwoman, or teacher but were often able to open their homes to boarders for extra income. Many of these women worked for the city's local hotels, particularly Read House (the former Crutchfield House of the antebellum era) and Stanton House. Men had much more variety in their choice of occupations, yet a majority tended to be general laborers at city industries such as Roane Iron Works, Chattanooga Iron Company, Hoyt's Tannery, and Montague's Fire Brick Works.[118]

Those individuals who either were free before the Civil War or began to establish businesses during the contraband period often acquired their own independent businesses after the war. William Lewis, a former hired slave who bought his emancipation in the 1850s, continued to run a blacksmith shop in the 1860s and 1870s and passed it along to the next generation of his family.[119] Jordan Carter ran a grocery store on Market Street, and

Henry Daugherty ran a shoe shop on Market and Sixth Streets. Two of the most prominent black-owned businesses in the 1870s were Jack Heggie's and James Henderson's Read House barbershop on Ninth and Market Streets and George Sewell's barbershop on Market and Seventh Streets.[120] Sewell capitalized on his social prominence and became a city alderman for the First Ward in 1871.[121] These businessmen were part of a small but growing class of property-owning, financially successful entrepreneurs.

Recreation and leisure activities were as essential in the postbellum black Chattanooga community as they had been in the antebellum and contraband periods. As the black urban sector expanded, the sites and types of recreational events became more varied. The churches were frequently the social center of black neighborhoods, and dances, dinners, and concerts were often part of church leisure activities and fund-raisers. First Congregational church often used concerts to raise money for church necessities, and a classical concert in 1867 enabled them "to put 31 good comfortable pews . . . in our chapel," thus connecting recreation to the financial stability of the community.[122] Fraternal lodges and benevolent societies held similar recreational functions, and by the late 1870s several such lodges existed in Chattanooga, including the Grand Council of the Odd Fellows, the Chattanooga Band of Hope, and the Young Men's Christian Association.[123] Churches, lodges, and societies held parades and festivals around major holidays. Chattanooga was known for its May festival parade, and blacks were very involved, especially with music. The Chattanooga Colored Brass Band provided the musical entertainment for several lodge parades and often traveled to engagements outside the city.[124]

Leisure activities began to be separated by a slowly growing internal class division in the black community. Although church and citywide events drew all Chattanooga blacks together, the new group of businessmen often attended lodge events, while day laborers often additionally spent their leisure time in local saloons and eating houses. By 1879, one of the few saloons that blacks patronized was the black-owned John Lovell's saloon on Carter Street.[125] While music at a benevolent society event might be classical—featuring, for example, the black lyric soprano Elizabeth Taylor Greenfield, "the Black Swan"—musical entertainment in the saloon would stem from the frank, bawdy folksongs of the boatmen or railroad workers.[126] Music still flourished around labor activities, and although blacks such as the Chattanooga residents Benjamin Holmes, Issac Dickerson, and Hinton D. Alexander began to study classical Western styles of music, worksongs and street cries were still heard in the streets of Chattanooga.[127] All genres of black recreational life illustrate how multifaceted the Chattanooga community had become after the Civil War: the lodge meeting was as important a site for the development of black culture as the church or the workplace.

As the 1880s approached, the black Chattanooga community had effectively made the transition from rural and urban slavery to urban quasi-freedom. Emancipation had only garnered African Americans quasi-freedom because the end of physical bondage and the removal of chains did not include the dismantling of racial discrimination or protection of black humanity in a "New South." The black populace had expanded its business, religious, educational, and recreational institutions throughout the immediate post–Civil War years and built on the new opportunities for an independent and fairly autonomous community that the contraband period had afforded. In the process, black labor had helped to make Chattanooga a flourishing city in the postwar South. The black community would grow more vibrant and face many more challenges as the city's population doubled in size within the last two decades of the nineteenth century—a period of growth that would welcome newcomers from throughout the South, including the family of Bessie Smith.

2

"THE FREEST TOWN ON THE MAP"
BLACK MIGRATION TO
NEW SOUTH CHATTANOOGA

Hold that engine, let sweet mama get on board,
Hold that engine, let sweet mama get on board,
'Cause my home ain't here, it's a long way down
    the road.

Come back, choo-choo, mama's gonna find a berth,
Come back, choo-choo, mama's gonna find a berth.
Goin' to Dixieland, it's the grandest place on earth.

    —BESSIE SMITH, "Dixie Flyer Blues"

In the aftermath of Reconstruction in the 1880s, the South attempted to reconfigure itself politically, economically, and socially in the wake of the removal of federal troops from the region. For Chattanooga, specifically, the 1880s saw a boom in its population and the development of industry. The city's population had doubled since 1870, and Chattanooga became one of Tennessee's larger cities, its residents numbering nearly thirteen thousand.[1] As early as 1868 the city's residents had encouraged northerners and southerners to "come to Chattanooga," and by 1880 the city was well on its way to transforming itself into one of the premier cities of Tennessee and the southeastern United States. The businessman and former mayor John T. Wilder predicted that the city would be the "freest town on the map."[2]

While the new decade brought the promise of prosperity for Chattanooga and other southern cities like Atlanta and Memphis, the era did not hold this same promise for the significant portion of the South's residents who were African American. Blacks, who largely resided in rural areas, bore the brunt of Reconstruction's aftermath. The removal of federal troops meant the end of overt federal protection for the few legal rights freedpersons had amassed with the passage of the Fourteenth and Fifteenth Amendments.[3] The return of southern Democratic rule ended many African American forays into local, state, and federal politics. Slavery was over, yet the sharecropping system still robbed former slaves of their economic freedoms and the right to control the product of their labors. Furthermore, racial violence erupted throughout the South, as white supremacist groups such as the Ku Klux Klan and the Knights of the White Camelia sought to restore control over the newly freed African American population through fear and physical intimidation. This violence, combined with the lack of economic and civil freedoms, prompted many southern blacks to attempt to escape their plight through migration North and West. Many African Americans who chose to migrate within the South pushed toward the growing urban southern centers. Chattanooga, a newly emerging industrial center of the Southeast, became one of the destinations for transformation and renewal.

The Chattanooga black community was greatly altered as a result of the wave of migration between 1880 and 1910. Migration redefined the social dynamics of the black community and allowed African Americans to become integral players in shaping the Chattanooga urban landscape. This environment drew black families like Bessie Smith's and hundreds of others to the city. The city landscape also created the conditions that fostered the rise of a blues culture, for the increase in the black population coincided with official implementation of Jim Crow segregation conditions.

Overview of Chattanooga in 1880

Although Chattanooga had begun to rebuild itself in the decade after the devastating Civil War, and black Chattanoogans had built the foundations of an independent community, the city did not experience a vast measure of expansion until the 1870s came to a close. When Adolph S. Ochs, the founder of the *Chattanooga Times* and the future owner of the *New York Times,* initially entered the city as a young man in 1878, he remarked that Chattanooga was a frontier town of "nothing but the most miserable dirt roads . . . and only a crude ferry operated by an old mule on a treadmill bridged the river."[4] Yet after surviving a disastrous flood in 1867, a national economic panic in 1873, a devastating fire in 1877, and a crippling bout of yellow fever in 1878, the city residents built new industries and rebuilt a railroad and river-transportation system that gave the city "the most ample connections with all points of the country."[5] By 1880, local residents hungered for a more modern image, a new start in the wake of Civil War turmoil, and the opportunity to be a city of the New South.

During the immediate aftermath of Reconstruction, urban southern promoters such as the Atlanta journalist and city leader Henry Grady used the label "New South" as a "rallying cry." As the southern historian C. Vann Woodward maintained, the term suggested that the South would rise up from its defeat in the Civil War and what many considered to be the injustice of Reconstruction politics to move toward a new industrialism.[6] Historian Howard Rabinowitz further asserts that advocates of the New South sought to convince "northern audiences that the region had broken completely with its past" and "southerners that they could experience change and still be true to their essential 'southernernness.'"[7] Chattanooga in the 1880s can be viewed as a city of the New South, for it strove to become an industrial and transport center and definitely did not exhibit the separatist, southern-nationalist tendencies and strict social hierarchies often associated with the pre–Civil War South.[8] Yet it remains questionable how "new" Chattanooga was in regards to race relations, racial tolerance, and traditional southern social hierarchies.

As one of the three largest cities in Tennessee and the twentieth largest city of the postwar South, Chattanooga did not have homogeneous residential demographics in the 1880s.[9] Its population was diverse and complex, as former Confederates, Unionists, southern merchants, northern industrialists, native white Tennesseans, European immigrants, and African Americans all shared the city streets. As the site of some of the most pivotal battles in the Civil War, particularly the Battle of Chickamauga, Chattanooga had been a momentary home to thousands of northern Union soldiers. After the close of battle, Chattanooga retained many of these soldiers, who remained due to the industries that developed as a result of military fortifications. Hence, just as the territory of Ross's Landing evolved into Chattanooga city because of the influx of military personnel involved in Cherokee removal in 1830, so too did a more cosmopolitan Chattanooga result from Civil War and Reconstruction activities. Consequently, by 1880 Chattanooga was "about equally divided between settlers from the northern and from the southern states."[10]

A primary reason that northern Unionists remained in the area is that many of the southern-born residents desired their presence. City boosterism began early in Chattanooga, and in the aftermath of the war, local newspapers issued advertisements like the following:

> The people of Chattanooga, . . . feeling the necessity of immediately developing the vast mineral resources surrounding them, by which they can place themselves on the high road to wealth, prosperity, and power, extend a GENERAL INVITATION to all CARPET-BAGGERS to leave the bleak winds of the North and come to CHATTANOOGA. . . . Those who wish to come can be assured

they will NOT BE REQUIRED TO RENOUNCE THEIR POLITICAL AND RELIGIOUS TENETS, as the jurisdiction of the KLU KLUX [sic] and other vermin does not extend over these parts.[11]

Although a substantial number of prominent white southern-born citizens, such as Rev. Thomas McCallie and William Crutchfield, had returned to the city, one can interpret from this advertisement that the remaining Chattanooga residents desired a more diverse and populous city.[12] Additional citizens and the investment capital they could offer were necessary to restore and transform Chattanooga into a thriving industrial city of "wealth, prosperity, and power," and regional, political, or religious prejudices could not and often did not overshadow this need. As a result, according to the noted Chattanooga historian James Livingood, the city's seemingly tolerant atmosphere attracted such rising northern industrialists and innovators as John T. Wilder, Hiram Chamberlin, Dwight P. Montague, Ewing O. Tade, and Henry D. Wyatt, each of whom would be instrumental in developing the iron, manufacturing, and educational enterprises in the remaining decades of the century. Wilder and Chamberlin pooled resources and formed the Roane Iron Company, while Montague, a Cornell graduate, created the Montague Brickworks Factory. Tade aided in the development of the Howard Free School, and Wyatt founded Chattanooga High School. The figures are examples of the Ivy League–educated, northeastern residents who relocated to the South after the war.[13]

Like other enterprising city leaders of the New South, Chattanoogans extended their solicitations for new residents to European immigrants as well. Although Chattanooga did not have a state bureau of immigration office, as did other cities like New Orleans and Charleston, Tennessee was a member of the Southern Immigration Association of America (SIAA). The SIAA began a campaign in the early 1880s to capitalize on the new waves of European immigration and create pools of labor to complement working-class whites and African Americans. The mission of the SIAA was more fully explicated in the opening ceremonies of its first annual conference:

> "[Our goal is] to devise those measures which will place us on an equal footing with the North and East in the interest of American immigration. Our ports of entry, New Orleans, Norfolk, etc., are to be made points of destiny for the emigrant and the wonderful resources of our own Southland are to be brought out in prominent contrast with the already crowded centers of the North and East and the less genial climate and productive soil of those sections which hitherto have laid the largest claim upon foreign immigration."[14]

While further investigation is necessary to determine the SIAA's particular activities in Chattanooga, it is apparent from census reports and the variety of ethnic institutions that arose in the mid 1880s that city leaders did indeed make Chattanooga appealing to European immigrants. As early as 1881, the city directory listed St. Peter and St. Paul's Catholic church, a German Lutheran church, a synagogue, and associations like the Hebrew Benevolent Association and the Hebrew Ladies Benevolent Association.[15] Although Chattanooga did not experience a tremendous wave of European immigration, a sizable number of immigrants from Canada, Ireland, England, Scotland, Wales, Germany, Switzerland, Sweden, Russia, Hungary, Ireland, France, and Italy made the city their home. The number of foreign-born whites in the city grew from 719 in 1880 to 2,096 in 1890.[16]

African American migrants joined this milieu of southern and northern whites and European immigrants in significant numbers. The black population more than doubled between 1870 and 1880, from 2,221 to 5,085, and would continue to rapidly multiply between 1880 and 1910.[17] Manuscript census schedules and local oral histories reveal that migrants who traveled to Chattanooga in the 1880s and 1890s were a mix of sharecroppers, general laborers, and small-business professionals from Alabama, Georgia, and western and middle Tennessee. Like most migrants from the Deep South states, the city's new citizens sought economic opportunity and relative freedom from racial violence.

The Road to Chattanooga

The story of the migration path to East Tennessee and Chattanooga is an interwoven narrative of census statistics and vibrant individual local histories. Overall, between 1870 and 1890 a total of 10,342 African Americans resettled in the area.[18] These African American migrants were instrumental participants in the urbanization of the South. They were among over five million persons who resettled in southern cities between 1880 and 1910.[19] Although the actual numbers of new black residents entering Chattanooga were not massive, they are significant in that they created a visible shift in the city's social landscape. In 1890, African Americans were approximately 43 percent of the Chattanooga population and 33 percent of Hamilton County's population.[20]

While the motives that prompted African Americans to leave their rural southern roots were similar, each migrant experience of travel and relocation was distinct. Migrants traveled in groups of ten to fifteen by train, horse, and wagon, or even by foot if no other method could be acquired.[21] Some migrants initially traveled as individuals and sent for other family members later, while others relocated with their entire immediate family. Many made a direct move from their place of birth to Chattanooga, and additional migrants settled in Chattanooga after frequent moves between small towns in the Deep South states. The exact location of origin and neighborhood of resettlement also varied from person to person, as revealed in the Chattanooga migrant narratives.

Some African American migrants settled on the immediate outskirts of Chattanooga rather than in the heart of the city. Tena Thomas Suggs recalls that her grandfather and grandmother, Paul and Tena Bell Thomas, moved from Livingston, Alabama, in the early 1900s and resettled in the Lookout Mountain community directly above downtown Chattanooga.[22] The Thomases apparently followed a migration pattern in which entire families relocated together and reestablished the community and family connections held in their former home to help them navigate the new geographic and economic setting of their new home. The Thomases were joined by other families from Livingston, including John and Josephine Speight, Will and Rosa Moore, and Ike and Nannie Moore, who all resettled on Lookout Mountain by the 1890s.[23] By the early 1900s, migrants from Georgia, middle Tennessee, and South Carolina joined the Livingston families in the African American Lookout Mountain community.

Other African Americans relocated to black neighborhoods within and surrounding downtown Chattanooga. For example, G. L. Nelson, a cotton sharecropper from Marietta, Georgia, settled in Chattanooga in 1892 after having lived in Alabama and Maryville, Tennessee. He later married and had a family with a native black Chattanoogan woman, Delia Elder, and became a prominent educator and local politician.[24] A native Mississippian, Charles Grigsby, traveled alone and settled in West Chattanooga in 1888, and E. D. Wisdom, a general laborer from Jackson County, Alabama, traveled to Chattanooga in 1886. Wisdom, like Nelson, found his mate within the existing black Chattanooga community and raised a family of four near the downtown area.[25] Vilma Scruggs Fields, the director of the Chattanooga African American Museum, stated that her relatives, Charles and Bertie Scruggs, traveled as a family unit of ten from West Tennessee and settled in the racially mixed neighborhood of Hill City (now known as North Chattanooga) in the early 1890s.[26] William and Laura Smith, Bessie Smith's parents, were also part of the family-chain migration pattern, for they reportedly traveled as a unit of nine from Lawrence County, Alabama, in the late 1880s and settled at the foot of the Cameron Hill neighborhood in West Chattanooga.[27]

Labor Opportunities

The narratives of these various African American individuals and families all identify labor opportunities as one of the primary factors that brought them to Chattanooga and its suburbs. The possibilities for employment in Chattanooga in the latter portion of the nineteenth century were more numerous than they had been in past decades for whites and African Americans, and the employment boom was directly linked to Chattanooga's growth as a flourishing industrial city. The editor of the *Chattanooga Times,* Adolph Ochs, predicted that the city would become a great industrial center, "a second Chicago," as the century closed.[28] Tour pamphlets remarked that "it is now generally conceded that the 'Chattanooga mineral district' is one of the richest in coal, iron, and copper in this entire continent."[29] While these claims are hyperbolic, several new industries lined the Tennessee riverside. By 1890 there were 110 factories in the city, and they employed 4,800 Chattanoogan men, while by 1910 there were over three hundred factories employing twenty-one thousand men in the city.[30] These factories manufactured a variety of goods, including iron, steel, textiles, lumber, pharmaceuticals, and leather products. The fledgling companies of the 1870s were joined by Citco Furnace Company, Chattanooga Machinery Company, Loomis and Hart Manufacturing Company, Montague's Clay Pipe Works, Scholze Brothers' Tannery, Chattanooga Medicine Company, and Lowe's Mineral Paint Mill, among others.[31] The city prided itself on being the first location in the southern states to produce Bessemer steel in its Roane Iron Works company in 1887, and by 1899 Benjamin Franklin Thomas opened the first Coca-Cola Bottling Plant, a company whose international recognition would eventually offer the city a noted place in American business history.[32]

African Americans labored in nearly every facet of Chattanooga's new industries, including the production, distribution, and consumption of goods. Just as they had in the decades immediately following the Civil War, African American men worked as general, unskilled laborers in all the city's predominant factories. Yet the surge in population created more opportunities for African Americans to work as skilled artisans and service professionals for the expanding population. African American men continued to work as draymen, tailors, and carpenters, and a substantial number found work as blacksmiths, shoemakers, and barbers.[33] The extension of the railway system with the emergence of the Nashville and Chattanooga, East Tennessee, Alabama Great Southern, Memphis and Charleston, Cincinnati Southern, Union, and Lookout Mountain rail lines created even more jobs for African Americans as yard masters, general laborers, brakemen, cooks, and porters.[34]

Hotels, restaurants, boarding houses, and wealthy private families continued to utilize the domestic services of African American women, and city directories noted several African American female laundresses, waitresses, cooks, seamstresses, and domestic servants.

One of the most significant changes that migration brought in terms of African American labor was the emergence of clearer class distinctions within the black community. Although a small group of predominantly free-born, property-owning entrepreneurs emerged in the 1870s, the following two decades witnessed the increased growth of a black professional or "business class," as well as the increase of a working-class population. The New South historian Don Doyle uses the term "business class" to "avoid the more amorphous expression 'middle class,' which does not properly identify the greater wealth and social status his [New South businessmen] claimed."[35] In reference to Chattanooga, "business class" denotes the group of African Americans who developed and owned or partially owned their own businesses, be it a saloon or law firm, while "working class" refers to the large number of skilled and unskilled laborers who worked for the factories or the service industry in the city.[36]

The number of black professionals in Chattanooga increased in part because lawyers, doctors, dentists, clergymen, educators, and entrepreneurs were also included in the migrant pool of rural workers and day laborers. The native Chattanoogan Vilma Fields's recollections of her own family's migration supports the view of a growing business class. Fields remarks that the African American settlers, including her ancestors, who relocated in Chattanooga in the 1880s and 1890s included doctors, lawyers, and skilled artisans who "had some money" and "owned small homes" prior to their arrival to Chattanooga.[37] These migrants soon opened independent businesses that complemented the successful, established African American businesses developed by freedmen in the initial aftermath of the Civil War.[38] Henry Ferguson, Jeff Reynolds, and Mrs. N. Morton are only a few examples of the new Chattanooga residents who became entrepreneurs in the late 1880s and 1890s. Ferguson, a North Carolina native, came to Chattanooga as a contractor in 1885 and established his own firm in the city shortly thereafter. The Adairsville, Georgia, native Jeff Reynolds settled in the city in 1888 and worked as a hotel employee before he developed his own grocery store on 526 East Ninth Street. Mrs. N. Morton, a native of McMinnville, Tennessee, relocated to Chattanooga in 1897, and by 1904 she had established a grocery store and restaurant on Boyce Street.[39] These clearer class distinctions would be accompanied by a sense of class conflict within the black community that influenced the sociocultural actions of black Chattanoogans.

Black migration to Chattanooga created several new civil service and city government job opportunities that were often denied to African Americans in other portions of the South. As the African American population grew to over a third of the city's population, it represented a considerable voting bloc in terms of city elections. Whereas southern Democrats had regained much of their political power throughout many of the South's state and local governments, Chattanooga (as well as Tennessee's two other predominant cities, Memphis and Nashville) remained a Republican stronghold for mayoral and city-council posts until the mid 1880s.[40] Much of the success of the Republican party can be attributed to the loyalty of politically aggressive African American voters. To ensure black votes, the Republicans operated a patronage system that allotted several positions for African Americans in city government and civil service in exchange for voter loyalty.[41] Thus, until the late 1880s, when Democratic politicians were able to use discriminatory politics to weaken their power, African American voters skillfully wielded the patronage system to become aldermen, firemen, police officers, justices of the peace, deputy sheriffs, and other civil servants. By 1882 there were seven black officers in the twelve-officer police force and several black fire fighters on the volunteer force.[42] Until the early 1900s, city voters elected a number of African Americans to the city council and the state legislature, including G. L. Nelson, Styles L. Hutchins, William C. Hodge, and Hiram Tyree.[43]

Gender differences in labor opportunities were also made more apparent as a result of urban migration. Male migrants arrived in Chattanooga and found work and political leadership positions much more frequently than female migrants. Although there were more opportunities afforded women in the city than on the rural plantation, they were still relegated to "female-friendly" jobs that mirrored some of their sharecropping duties— cooking, clothes care and production, cleaning, and child care—yet now they performed these services inside the home for their own families and outside the home for wealthy whites. The discrepancy in labor opportunities is made even clearer when examining people who were praised by Chattanooga African Americans as the entrepreneurial leaders of the community. In newspapers and local histories of the early 1900s, African American men were clearly at the forefront of discussion, while only a few African American women, such as the dentist O. L. Davis, the restaurateur N. Morton, the classical musician Maude Browne, the educator Bell Washington, the society matron Nancy Barge, and several photographed but unnamed Howard High School and Montgomery High School teachers were lauded by their contemporaries for their labor efforts.[44] Although Chattanooga African Americans heralded N. Morton as an example "of what can be accomplished by our women of today without the aid or assistance of any one," women's labors were often separated and perhaps seen as less pivotal than those of men.[45] Nonetheless, Chattanooga African American women were far from powerless or completely subservient and prospered economically and socially despite societal restrictions, as an examination of Bessie Smith's family will illuminate.

Material Wealth

Increased access to material wealth was another significant factor prompting black migration to the city. African Americans who had been prohibited from buying farms or land because of the financial inequities of the sharecropping system and racial discrimination were finally able to use the savings they accumulated from their new industrial or service jobs to buy property in Chattanooga. As the scholar of black business development Robert Kenzer notes, post–Civil War black entrepreneurial ventures tended to succeed and persist longer in East Tennessee than in other regions of the state because they were established earlier, captured the market before other black firms in the state, and were more diversified.[46] Business owners used the profit from these ventures to buy more commercial property and single-family homes. Further evidence that African Americans had greater access to material wealth in Chattanooga can be found in biographical sketches of some of the city's black professionals: Thomas Elder Jr., D. T. Edinburg, and Rev. G. W. Parks. The former boot black Thomas Elder saved his profits from his boot-black stand and eventually bought a home and a grocery and merchandising store. Elder had property and capital worth over two thousand dollars by 1904. The former iron-factory laborer D. T. Edinburg opened a contracting firm in the late 1890s; by 1904 he had accumulated over four thousand dollars in property, including a large Victorian-style home. The pastor of First Baptist church in the early 1900s, Rev. G. W. Parks, purchased at least two large personal homes in downtown Chattanooga with his prior earnings as early as 1902.[47] Although these African American men were far from wealthy by elite white standards, they are examples of migrants who rose from meager beginnings to become entrepreneurs and property owners.

The success of individuals like Elder, Edinburg, and Parks again illustrates how migration made class distinctions more visible within the African American community. Although black professionals purchased businesses and lived in large single-family homes, financial restrictions prevented members of the working class from taking advantage of these opportunities. Lower-income residents often rented rooms together in residences owned by prosperous entrepreneurs. For example, the 1899 city directory lists four single individuals, two males and two females, who lived in the rear of the African American A. D. Evans's shoemaking business.[48] Large families occasionally shared homes, while single individuals often lived in poorly assembled alley dwellings or in the attics and basements of their white employers.

The demographics of the city were altered as a result of black urban migration. Former all-white neighborhoods now listed one or two black families in the manuscript census records, usually because laborers boarded with their employers. As more African Americans streamed into town, a primarily black residential area could emerge between a native white community and a European immigrant enclave.[49] After 1890, two of the city's seven wards, Wards 4 and 7, were predominantly African American, and no ward was completely without a black presence.[50] Predominantly African American alley communities such as Posey Row, Allin's Row, Warren's Alley, or Brown's Alley were often adjacent to larger homes on main residential streets.[51] African Americans also lived in the outskirts or immediate suburbs of Chattanooga; notable black neighborhoods in the city's suburbs included Cedar Grove, Churchville, Fort Cheatham, Rosstown, Bushtown, and portions of Orchard Knob and St. Elmo.[52]

Unfortunately, the overall increase in the general population exacerbated several existing housing problems throughout the city. Just as poverty and the increased population of the post–Civil War period forced African Americans and poor whites into the shacks of the contraband settlement, rapid post-Reconstruction migration pushed impoverished migrants into shoddy housing along the margins of the city. Some of the devastating effects of rapid migration are evident in the following account of a visitor's tour to Chattanooga in the 1880s:

> "The city contains many fine residences, but their beauty is marred by the many shanties that have sprung up around them thick . . . with their low thatched roofs and stick chimneys—dining room, bedroom, parlor and kitchen all combined. The number of inhabitants of each hut is hard to estimate unless it is a warm, sunny day, when they appear as thick as June bugs in harvest time.
>
> The sanitary condition of the city is bad. Cows and hogs roam the streets seeking what they may devour; streets and alleys are in a deplorable condition. Language cannot fully describe the condition of the streets as they are at present."[53]

While the author of this letter describes the impoverished dwellings as disruptions of the city's beauty, his comments fail to illustrate how the residents of these "shanties" and "huts" survived in their "deplorable" conditions. As the population steadily grew, poor African Americans and whites lived in small, tenement-like shacks or small "shotgun" (all rooms aligned in a row) housing. Business owners often funded the building of shoddy housing near warehouses, tanneries, packinghouses, and other industrial environments to quickly house their growing number of employees. Consequently, many factory workers lived in dwellings with poor ventilation, heating, sanitation, and plumbing under clouds of industrial smoke.[54] Don Doyle contends that throughout the urban South, African Americans suffered a mortality rate that was twice as high as that of whites due to "poverty, filth, and poor health care."[55] These conditions slowly began to improve with the development of new utilities by the 1890s and a considerable decrease in migration to the city in 1900.[56] Living in an urban environment allowed many residents to enjoy the benefits of indoor plumbing, gas lighting and heating, and electricity at a time when few of these amenities were available in the rural regions and towns of the South. However, poverty and discrimination prevented many, particularly poor white and African American urban residents, from sharing in the modern conveniences of the city.

Educational and Recreational Opportunities

Although migrants struggled with housing conditions in the city, they did enjoy the educational opportunities Chattanooga had to offer. Howard High School continued to thrive in the two decades after its inception, despite disputes with the city government over the physical location of the school. As early as the mid 1880s, Howard's and the other African American Hamilton County schools' curricula prepared graduates to pursue higher education. Many of the graduates went to such prestigious African American schools as Howard University, Fisk University, Atlanta University, Spelman Seminary (now Spelman College), and Meharry Medical School. Some Howard High School graduates, including Bell Washington, John Waller Williams, and H. B. Lewis, remained in the Hamilton County school district and the Chattanooga community as teachers after completing their secondary education.[57] While Howard was the only public secondary school for black residents, African Americans built more primary schools between 1880 and 1900, including the Montgomery Avenue School, East Fifth Street School, and East Eighth Street School.[58] Rapid migration increased the Chattanooga population so greatly that by the early 1900s there was a black primary school in every African American residential neighborhood.[59] While white schools outnumbered and were better funded than their African American counterparts, significant numbers among the black community took advantage of all that the educational system afforded them.[60] Over a third of the student and faculty population in the 1890s was composed of African Americans.[61]

As with every other realm of Chattanooga black-community life, recreational and social institutions were transformed by the increased African American population. African American churches continued to be a hub of social as well as spiritual activity, and the select churches founded in the 1870s—First Baptist, First Congregational, and Tompkins Chapel AME Zion—were joined by a host of other places of worship, for as new black residents flooded into town, they often brought their church and pastor with them. Furthermore, theological, class, and personal disputes sparked the division of long-standing congregations into separate and distinct entities. Ultimately, the 1880s and 1890s gave rise to the building of over twenty-seven churches in various denominations, including St. James Baptist, Grace Memorial Methodist, Monumental Baptist, Leonard Street Presbyterian, and Warren AME churches.[62]

Each African American neighborhood institution aided the surrounding, often newly arrived black community in adjusting to urban life. Congregations took part in many of the same social and recreational functions that churches devised in the 1870s. Attending church was not reserved only for Sunday, and parishioners occupied themselves with community-service meetings, deacons' meetings, choir rehearsals, Bible study sessions, and Sunday school classes.[63] Church members often visited other churches to attend holiday festivals such as the Christmas Tree Festival at Mt. Param Baptist church or the Shiloh Baptist church Christmas cantata.[64] Other church-sponsored socials, concerts, sporting events, and guest lectures all increased church funds and allowed new residents to meet more established black residents.

Fraternal lodges and benevolent organizations grew much in the same way as African American churches during this period. Lodges provided a recreational home for many of the city's black professional and select working-class residents. City residents supplemented the three or four lodges created immediately after the Civil War with several chapters of the Knights of the Wise Men of the World, the Prince Hall Masons, the Knights of Pythias, and the Knights of Templar.[65] As African Americans moved throughout Chattanooga's suburbs, so too did the lodges. These organizations generally met twice a month and performed various community-outreach tasks. They also hosted a number of recreational functions and festivals, and the opening festivities of a new lodge were often noted as an African American entertainment highlight of the year.[66]

Saloons were additional sites of recreational culture that flourished during this period. At these venues, primarily male patrons were often able to dance, listen to music, play billiards, cards, or pool, and generally socialize outside the confines of a church or lodge. John Lovell's saloon, formerly the only place of its kind for African Americans in the city, faced the competition of J. C. Cook, Marshall and Reynolds, Slayton and Maudlin, Taylor and Groves, and Whitener and Company saloons by the end of the nineteenth century.[67]

The Rise of Jim Crow and Its Effect on Race Relations

The persistence of racial discrimination and the formal implementation of segregation during this period greatly challenged and shaped much of the progress that migrants and the general Chattanooga black community experienced as a result of the 1880 migration surge. White Chattanoogans had encouraged African American migration initially because they needed laborers to transform the city into an urban industrial center, a true New South city. As African Americans grew to be a substantial portion of the population and moved outside of the role of laborers, many whites began to resent the power they wielded in the local legislature and their fundamental presence in the city.[68] As the historian Joseph Cartwright maintains, the 1880s witnessed a shift among the attitudes of whites toward African Americans in the Tennessee cities of Nashville, Memphis, Knoxville, and Chattanooga from "benign paternalism" to "overt hostility."[69] In Chattanooga, whites, particularly white Democrats, expressed this hostility in the arena of local politics.

Disgruntled by their inability to wrest local control from the Republican party, white Democrats began to speak out against African American suffrage and the Republican patronage system in the early 1880s. The *Chattanooga Times* editor John MacGowan led the charge against African Americans in print, criticizing black civil-service appointments as devices merely "to keep the negros [*sic*] solid for the Republican ticket."[70] McGowan continued to challenge the capabilities of black police officers, aldermen, and school board officials based on the "peculiarities of the negro character" and his belief that African Americans lacked the "judgment" for such positions.[71] Fueled by these and their own personal racist sentiments, white Chattanooga Democrats sought to pass a bill in 1883 that would override the city's charter, thus turning the city government to state authority, effectively ending ward politics, black suffrage, and Republican control.[72] The charter bill failed, but a compromise was reached in March 1883 calling for city-council candidates to post a ten-thousand-dollar bond to run for office, a registration law, a poll tax, and the appointment of city police through a governor-appointed state commission.[73] By 1890, the assault on African American political participation rose again as white Democrats passed a bill that allowed for a literacy clause and a one-dollar poll tax throughout the state. Locally, Democrats redistricted the city's wards, confining black political power to the two wards in which African Americans were a clear majority.[74] Consequently African Americans lost most, but not all, of their civil-service positions and much of their voting power.[75]

African Americans struggled with the implementation of legal segregation in public spaces at the same time that they faced disenfranchisement. De facto segregation already existed in much of the city; African Americans attended separate schools and churches and went to separate restaurants, saloons, and eating houses. Formal segregation began in 1881, when the Tennessee state legislature mandated that African American and white passengers occupy separate railroad cars.[76] For some local white citizens, racial segregation was only a step toward the goal of the total expulsion of African Americans from the region. A brief discussion of the African American presence in a late-1880s city tour guide explores this desire for the expulsion of black Chattanoogans:

> The negro problem is creating some anxiety among thoughtful citizens, but the influx of Americans from the North, and of foreigners from Germany and Ireland will solve that problem.
>
> The writer will not live to see the pressing southward of that *unfortunate* race by this invasion from the north and from beyond the seas. But the negro has been pressed southward from New England and his destiny is as assuredly southward as the Indian's destiny westward. Within fifty years the negro will be as infrequent in the valleys of Chattanooga and Lookout as he now is in the valley of the Gennessee in New York.[77]

The rise in racial hostility in print discussions of African Americans coincided with a rise in racism in everyday interactions. Unless they were employees, black Chattanoogans could only enter the famed Read House "fearful of the consequences [of racial hostility]."[78] In the 1890s, a black railroad passenger, Andrew Springs, traveled from North Carolina to Fisk University; on his layover in Chattanooga, he was severely chastised by the local police for not using the correct racially designated water-drinking cup.[79] Incidents like these became commonplace in the city and by the early 1900s were followed by the spread of legal segregation to most other public facilities throughout Chattanooga, including hotels, theaters, and streetcars.[80]

Black Chattanoogans responded to the loss of political influence, disenfranchisement, and segregation in a variety of ways. Initially, African Americans used the legal system as a resistance measure against segregation. The experience of Georgia Edwards is an example of resistance through legal means. In the early 1900s, after being forced to endure poor facilities in the second-class car of the Nashville, Chattanooga, and St. Louis railroad when she had purchased a first-class ticket, Edwards filed a complaint with the Interstate Commerce Commission (ICC). Although the ICC did not rule against segregation, it did order the railroad to make the facilities in the segregated cars more equitable.[81]

When the legal system did not completely produce the results African Americans desired in their fight against segregation, they resorted to boycotting and protesting racial inequalities. When the city segregated the local streetcars in 1905, African Americans attempted to boycott the streetcar line. Led by Randolph Miller, the outspoken editor of the local black newspaper, *The Blade*, boycotters created their own hack line to transport passengers who did not patronize the streetcars in July 1905. The hack line consisted of three horse carts that would transport people from the black neighborhoods of Bushtown, Fort Cheatham, Churchville, and St. Elmo to the center of downtown for five to ten cents a ride. A few weeks into the boycott, nine black businessmen, including Miller, formed the Transfer Omnibus Motor Car Company and hoped to expand the hack service into a motor-car service.[82] Because of the lack of investment and the harassment of hack drivers by Chattanooga police, the Transfer Company failed, but other hack line services operated until the 1920s. The boycott also collapsed by the end of that summer due to the lack of public support by black Chattanooga residents.[83]

Aside from legal measures and public protests, African Americans in Chattanooga reacted to discrimination and racist segregation by becoming a self-sufficient community. Although this move inward combined with the decrease in public displays of protest might suggest that many black Chattanoogans simply accommodated segregation and racism, this was not the case. African Americans concentrated on building their own city within the city of Chattanooga and on developing a strong economic base as independent from whites as possible.[84] All members of the community had to work together to develop and maintain the vast array of businesses, an admirable task that was commented on in the national black press:

> It is simply amazing to note the progress of the people of Chattanooga, with their splendid business enterprises, standing as a monument to their thrift

and energy. I was simply amazed when I was informed that a greater portion of them came from the lowest positions as menials on the farms and on the railroads, in the mines and in the foundries. . . . This much can be said of the business Negroes of Chattanooga, that they rank head and shoulder with those of any city of similar size in the country.[85]

The select businesses African Americans created in the early 1880s were supplemented in the 1890s and 1900s by nearly every other conceivable business enterprise. The city soon housed black-managed and -owned drug stores, shoe stores, print shops, funeral parlors, blacksmith shops, barbershops, restaurants, saloons, laundries, theaters, hotels, hospitals, grocery stores, bakeries, and confectionery shops.[86] African Americans even developed their own manufacturing plants, including the Enterprise Manufacturing Company, the Chattanooga Car and Machinery Manufacturing Company built in 1903, and the Rising Sun Manufacturing Company developed in 1900 and built in 1903. For a time these companies produced car parts, machine mechanisms, general hardware goods, stoves, grates, fenders, and hollow ware. The manufacturing companies were even fueled with raw material from the black-owned Jackson's Wood and Coal Yard.[87]

Part of building a self-sufficient community included creating a local black press to communicate with African Americans in Chattanooga and throughout the South. The local white press, including the *Chattanooga Times* and the *Argus,* rarely covered events in the black community unless they concerned black crime. Hence, African Americans developed their own newspapers, including *Justice,* published by Horn and Wilson in 1887, and the more successful *Blade,* founded and published by Randolph Miller between 1898 and 1914.[88] The black press bolstered the community by encouraging readers to patronize black businesses that advertised in the newspaper and by criticizing racial injustices in the city.[89] Miller was especially adept at challenging the increase in Jim Crow laws, stating in 1905 that "they [whites] have moved our school to the frog pond, they have passed the Jim Crow law . . . and in what thunder more will they do no one knows."[90]

Prelude to the Dawn of Blues Culture

African Americans did not know what more horrific injustices lay ahead in their struggle against racial oppression, and this reality was one of the foundations of blues culture. In the newly built saloons, eating houses, and pool rooms, part of the more independent black community, African Americans

Black businesses: Union Hotel, Chattanooga, 1899. Library of Congress, Prints and Photographs Division, LC-USZ62-72435.

Funeral home of G. W. Franklin, 1899. Library of Congress, Prints and Photographs Division, LC-USZ62-109101.

could express their confusion, anger, and doubt free from the gaze of white society and away from the confines of more conventional black social environments like religious institutions and fraternal societies. The development of saloons and other future sites of blues culture was on the rise by the late 1890s, at the same time that African Americans in Chattanooga endured the brunt of Jim Crow oppression. This growth suggests that the recreational environment was becoming an important refuge for African Americans as they contemplated how their migration to Chattanooga had brought them so much in terms of political, economic, and social advancement but was now threatened with destruction due to the institutionalization of racism and discrimination.

The arrival of the twentieth century brought dramatic changes in the African American community of Chattanooga. The migration boom had provided employment, educational, and standard-of-living improvements for many black migrants who had fled the poor economic conditions and escalating racial violence of the lower South. Yet migration also more clearly revealed class distinctions and gender inequities within the black community and forced impoverished migrants to struggle with the overcrowded, often unsanitary conditions of city life. Clearly, white city leaders' expectations that the city would be the "freest" on the map were not met when it came to race relations. Ultimately, migration was yet another occurrence that prompted many white Chattanoogans to officially weaken African American access to political power and social equality, which resulted in the creation of an African American community very much removed from the white community. It was in this separate African American community in Chattanooga that William and Laura Smith set up their home and gave birth to a girl named Bessie in 1892.

THE EMPRESS'S PLAYGROUND
BESSIE SMITH AND BLACK CHILDHOOD
IN THE URBAN SOUTH

My mama says I'm reckless, my daddy says I'm wild,
My mama says I'm reckless, my daddy says I'm wild,
I ain't good looking, but I'm somebody's angel child.

—FRED LONGSHAW (sung by Bessie Smith),
"Reckless Blues"

In the rural Deep South in the 1880s, many African American families experienced a period of tremendous upheaval. Prompted by racial strife and economic loss, they packed up their meager belongings in well-worn trunks and traveled by wagon, train, and foot to southern urban areas in search of a better life. The Smith family of northern Alabama was among these migrants. Just as thousands of black residents from Georgia, Alabama, Mississippi, and the Carolinas marked a path to the centers of urban South, William and Laura Smith made their way to Chattanooga, Tennessee. Their six children joined them for the journey between the late 1880s and early 1890s, and by 1891 Laura Smith, at age forty-one, was expecting yet again. Laura gave birth to her youngest child, Bessie, in the late spring of 1892.[1] It was the talent and enduring legacy of this last child that would assure the Smith family a noted place in Chattanooga history.

Long before Bessie Smith was the "Empress of the Blues," she was "somebody's angel child," a daughter of migrant parents who endeavored to raise their children to the best of their ability and with the local community's resources. Chattanooga experienced increasing racial tension in the 1890s and early 1900s. The city possessed a thriving African American business-class population and an even larger population of impoverished African Americans. In this racial climate, the young Bessie would have to learn how to negotiate the city's schools, streets, and social mores about the proper place for working-class African American women.

The Smith family's encounters serve as a window into the environment of working-class African American families in the urban industrial South. Exploration of Bessie Smith's religious, labor, educational, and recreational activities as well as her exposure to women's ways of work illuminate the social landscape of black Chattanooga, which provided the foundation of her childhood and adolescence.

Blue Goose Hollow

The Smith family arrived in Chattanooga sometime prior to Bessie's birth, between 1885 and 1892.[2] As early as 1886, a William Smith appeared in the city directory, residing at 25 Hill Street in the same West Chattanooga neighborhood in which Bessie would spend many of her early years: Blue Goose Hollow.

A few miles away from Blue Goose Hollow, during the period of the Smith family's migration, the local government began investing a great deal of capital and organizational effort into transforming Chattanooga into a national tourist destination. The famous Civil War battlefields of Chickamauga and Missionary Ridge as well as the National Cemetery, filled with fallen Union and Confederate soldiers from throughout the nation, lined the borders of Chattanooga. Veterans, led by the former Union commander Henry Boyton, desired to turn these sites into a national military park that would memorialize Civil War veterans, raise the national visibility of Chattanooga, and draw thousands of visitors to the city.[3] In 1895, between forty and sixty thousand patriotic visitors flooded into Chattanooga for the dedication of the park, proving that the $215,000 dollars invested in the National Cemetery alone had been wisely spent.[4]

In stark contrast, local government officials invested a great deal less in working-class residential neighborhoods in West Chattanooga. A local tourist map in 1886 carefully noted all the prominent industries in the area, including the Chattanooga Iron Company, Roane Iron Works, and the Montague Clay Pipe Works, industries staffed by many laborers in the African American community. Yet the streets of the predominantly black neighborhood of Blue Goose Hollow, which lay in the midst of these industries, were not even named on the map.[5] Composed of a cluster of streets between the Tennessee River and the railroad tracks, Blue Goose Hollow lay at the base of Cameron Hill. The longtime Chattanooga resident George Connor described Cameron Hill in the following manner: "[A]scend to the summit of Cameron Hill by the road on the eastern brow. While you ascend, the prospect widens and brightens until the valley of Chattanooga, with its prosperous city, its bright painted suburbs, its forest of brick and iron smoke stacks, its vineyards and orchards and majestic river lies beyond and behind you; a beautiful panorama, full of color, life and promise for the future."[6] Connor vividly describes a vibrant and thriving city from his vantage point at the summit of Cameron Hill. The residential neighborhood on the hill contained the residences of some of the city's most successful entrepreneurs, including The *Chattanooga Times* publisher Adolph Ochs's twelve-room Georgian-style home on the corner of Fifth and Cedar Streets.[7] However, at the base of Cameron Hill, in the midst of the "forest of brick and iron smoke stacks" that Connor noted, lived the poorly housed workers whose labor contributed largely to the "prosperous city" and its "promise for the future."

Unlike several other black neighborhoods, such as Bushtown, Rosstown, or Cedar Grove, which were in Chattanooga's suburbs, Blue Goose Hollow was within the immediate confines of Chattanooga and was not isolated from the benefits and the detriments of urban living. It was close enough to the industrial plants that workers would not have to travel far to their place of work, and it was also on the streetcar line that could bring Blue Goose Hollow residents directly to downtown stores, churches, and offices. Yet Blue Goose Hollow was also subject to the crime, unsanitary conditions, and shoddy housing that came with life in a developing urban center. Blue Goose Hollow was predominantly populated by African Americans and a handful of lower-income white residents.[8] The neighborhood was what Gwendolyn Smith Bailey, Bessie Smith's great niece, described as the "poorest part of Chattanooga" where "houses were scattered amongst the fruit trees" in an almost wooded environment.[9] The longtime resident and descendant of generations of black Chattanoogans Vilma Fields characterized the area as a neighborhood of "medium to poor income," full of "shotgun houses" where residents "scuffled to send their children school."[10] Here in these scattered shacks of the "squalid negro settlement," as one 1890s visitor referred to the area, the Smiths made their home.[11]

By 1890, the migrant Smith family consisted of William Smith, aged between forty and fifty, Laura Smith, forty, and their six children: Bud, Andrew, Viola, Tennie, Lulu, and Clarence, ranging in age from their late teens to five years old.[12] As migrants, William and Laura's first concern after settling in

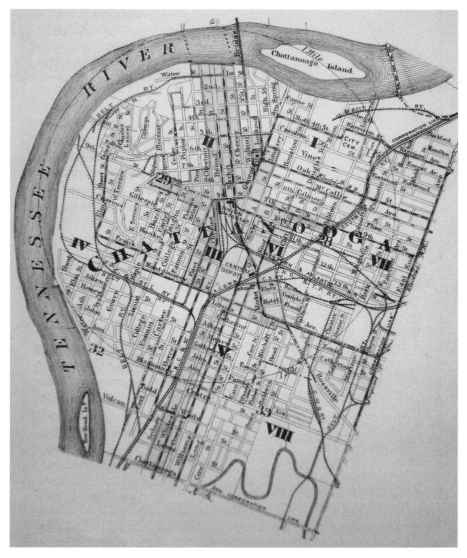

Chattanooga City, 1889. From *Atlas of the City of Chattanooga, TN and Vicinity,* 1889.

Blue Goose Hollow was finding employment, as the hope of economic opportunity is what had beckoned migrants to Chattanooga in the first place.
To sustain their large family, they both needed stable employment to ensure
as much income as possible. Although William and Laura Smith would not
live to see Bessie completely through her childhood, their labor activities

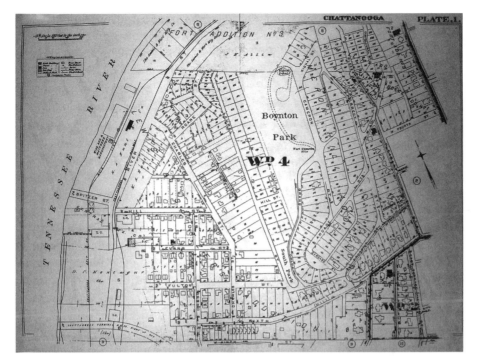

Map of Blue Goose Hollow. From *Plat Book of Chattanooga, TN.*

would have a great deal of influence on the type of household in which she was raised and on the siblings who would help raise her through adolescence as the first decade of the twentieth century came to a close.

Labor and the Smith Family

WILLIAM SMITH

According to prominent biographical studies of Bessie Smith, including Chris Albertson's *Bessie* and Carman Moore's *Somebody's Angel Child,* William Smith was a part-time or lay Baptist minister and a day laborer.[13] While William Smith's calling as a clergyman would decidedly affect the Smith home, his primary occupation in Chattanooga was that of a factory laborer. As a former slave of rural Alabama, agricultural labor on a plantation or farm would have been familiar to William, while industrial labor might have been an adjustment for him to make.[14] The long hours of labor would have been familiar, but he would have had to become accustomed to the specific and individual tasks manufacturing industries required. Apparently, he made this adjustment, for his first appearance in the Chattanooga city directory lists him as a laborer at the J. T. Cahill Plant, a prominent iron foundry.[15] He served as an iron worker at the Cahill Plant for a few years, worked intermittently as a day laborer, and then continued as a iron worker at Montague and Company (the Montague Clay Pipe Works) and finally the Chattanooga Plow Company. By 1898, William rose from the ranks of unskilled or semiskilled general laborers to become a skilled grinder at the Plow Company.[16]

Fortunately for the financial welfare of his family, William obtained one of the prized industrial and manufacturing jobs for which Chattanooga was known relatively soon after he settled in the city. Industrial jobs were particularly sought-after by incoming migrants because they offered greater wages than previous sharecropping jobs and the hope that employees might gain some autonomy, save earnings, and perhaps later own small businesses.[17] The labor tasks of manufacturing could be just as arduous as those of agricultural production, but industrial labor allowed workers to collect more of their earned income than sharecropping. Nonetheless, it was strenuous and hazardous for all workers in the factories of the 1890s, particularly for a middle-aged man like Smith. Roland Hayes, a noted African American classical tenor, lived and worked in Chattanooga as an adolescent during the 1900s. He vividly recounted his tenure at the Price and Evan Sashweight Foundry in 1900:

> "From early morning until three o'clock that afternoon we unloaded scrap iron from freight cars and wheeled it into the foundry. Then we went to work for the rest of the day at the cupola where scrap iron and pig iron were melted for casting. . . . That was our work every day thereafter. I carry today on my feet and legs the scars of many a burn from molten iron, which had the habit of exploding in every direction when it was spilled upon the damp earth. Time and again my flesh was burned *to the bone*."[18]

Hayes's experiences were common in an environment that was focused on output and profit but not necessarily equally concerned with the safety of its workers. Later in that same year, 1900, Hayes was also accidentally caught in and trapped beneath one of the conveyor belts he was loading and spent several months recovering from broken bones and lacerations.[19] Although Hayes was only fifteen when he experienced these work-related accidents and had youth to aid in his recovery, older workers like William Smith faced the same dangers, and neither the young or the old had the benefit of company-subsidized medical insurance.

Like many other laborers of the post-Reconstruction age, Chattanooga industrial workers not only faced hazardous conditions but low wages. Hayes recalled that he only earned eighty cents per day as a foundry worker, and the Tennessee historian Lester Lamon recounts that adult workers could only expect to earn between one dollar and $2.50 per day on average.[20] The true plight of working-class Chattanoogans is more fully illuminated by the historical statistics. Nationally, a construction worker earned an average of $593 a year in 1900, while laborers at the low end of the Tennessee scale in 1900 earned $260 a year ($5,665 in 2003 dollars).[21] Although some laborers were able to advance, invest their earnings, and open their own profitable businesses, as evidenced in the discussion of the rising Chattanooga black business class of the early 1900s, most laborers were barely able to sustain the needs of their families. With the birth of Bessie, William Smith had to house, feed, and clothe his ten-person family with his base meager income of approximately twelve dollars per month. Given that rent could cost from six to twelve dollars per month, not much income was left for anything else.[22]

The problems laborers endured due to insufficient wages were further compounded by the unstable nature of factory jobs. General industrial labor was not an occupation in which you could often settle with one manufacturing firm and expect to retire in that firm. In the twelve-year period between 1886 and 1898 alone, William worked for three companies and performed day labor in the periods when he was not listed with any particular company. Furthermore, in the early 1890s Chattanooga experienced an apparent downturn in factory employment. A local police official, Capt. J. L. Price, noted a sudden surge in out-migration from the city and remarked:

> The fact is the business enterprises and the manufacturing concerns of Chattanooga have been doing so badly during the year that they have been obliged to cut down their force, of employees, or in many cases to close up altogether. This has thrown hundreds, I may almost say, thousands of men out of employment, the majority of them being negroes. The result has been that these poor fellows have not been able to pay their rents, and scarcely to find food for their families.[23]

Although the downturn of Chattanooga industries in the early 1890s did not result in the mass "negro exodus" from the South that Price predicted, the closure of some factories did worsen the financial situation for many African American migrants.[24] The combination of the general depression throughout the South as a result of plummeting cotton prices and the demise of the Chattanooga real estate boom of the 1880s forced many business owners to cut costs.[25] Cutting costs meant firing industrial workers, a majority of whom were African American males.

The financial situation of industrial workers in the city improved as the 1890s progressed, and the Smith family did not flee with the several hundred other African Americans who left Chattanooga in search of employment alternatives.[26] Many of the remaining factory laborers faced the threat of further reductions of their already paltry salaries. An example of how several African Americans reacted to this threat can be seen in the labor practices of the Chattanooga Foundry and Pipe Works. In 1898, fifty African American workers refused to work and effectively shut down the foundry for a time in response to the foundry's call for a 3 percent pay cut. The Foundry and Pipe Works maintained that they would subsidize a general insurance fund from lost wages.[27] Although insurance was necessary, especially in light of the hazardous conditions of factory labor, a 3 percent pay cut would reduce already miniscule incomes earned by the average black worker—a 3 percent decrease in an annual salary of $650 was nearly equal to a week and half's wages. While the *Chattanooga Times* implied that the strike was not representative of "hard times" but rather of great "job prosperity in South Chattanooga," prosperity seemed to be a rather relative concept for the worker whose employment did not ensure financial stability.[28] However, despite these problematic job conditions, William managed to obtain work from the initial period of his family's migration until his death sometime between November 1899 and June 1900.[29]

William Smith's formal occupation as an industrial laborer was fundamental to the financial maintenance of the Smith home, yet his other occupation as a part-time Baptist minister was equally significant to the shape of the Smith household. The journalist Sara Grimes contends that William was previously a Baptist minister in Lawrence County, Alabama, prior to the family's migration to Chattanooga.[30] However, none of the fourteen Baptist churches in the 1892 city directory list William as a pastor.[31] He might have been a lay minister (a nonordained pastor who delivers sermons and is a church leader) or a deacon in one of these congregations. Regardless of William's specific leadership position, his involvement in any aspect of the Baptist church would have had a decided effect on how he raised his children.

Many of the low-income migrants who made Chattanooga their home chose to go to a church that an already previously established family member attended and/or one that reflected their class and social status. Roland Hayes remarked that upon relocating to the city, his aunt, the Chattanooga resident Harriet Cross, took his working-class family to the long-established, "widely influential" First Baptist church.[32] However, Hayes felt that the "stylish colored people" with "straight hair and store clothes" of First Baptist made him and his family feel "loutish and out of place."[33] The Hayes family soon joined the Monumental Baptist church, founded in 1892 by a group of First Baptist parishioners who split from the congregation.[34] Likewise, the Smith family might have attended a church that reflected their migrant status and was near the Blue Goose Hollow community. It can be determined from city directories and maps that one of the few black Baptist churches in West Chattanooga in the 1890s was the Pleasant Grove Baptist church (later renamed Second Baptist church), which remained a pivotal force in West Chattanooga and currently exists as the Second Missionary Baptist church of Chattanooga.[35] Although general church histories from this period have been documented, church membership rolls have been inconsistently preserved; without further documentation, speculation suggests that the Smith family attended Pleasant Grove, for it was only blocks away from their Charles and Cross Street residence.[36] Early congregants of the church were also laborers in many of the same factories where William Smith worked, including Montague and Company.[37]

As congregants of a Baptist church, William Smith, along with his wife Laura, undoubtedly would have been encouraged to organize their home and family in accordance with African American Baptist theological tenets. According to the proscriptive black Baptist teachings of the late 1800s, in every "well-ordered home" was "a model school, a Christian church and a regular form of government." Hence the home was meant to be a "miniature domestic kingdom" that reflected Christian principles.[38] Sunday services would have only been one reflection of the Smiths' spirituality, and church functions and meetings would have been an integral part of daily life. The centrality of the church in an African American religious home was noted in the observations of the scholar W. E. B. DuBois. After traveling through the South, DuBois witnessed the varied functions of an African American Baptist church in the early twentieth-century South and remarked:

> The Negro church of to-day is the social centre of Negro life in the United States, and the most characteristic expression of African character. Take a typical church in a small Virginian town . . . various organizations meet here—the church proper, the Sunday-school, two or three insurance societies, women's societies, secret societies, and mass meetings of various kinds . . . employment is found for the idle, strangers are introduced, news is disseminated and charity distributed. At the same time this social, intellectual, and economic

centre is a religious centre of great power. . . . [T]he Church often stands as a real conserver of morals, a strengthener of family life, and the final authority on what is Good and Right.[39]

As the church was such a central force, William's weekly activities may have included church board meetings, Sunday school, and any other meetings of social organizations that were affiliated with the church. While William was considered the head of the household according to Baptist teachings, Laura Smith would have been responsible for the spiritual maintenance of the home, and "intrusted with the care of rearing souls [children] for God and humanity."[40] At church Laura may have been part of a women's circle, Sunday school, Bible study, or music ministry. Within the home, she would have been expected to promote a strong faith in Jesus Christ among her children and may have led them in prayer and instructed them in scripture recitation in keeping with the Baptist tenet that the Bible was the "only rule or standard of faith and practice."[41] According to church teachings, William and Laura were responsible for running a loving but disciplined home in which they discouraged their children from immoral behavior such as fornication, gambling, drunkenness, profanity, and inappropriate dancing.[42] Finally, a church that served the needs of the African American community might have also been involved in race politics and supported uplift work, including literacy training, the promotion of select political candidates, and speaking out against local instances of racial injustice.[43] While there is no explicit evidence that the Smiths were directly involved in these actions, their attendance at Chattanooga Baptist churches would have made them familiar with such community activities.

Out of all the services and teachings that the Baptist faith offered, what would have been of utmost importance to a young Bessie Smith in her later years would be the music ministry. William and Laura's involvement with the church, however small, would have exposed Bessie to African American hymns, spirituals, and shouts and the power that music can have on an attentive audience. Just as it had been in indigenous African, colonial, and antebellum black religious worship, song was essential in the post-Reconstruction black church. Music played a fundamental part in the organization of a Sunday service, and it aided in the oral transmission of biblical scripture (particularly for the partially or nonliterate) and in the worship and public praise of God.[44] Building upon traditions borrowed from psalm lining in white colonial churches, which slave masters eventually allowed their enslaved laborers to attend, black Protestant churches of the 1900s often included congregational singing.[45] If the church had no or few instruments, the congregation would have learned hymns like "Amazing Grace," "What a Friend We Have in Jesus," "I Love the Lord," or the spirituals "Were You There" and "Jacob's Ladder" through a lining-out method. In "lining out," a song leader sings the first line of the song, and the congregation repeats it, often in their own vocal range. The music scholar and composer John W. Work offered a vivid description of this type of collective singing and remarked, "each singer derives his personal melody . . . and adds to it his own melismas, interpolations, and in many instances his own principles. . . . [W]hen a hundred aroused singers so intone, the resultant sound is indescribable."[46] Also referred to as the "Dr. Watts" method in reference to English minister Dr. Issac Watts, the author of the colonial collections of hymns, *Hymns and Spiritual Songs* (1707), lining out enabled a congregation to learn songs through an oral tradition even if it could not interpret a written hymnal.[47] If instruments such as an organ or piano were present, the congregation often followed along with the instrumentalists using song texts like Marshall W. Taylor's *A Collection of Revival Hymns and Plantation Melodies* (1882) or the *Soothing Songs Hymnal* (1891), which reproduced the text, melody, harmony, and vocal dynamics of songs in written sheet music.[48]

The musical worship practices of black Baptists shared many similarities with other black Protestant groups. While each sect in the city valued the distinct characteristics of their own congregations, Baptists, African Methodist Episcopal (AME), African Methodist Episcopal Zion (AME Zion), Congregational, or Presbyterian worshipers might have cause to visit each other's services during holidays, graduations, or other community events.[49] Hence, Bessie might have also been familiar with the music practices of the African American Methodists, the other prevalent Protestant group in the black Chattanooga community.[50] The marked difference between the Baptists and Methodists in music ministry was the Methodist use of the Richard Allen Hymnal, the *Collection of Spiritual Songs and Hymns Selected from Various Authors* (1801), and later the AME Hymnal (1818).[51] Allen, the founder and first bishop of the African Methodist Episcopal church, crafted his hymnal with the express purpose of collecting hymns that directly spoke to the African American experience, thus bolstering his mission to form an autonomous black Methodist church that focused on the unique needs of its congregants. Although hymns from the AME Hymnal would have initially been lined out, by the mid 1800s Bishop Daniel Payne led an attempt to "civilize" black worship by denouncing the singing of spirituals, ring shout, and other overtly demonstrative displays of spiritual expression as a "heathenish way to worship."[52] Payne subsequently supported the institution of choral singing and Western instrumental accompaniment in the AME service. While not all churches abandoned their traditional music practices, by the 1890s many AME churches had a formalized church choir that led the hymns from written sheet music to accompany the weekly service. Through shared fellowship, the Smiths could have been equally familiar with the congregational singing of local Baptist churches and the choirs of AME and AME Zion churches, all of which garnered the attention of the local black press, who often noted when a church's music ministry "delighted the audience" or "rendered excellent music."[53]

Although the traditional Christian faith expressed in African American sacred music would be manifest in varied ways throughout Bessie's later years, what would have been greatly significant to Bessie may not have been the text of the songs but the manner in which the songs were received by a spirit-filled audience.[54] A truly moving sermon or song could cause members of the congregation to vocally interact with the pastor or the singer, as evidenced in William Wells Brown's observations of a Tennessee church in the 1880s: "The church was already well filled, and the minister had taken his text. As the speaker warmed up in his subject, the Sisters began to swing their heads and reel to and fro, and eventually began a shout. Soon, five or six were fairly at it, which threw the house into a buzz. Seats were soon vacated near the shouters, to give them more room."[55] Although Brown concluded from these observations that African Americans were too steeped in folk religion and revivals, which could be "injurious to both health and morals," his descriptions capture the spiritual power that music and the call-and-response aspect of a sermon can have in African American worship services.[56] As Bessie witnessed the parishioners possessed by the Holy Spirit who clapped and responded to the church sermons with "amens" and "hallelujahs," it foreshadowed how a secular blues audience could be moved by a performance. Bessie would not necessarily have been conscious of this relationship between religious worship and secular performance, but the setting itself and the manner in which a sacred-music soloist delivered his or her song would remain familiar to young Bessie and form a foundation for her musical training in Chattanooga.

Ultimately, the six or seven years that William Smith had with his youngest child would have some influence on her, however small. Although it is difficult to determine anything about William and Bessie's interpersonal relationship, Bessie would have known that she had a committed and dedicated father in her early years. Whether or not she was acutely conscious of it, Bessie would have briefly observed a man with a strong work ethic who used what limited economic resources he had to provide his family with a better life than might have been had in rural Alabama. From her own experiences and the memories that family members shared with her, she would have also known a father who worked diligently whenever possible to keep his large family fed, clothed, and sheltered together under one Christian household. The importance of family unity would be further instilled in her by the examples of her mother and siblings throughout the rest of her childhood in Chattanooga.

LAURA SMITH

Bessie's personal interactions with her mother are as difficult to determine as those with her father, yet the effects of Laura's labor activities on the Smith family can be traced by exploring her work tasks in the context of working-class urban African American women of the period. Laura Smith's overall influence on the Smith household and Bessie's upbringing was equally as significant as William's, and perhaps even more, for Laura was present for a slightly greater portion of Bessie's childhood. Just as William Smith held the dual role of laborer and clergyman to economically and spiritually support the Smith household, Laura Smith held the combined roles of homemaker and child-rearer with that of domestic servant.

Migration would have mandated that Laura Smith make a transition from rural to urban life. As the wife of a plantation laborer, Laura would have been responsible for all the tasks needed to maintain a rural home, including planting and harvesting subsistence crops, preparing and preserving food, gathering water, obtaining knowledge of herbal medicinal remedies, cleaning and mending clothes, tending livestock, and general house cleaning. Additionally, like other sharecropping women in the rural South, perhaps Laura worked alongside men in the fields, picking cash crops such as cotton or tobacco and aiding other field laborers in getting this product ready for market. Housework and field work would have been done in addition to her primary task of bearing and rearing children—children who were greatly needed as laborers on the farm or plantation. Child care in a large family would have been no easy task when each child demanded individual attention, and there was simply not enough time to devote any one period entirely to child care or to house- and fieldwork. Ultimately, Laura Smith had to maintain a rural home with limited economic resources in a small living space and in the face of the injustices inherent in the sharecropping system.[57]

The specific adjustments Laura made in urban Chattanooga did not necessarily involve performing new labors but rather performing these labors in a new and somewhat foreign setting full of all the hazards that accompanied a developing city. Chattanooga possessed all the conveniences of a late nineteenth-century urban environment such as gas lighting, indoor plumbing, paved streets, and readily accessible transportation. In many aspects, the city was an example of what the New South could become in terms of new technology. Roland Hayes, in his account of his initial arrival in Chattanooga, described being awed by "the gas-lit avenues of a New Jerusalem."[58] Yet the modern amenities of the city did not generally extend beyond the business districts or elite neighborhoods. Out of the sixty-five miles of city streets, only six were paved by 1880, and there were no uniform sidewalks. Only 5 percent of the area's homes had indoor plumbing, and most people built outhouses or "privy vaults" four feet from their dwellings. The municipal government devised a trash-removal and street-cleaning system, but the refuse from street sweeping was "deposited on unimproved streets" or the unpaved streets in low-income areas like Blue Goose Hollow.[59] The city did not maintain clean drinking water, and there were no specific laws against disposing of human, household, and industrial wastes in the river.[60] Consequently, the low-income areas of the city, like Blue Goose Hollow, were often crowded, unsanitary areas where mud and trash collected in the streets after a flood or heavy rain and the conditions were favorable for the rampant spread of disease. Hence, while Laura Smith weathered the stress of maintaining a poor rural household, sustaining a large family in a small two- or three-room wooden home in the impoverished districts of a nineteenth-century city was equally taxing.

Like most homes that housed the low-income industrial laborers of the city, the Smith home was not large nor well built. A closer examination of such a home provides a glimpse of what Laura Smith and African American migrant women in general had to contend with in terms of housekeeping. The "little ramshackle cabin" that Bessie Smith acknowledged as her birth home was probably a two- or three-room wooden structure in which all the rooms lined up in a row—a shotgun house.[61] As the scholar Ruth Schwartz Cowan contends, in such a dwelling there would have been few furnishings, little storage space, and general cleaning would have been a "herculean endeavor."[62] In a household of ten, such as the Smith home, there was little unused space and nearly no privacy. A living or sitting room would also have substituted as a bedroom, storage room, and recreational area. Several Smith children would have had to share a bed or else sleep on pallets on the wooden floor, and that same bed would later have been converted into a chair or a surface to store clothes or other personal belongings. The kitchen might have served as a laundry room, bathing room, or play area during the winter months, as

An average Chattanooga working-class black home, 1899. Library of Congress, Prints and Photographs Division, LC-USZ62-72447.

well as the site of food preparation and consumption. The cast-iron stove was essential to food preparation but also would have been a significant source of heat in the noninsulated shack.[63]

Although the city had opened its first electricity plants as early as 1882, homes were not yet wired; as the Chattanooga historian James Livingood maintains, "[N]o one would dare to install such a dangerous genie in his own home."[64] Hence, the family would have had to use kerosene lamps and candles as the source of light for any nighttime activities. Laura Smith, like many other women in the fledgling urban South, lived within the vicinity of modern conveniences but still had to care for her home and family with few of the benefits of modern technology.

Perhaps the greatest challenge Laura Smith faced in her relocation to Chattanooga was child rearing or, more specifically, the birth of Bessie. At forty-two, childbirth was not an easy task, particularly as Laura had a history of failed pregnancies and child deaths. By the time of the 1900 census, she reported that she had had ten pregnancies, and out of these only seven children survived.[65] That she had children that survived past adolescence is an accomplishment in itself, at a time when the uncomplicated birth and survival of a healthy child was far from guaranteed. Laura's reproductive capabilities may have also been affected from her treatment as a young adolescent enslaved woman. Nonetheless, she matured to womanhood and childbearing age during an era when enslaved women toiled long hours with inadequate nutrition or health care and little protection against physical and sexual abuses.[66] Even in the aftermath of slavery, low-income women were often poorly fed, overworked, and generally fatigued, and this combination could lead to women receiving inadequate prenatal care.[67] The high infant-mortality rate was often so prevalent in the post-Reconstruction South that, as the historian Edward Ayers remarks, some children were not even named "until they were over a year old," in case they did not survive.[68] Fortunately, this was not a fate that befell Laura Smith with her final pregnancy, and she was able to see Bessie past infancy through her early childhood years.

Women's Ways of Work

Laura Smith's labor activities extended far beyond her own household. The low wages that African American male laborers earned necessitated that their female counterparts also work outside the home to financially support the household. Thus, while William toiled as a general laborer, Laura worked as a laundress. Despite the desire many African Americans had to protect their wives, daughters, and sisters from abuse by not having them work as domestics in white homes, African American women were always a significant part of the wage-earning labor force.[69] Unlike many native-born white women, who often performed wage work only before marriage, single, married, divorced, or widowed African American women often had to be wage laborers just so they and their families could meet their base subsistence needs.[70] Laura Smith joined the millions of African American women who took to private homes, hotels, boarding houses, stores, and street markets as wage laborers.

By 1898, the combined income from Laura's laundry work and William's factory labor allowed the couple to purchase a home at 100 Cross Street in Blue Goose Hollow. Although the house may have been as small and of as poor quality as the shoddy cabin of Bessie's birth, owning property was a definite statement of financial progress for the Smith family despite their low-income status. Paying a flat-rate monthly mortgage as opposed to rent saved the family money in the long run, for they invested money in the ownership of material property as opposed to paying six to twelve dollars monthly on property that would never be their own. Owning a home would have also provided the Smith family with a stable physical foundation in Chattanooga and alleviated the need to constantly move between rental properties when rent increased. With the 100 Cross Street home, the Smith family was on its way toward joining the group of African American migrants who became material property owners or entrepreneurs as a result of relocating to an urban environment. According to the scholar Loren Schweninger, by 1910, "[N]early one out of four blacks, excluding farmers and farm owners [in the upper and middle South], owned their own homes, about 25 percent greater than the ratio in the Lower South."[71] Hence, with their move out of Alabama, the Smiths became one of Tennessee's over eight thousand black homeowners in the 1890s.[72] For a fleeting few years, Bessie and her family would finally have had a measure of geographic and financial stability.

The years of geographic stability and family cohesiveness enjoyed by the Smith family would be greatly tested in the wake of William's death in 1900. Laura became part of the 20 to 25 percent of black urban women in the South who were widowed in the late nineteenth and early twentieth centuries.[73] In William's absence, Laura became the financial head of the Smith household for a family of nine including herself, despite the fact that her elder children, Andrew and Viola, were also employed.[74] It has not been determined exactly how the Blue Goose Hollow community helped the Smiths adapt to the loss of William or if a church or some African American benevolent organization provided for William's burial, as it was customary for many religious and social institutions to do.[75] Nonetheless, with the absence of her father, perhaps Bessie more consciously experienced and realized what it meant to be a laboring African American woman in the urban South, for she was enveloped in a household that was led by working black women.

As an African American woman with little formal education in a hierarchical society governed by race, laundry work was one of the few viable employment options available to Laura Smith. Although female educators, entrepreneurs, and other professionals existed in the Chattanooga African American community, the majority of black women in the city worked as domestics, cooks, child nurses, and laundresses either in private homes or in local city establishments.[76] Domestic work was a reality that many black women had no choice but to accept, and according to the African American domestic Cecelia Gaudet, "[T]he majority of people here [in the urban South] worked . . . and the majority of them made their living working for white people or washing and ironing for them. Everybody couldn't be teachers and that was the only thing for them to do."[77] The limited range of employment open to African Americans was further reflected in the classified section of the city's primary newspaper, the *Chattanooga Daily Times*. Under "Help Wanted—Female," there were often published advertisements seeking "a young colored woman that can do cleaning, pressing and repairing work" at a hotel laundry, or a "colored woman for general housekeeping" of a private downtown residence.[78] Of the few choices available, laundry work offered Laura the benefits of personal control and flexibility over her time, which made it one of the most prevalent occupational choices for African American working-class women throughout the South. African Americans comprised 64 percent of the laundry workers nationwide in the early 1900s.[79]

Black women selected laundry work as an alternative to other domestic occupations such as cooking or housekeeping primarily to elude the dilemmas that often accompanied live-in or day domestic labor. As a live-in domestic worker, a woman might be hired do to general housework but eventually be asked to cook, care for children, and perform any other task an employer might think of at any random moment in the day. As a resident within an employer's home, a domestic often had little privacy, for there was no "clock-out" portion of the day. One domestic worker, Viola Lomax-Winfield, recalls that her employer wanted her to put on a full uniform and apron simply to bring her a glass of water in the late evening, long after working hours should have been over.[80] Live-in work was often undertaken by unmarried women without children primarily because of the lack of personal time. Married women who were live-in domestic workers were often only permitted to see their husbands and children on their days off, which were at the discretion of the employer. Days off were sometimes so few that a live-in laborer reported to the *Independent* that she was only allowed to see her own children once every two weeks.[81]

Many married African American women with children often opted to work at day-labor domestic jobs, which proved little better than live-in positions.[82] Day laborers worked long hours, during which they were forced to leave their children and homes to care for their white employer's children and home. The Chattanooga pastor Rev. Joseph E. Smith noted that in 1897, the streets of Chattanooga in the early morning were filled with African American women "rushing to their places of work for the day" from which they did not return until "eight o'clock at night."[83] As there was no formal system of day care for working mothers, Reverend Smith witnessed small children (who could not be looked after by a neighbor or relative) left to their own devices for the day to wander the city streets.[84] Live-in and day workers toiled long hours for little financial profit, and employers often included food leftovers or "service pans" and castoff clothing as part of a domestic's wages.[85]

As laborers in a white household, one of the greatest hazards that African American female domestic laborers faced was the threat of sexual harassment by white male employers. Admittedly, some female laborers turned these advances to their advantage and gained extra material possessions from their relationships with white males. Yet, as an African American child-care worker in 1912 reveals, there was little protection against nonconsensual liaisons, and if the male relatives of an abused domestic laborer sought to address the employer's crimes, "the guiltless negroes would be severely punished, if not killed, and the white blackleg would go scot-free."[86] This same child-care worker further illuminates the overall plight of domestic laborers in the following public appeal featured in *The Independent:*

> "We poor colored women wage earners in the South are fighting a terrible battle. . . . On the one hand, we are assailed by white men, and on the other hand, we are assailed by black men, who should be our natural protectors; and, whether in the cook kitchen, at the washtub, over the sewing machine, behind the baby carriage, or at the ironing board, we are but little more than pack horses, beasts of burden, slaves! In the distant future . . . a monument of brass or stone may be erected to the Old Black Mammies of the South, but what we need is present help, present sympathy, better wages, better hours, more protection, and a chance to breathe for once while alive as free women."[87]

In contrast, laundry work allowed women to work in their own homes and thus be actively involved in raising their own children and maintaining their own households. Despite the benefits laundry work afforded, the work load of a washerwoman was no less rigorous than that of a domestic laborer or cook. Bessie Smith offered a glimpse of the arduous nature of laundry work in her 1928 recording of "Washerwoman's Blues":

> All day long I'm slavin, all day long I'm bustin' suds,
> All day long I'm slavin, all day long I'm bustin' suds,
> Gee my hands are tired, washin' out these dirty duds.

> Lord, I do more than forty 'leven Gold Dust Twins,
> Lord, I do more than forty 'leven Gold Dust Twins,
> Got myself a achin' from my head down to my shins.

> Sorry I do washin' just to make my livelihood,
> Sorry I do washin' just to make my livelihood,
> Oh, the washwoman' life, it ain't a bit of good.

Rather be a scullion cookin' in some white folks' yard,
Rather be a scullion cookin' in some white folks' yard,
I could eat a plenty, wouldn't have to work so hard.

Me and my ole washboard sho' do have some cares and woes,
Me and my ole washboard sho' do have some cares and woes,
In the muddy water, wringin' out these dirty clothes.[88]

As Bessie revealed, washing often resulted in a woman "achin' from her head down to her shins"; it was a task that had to be accomplished in the 1900s without the benefits of modern technology such as electricity or indoor plumbing. A laundress would gather clothes herself or have some relative tote the clothes from customers and carry them back to her own home. The actual washing was often conducted on Blue Monday, so-called because of the bluing, a chemical agent used to prevent clothes from yellowing that a washerwoman added to the rinse water.[89] However, Monday must also have become emotionally "blue" due to the drudgery of the process. Washing began by gathering and boiling several buckets of water in a large iron pot over a wood fire. The laundress then added soiled clothes, sheets, and linens to the water and soaked them before adding a soap agent and scrubbing each item against a washboard by hand. She then gathered more water, boiled it, and added bluing and the laundered clothes for the rinsing process. Subsequently, she twisted out the excess water and hung the laundry to dry on an outdoor line. The entire process ended with her smoothing out the cloth with stove-heated pressing irons, folding the items, and returning them to her customer by the end of the week.[90] For this tedious and physically intensive process, a washerwoman earned a meager profit. One domestic, Cecelia Gaudet, contends that no matter how skilled and efficient a washerwoman was, "the pay was small!" Gaudet knew laborers who "got a $1 a bundle, some 50 cents and 75 cents . . . and if they got a $1.50 that was big money!"[91]

The physical toil, meager wages, and emotional strife shared by working-class African American women in Chattanooga helped them to develop a community of women bonded in their knowledge of the ways of work. In her discussion of Atlanta domestics and washerwomen, the historian Tera Hunter maintains that "laundry work was critical to the process of community-building because it encouraged women to work together in communal spaces within their neighborhoods, forming informal networks of reciprocity."[92] Although there is no evidence that the washerwomen of Chattanooga formally organized an economic union as the Atlanta washing women did in 1881, domestic laborers created communal bonds in the city, and Bessie Smith, her mother, and her sisters were part of this network.[93]

Example of a laundress's work, 1900. Library of Congress, Prints and Photographs Division, LC USZ62-51058.

At the time that Laura Smith became the sole financial head of the Smith household, there were over a thousand female laundry workers in Chattanooga.[94] Although these women were scattered into different neighborhoods, their daily work practices were quite similar. While day domestics, cooks, seamstresses, and hairdressers went off to work, it was often the washerwomen who cared for their children. In return, these women who left their homes to labor might inform washerwomen about potential new customers. The young black working women of Chattanooga took pride in their work and saved their earnings when they could; decades later, some Chattanooga whites marveled enviously at the material possessions washerwomen were able to acquire.[95] Additionally, as washing was an occupation that allowed for greater overall family participation because it was carried out in one's own home, young women often learned the skills they would carry into their own jobs by helping their mothers sort clothes, boil water, fold clothes, and so on.[96] Undoubtedly, Bessie and her sisters would have helped their mother Laura in her daily tasks. More specifically, there is evidence that Bessie's elder sisters Viola and Tennie and Bessie herself incorporated their mother's domestic-labor skills in their own occupations. In later years, Viola took in laundry as her mother had and supported her siblings and her own children with her earnings.[97] By 1908, Tennie Smith was also noted in the city directory as a laundress.[98] Bessie worked in a commercial laundry in downtown Birmingham, Alabama, to supplement her meager earnings during her early vaudeville years.[99] Bessie grew to adolescence among a community of laboring women who possessed persistence, discipline, strength, and relative independence when compared with other domestic workers. Bessie would carry these qualities of persistence and a sense of independence, in addition to practical labor skills, into her later life.

Smith's Early Adolescence and Life in the Absence of Her Parents

The life that Bessie lived as a preadolescent girl was marked by the death of her mother, Laura Smith.[100] Although one can only speculate as to the emotions she experienced from the loss of her father and her mother in such a short time, her parents' deaths would certainly have affected how the household functioned. Much of what would have been familiar and secure would have been drastically altered.

In the aftermath of Laura's death, Bessie's eldest sister Viola, at age twenty-five took over as a financial head of the household.[101] She supported herself and her younger siblings, Tennie, Lulu, Clarence, and Bessie initially by working as a cook and later following in her mother's path as a washerwoman. Perhaps Viola began to take in washing to avoid being one of those women who invaded the Chattanooga streets in the early dawn hours between five and six.[102] As a washerwoman, Viola would have been in a better position to keep a close watch over her siblings, yet she would also have lost the freedom she had possessed as a single, childless woman. This change in the relationship between Viola and her siblings may have caused all parties some angst, as Viola was forced to take on responsibility for the family, and her sisters and brothers had to look upon her as an authoritative figure rather than merely an older sibling. The entire dynamics of the Smith household altered for Viola and her siblings as she fulfilled the role of mother. Not only did the guardian figures shift in the home but the physical notion of "home" altered in the aftermath of Laura Smith's death—by 1903, the Smiths no longer occupied the house on 100 Cross Street.[103] Throughout Bessie's time in Chattanooga as an adolescent, Viola moved from residence to residence, often boarding with others instead of renting or owning her own property, while Tennie, Lulu, and Andrew also appear at several different addresses in the local city directories.[104] Without the combined income of Laura Smith and her eldest children, it seems as if continued ownership of a home for the family as a unit proved difficult. By the age of ten, Bessie would have understood and endured the instability that poverty can induce.

Despite the dramatic shifts in the Smith home after their parents' deaths, Viola and Bessie's other siblings managed to see Bessie through to adolescence. As Viola was responsible for the rest of Bessie's upbringing in Chattanooga, she made sure that Bessie spent some time in the city's formal educational system. African American Chattanoogans believed deeply in the value of education, and Howard High School and several common schools were among the first institutions African Americans established in the early years of community development. The community as a whole shared a love of formal learning; over six thousand residents attended the Howard High School graduation in 1904 to support the school's fifteen graduates.[105] Clearly, the fifteen high school diplomas were not only significant to the graduates and their families but were seen as symbol of progress by much of the city's African American community. There is no record of Bessie attending school at any of the African American secondary schools in Hamilton County, but she did have the opportunity to be educated, if only briefly, as a student at the grammar school on West Main Street, originally known as Montgomery Avenue School.[106] There she would have learned the fundamentals of reading, writing, and arithmetic to help prepare her for the college-preparatory, rather than industrial, curriculum of Howard High.[107]

Bessie was fortunate to attend school at all, for many black children, including her eldest siblings, did not frequently have the opportunity in the early twentieth-century South. For many African American and low-income white children, the stages of childhood and adolescence were not protected periods of growth, learning, and minimum responsibility.[108] In the early 1900s, parents often required children to contribute to the family's income or domestic labor. In rural areas, children were expected to help in the production of subsistence and cash crops, and these labor tasks often shortened the time a child could attend school or prevented him or her from attending classes at all. In urban areas of the South, some laws limited child labor, such as the Tennessee act of 1893 that made it illegal to hire "children less than 12 years of age" to work in any "workshop, mill, factory or mine in the state."[109] Nonetheless, families often found ways to circumvent such laws if they desperately needed the income their children could provide. There were few laws that restricted the age at which young girls could be hired for private domestic employment.[110] Hence, in large families some children would have had to work to afford younger children the opportunity to attend school. Such was the case with Bessie and her siblings. The elder Smith children—Viola, Andrew, Bud, and Tennie—who experienced childhood in rural Alabama had no record of formal education and were reportedly illiterate. In contrast, the younger Smith children—Lulu, Clarence, and Bessie—who lived much of their youth in Chattanooga, all spent some time in Chattanooga schools.[111] Hence, Bessie was able to acquire literacy in part because her parents moved the family to the urban South.

Attending school did not occupy all of Bessie's time. Like any child, she probably longed for recreation and amusement, and she searched outside her home to find them. Bessie may have engaged in church social activities when her parents were alive or participated in school-related recreation activities during her months as a student at Main Street School. However, Bessie spent the majority of her recreation and leisure time in the public landscape of Chattanooga. As a youth, Bessie was drawn to the sights and sounds of Chattanooga streets, which offered her some escape from her destitute living conditions, the world of domestic labor, her family, and school. Bessie initially used the streets of Blue Goose Hollow and beyond as her playground, for there were simply too few places for children to play in the urban environment. Although William Wilson and other African American citizens had established a black branch of the Young Men's Christian Association to provide a recreational and educational outlet for young men by 1903, few other independent recreational centers existed for black youth until sometime after 1910.[112] The African American branch of the Young Women's Christian Association was not built until 1917, and the main black park, Lincoln Park, was not developed until the 1930s.[113] Hence, the riverfront, open fields, and streets became the playground for Chattanooga's black children. Bessie's need to turn outside of the home for amusement can be made more clear when observing how the sociologist William H. Jones describes the conditions of the urban, poverty-stricken black home of the era: "The poorly furnished, unclean, or untidy home cannot act as an ideal rendezvous for the weary members of the family. Hence they can hardly be regarded as true centers of recreation. Two or three small, poorly lighted and heated rooms and a hall do not lend themselves readily to privacy, comforts, and home parties."[114] Bessie's Blue Goose Hollow home would have been similar to the Washington, D.C., alley dwellings described by Jones. Plagued by the crowded conditions of the shack she shared with as many six other people at a time (including her sister-in-law and later her niece), Bessie probably took off to the city's streets, moved by how they promised to "satisfy to some extent the craving for new and thrilling life."[115] In search of this "thrilling life," some youths engaged in whatever childhood games their imaginations could devise, while many others used the city's surrounding fields to play baseball, football, and other sports.[116] Reportedly, among the pastimes Smith enjoyed as a young child was rolling skating, which she used as transportation to travel around the few paved paths of the city.[117] Many of Chattanooga's streets were far from an ideal playground, for crime in downtown Chattanooga was often rampant.

Reports of criminal incidents laced the pages of the city's newspapers on a weekly basis. Violent domestic disputes, drunken brawls, disorderly conduct, and robberies—crimes induced by poverty and human nature—were only a few of the incidents that made headlines in both white and black newspapers. On any given day, one could witness a "lively fight" between a man and his wife in which the "man was well beaten," see several women engage in a "free fight" on Ninth Street, or hear about a young black girl who was "accused of having stolen a purse of gold."[118] Bessie would have known about or perhaps even witnessed these criminal incidents as she moved about Blue Goose Hollow or traveled to school. Yet local community disturbances were not the only crimes that threatened the safety of Chattanooga's citizens.

Although Chattanooga was not as plagued with racial violence as the rest of the South, it was not free from interracial tension and the subsequent crimes that could ensue. General misunderstandings between white and black residents could often result in physical violence when white citizens attempted to remind African Americans of their inferior "place." In March 1898, two white clerks at Anderson's drug store assaulted a prominent African American physician, Dr. A. J. Love, after he apparently complained about the disrespectful tone in which he was being spoken to.[119] In that same month, a local white fireman, Martin Hackett, shot a black waiter, John Rutledge, when Rutledge failed to give Hackett a napkin with lunch.[120] By 1906, such violent occurrences culminated in one of the worst incidents of mob violence in Chattanooga's history. Ed Johnson, an African American laborer, was accused of raping a young white woman in St. Elmo, one of the city's outlying suburbs. Although the victim could not confirm the identity of her attacker, the police arrested Johnson, charged him with rape, and had him stand trial for the crime. Before any sentence could be legally carried out, an angry white mob tortured and lynched him at the Walnut Street Bridge in 1906. Johnson's murder was one of the few lynchings that occurred in Chattanooga, during a period in which lynching plagued much of the South.[121] Yet such terrible displays of violent savagery threatened the stability of race relations in the city. These threats were only tempered by the black and white community's general abhorrence for mob violence.[122]

It was within this environment of strife that Bessie had to learn to negotiate the streets as a young African American woman. The legendary stories of her aggressive behavior and her willingness to engage in physical fights with those who crossed her perhaps stemmed from the survival instinct she had to maintain on the hostile streets of her youth. At ten or eleven, she would have had to adopt a cautiousness and sense of adventure that protected her from being trapped by the crime in her own neighborhood. She would have also had to observe a primary unwritten rule of African American behavior—deference to whites in public—and have a basic knowledge of which parts of the segregated city were closed to her.[123] Apparently, Bessie learned to negotiate the ills of the segregated urban environment fairly rapidly, for by the early 1900s the street was not only her playground but her stage.

By the early 1900s, Bessie Smith had lived through many of the experiences that would serve as a foundation for the young woman she was to become. She had been exposed to the music and teachings of the black Baptist church, learned the ways of women's work, survived her parents' deaths, and endured the poverty and crime of the urban environment. The community of women that surrounded Bessie would have provided her with several examples of what it meant to be a wife, mother, laborer, and woman. She could have chosen to mirror herself after the women she saw in her home and Chattanooga neighborhood, yet she sought another, vastly different option of the woman she wanted to become. At an early age, Bessie set off on a path that was unique, daring, and a contrast to all she had known and she began by absorbing the music, dance, and adventure of the city's Ninth Street, the "Big Nine."

LIFE ON "BIG NINTH" STREET
THE EMERGING BLUES CULTURE
IN CHATTANOOGA

The streets of a city are the exhibition halls of its
citizens. Walking through these public halls all phases
and conditions of life may be seen and the character and
civilization of its people judged.

—REV. JOSEPH E. SMITH

I take your East Ninth Street to my
Heart, pay court on your Market
Street of rubboard players and organ
Grinders of Haitian colors rioting
And old Zip Coon Dancers
I want to hear Bessie Smith belt out
I'm wild about that thing in
Your Ivory Theater
Chattanooga
Coca-Cola's homebase
City on my mind.

—ISHMAEL REED, "Chattanooga"

While the first of this chapter's epigraphs, written in 1897 by the African American pastor of Chattanooga's First Congregational church, refers to the streets of all urban landscapes, the second, a poem by the Chattanooga native Ishmael Reed, reveals that the greatest "exhibition hall" of Chattanooga in the early twentieth century was the vibrant Ninth Street. Stretching from the banks of the Tennessee River and the Union Railway lines through downtown to the edge of the famed National Cemetery, Ninth Street was a microcosm of the city's commercial and social offerings as well its diverse population.

On West Ninth Street, the impoverished African American residents of Blue Goose Hollow could cross paths with the elite white socialites of Cameron Hill as they all traveled into the heart of the city. Some blocks further down Ninth was the commercial district, where "bankers and brokers, merchants and manufacturers, lawyers and doctors, and yes even politicians [could meet] on common ground."[1] Around the bend in Ninth just past Union Station and the elegant Read House hotel, the heart of downtown black Chattanooga—East Ninth Street—came into sight. Although many of the commercial establishments of East Ninth catered to African American customers, a visitor could find Charles Zegelbaum's jewelry store, C. J. McFarland's shop, and Shweidelson Brothers' ladies' tailors in the same block as the offices of the African American lawyer J. W. White and the black hairdresser J. T. Higgins.[2] In the midst of this medley of shops, professional offices, restaurants, and boarding houses lay the saloons and theaters that brought some of the most popular musical fare of the period to the city. It was in the streets and sidewalks in front of these social establishments that an adolescent Bessie Smith made her first public performances and encountered a musical entertainment culture that contained elements of all the African American musical genres of the late nineteenth and early twentieth centuries, from worksongs to minstrelsy, "coon" songs to black vaudeville.

Origins of Ninth Street

The adventure offered on Ninth Street called to Chattanooga residents as early as 1900. The twentieth-century status of East Ninth Street as a vibrant hub of black life can be traced to the early years of the city's development. Prior to the Civil War, the area had been primarily waterlogged land that contained a pond used by local women for washing clothes.[3] After the Civil War and emancipation, freedpersons settled in the area and eventually purchased small plots of this land, largely because of its "undesirability" to the general white population. As the black population grew in size, the East Ninth area became a hub for the newly built African American churches, businesses, and professional offices of the late 1890s.[4] As the twentieth century dawned, the area became a foundation of the downtown activities of African Americans and housed the institutions of the relatively self-sufficient community. It was the vast number of such institutions, including drug stores, physician's offices, restaurants, boarding houses, and churches, that led several residents to later refer to East Ninth as the "Big Nine"—a street that predated and, in many black Chattanoogans' eyes, rivaled Memphis's Beale Street.[5]

Just as Beale Street had been home to the musical and recreational activities of Memphis blacks, East Ninth Street was a center of entertainment as well as commerce for African Americans in Chattanooga. The area's theaters, eating houses, and saloons hosted many of the nation's traveling revues as well as aspiring local entertainers. Remarkably, the early boom period of Ninth Street (approximately 1900–17) coincided with a historical moment in which several African American musical genres were on the rise.[6] By the 1900s, locally rooted worksongs and folk ballads merged with the golden age of black minstrelsy, ragtime, the dawn of black vaudeville theater, and a brass band movement to create an emerging blues-music culture. It was during this period that Bessie Smith became aware of the secular musical life of the city.

Overview of Black Musical Culture, 1890–1910

Before examining Smith's forays into Chattanooga's black musical culture, it is important to survey the origins of each of the rich musical traditions that coalesced in the city. The nonprofessional music traditions of worksongs, boat songs, and street cries that were present in the colonies in the antebellum

Market Square, corner of Ninth and Market Streets, Chattanooga. Library of Congress, Prints and Photographs Division, LCD4-19992.

era and the initial emancipation period continued into the early twentieth century, although laborers adjusted their songs to the new types of work of the urban environment. As discussed in chapter 1, laborers used worksongs to measure out the beats of manual work. Railroad workers or convicts forced into labor on chain gangs often used worksongs as they laid railway ties or labored at road repair. Similarly, boatmen, the laborers who worked at the riverfront docks, also sang worksongs to lessen the tedium of manual labor and to move the pace of loading the flatbed boats along. In the areas where water trade and transportation were still viable, boatmen's cries could be heard during the workday. In some cities, boat songs mingled with vendors' street cries, song phrases street merchants used to advertise their products. Although the number of street vendors lessened as retail stores began to sell more goods in the urban environment, one could still hear hawkers singing about everything from produce to tinware. Overall, the music that accompanied black labor formed a secure foundation for the advancement of secular African American musical culture.[7]

The music from the brass band movement of the late nineteenth and early twentieth centuries bridged the gap between amateur and professional African American music of the era. As the dawn of the 1900s approached, the music of a brass band could be heard in many regions throughout the nation at events as varied as holiday parades or the opening of a local shop. The surge of popularity in band music in the late nineteenth century was connected to the prominence that military bands had held during the Civil War. This new interest in brass bands was subsequently connected to an increased interest in music instruction in the early 1900s.[8] In this era before modern recreational outlets, playing and listening to music within the home and local community served as a primary method of entertainment for middle- and low-income individuals alike, and various ethnic, religious, and social organizations sponsored band ensembles throughout the country.[9] The members of traveling brass bands were often not professional musicians. Depending on the institution organizing the band, members could be shopkeepers, steel workers, hack drivers, or lawyers in daily life but celebrated trumpet or trombone players in the Labor Day Festival or local high-school commencement ceremony. Participating in a band gave an amateur musician a sense of pride, joy, and recognition as well as an identity apart from the constraints of daily life.

African American brass bands entertained at such community functions as funerals, church socials, festivals, and holiday parades and were often sponsored by fraternal and benevolent organizations, schools, and churches.[10] Musicians from regional amateur bands often made their way into professional traveling troupes. Conversely, a musician on break from a minstrel show, theater orchestra, or circus band might join the community band to maintain his or her skills. The local amateur band played a particularly significant role in the history of the brass band movement in New Orleans. At the picnics, parties, and funeral marches of New Orleans society, cornet, clarinet, and trombone players in the brass bands of the early 1900s experimented with the polyphonic sounds and rhythmic phrasing that provided a foundation for jazz music.[11] Brass bands could be found throughout many of the working-class neighborhoods of the city, and their syncopated sounds drew in many listeners, according to the New Orleans native and gospel music pioneer, Mahalia Jackson:

> I saw lots of the famous New Orleans brass bands when I was growing up. They advertised the fish fries and the house-rent parties and played for the secret order lodge dances and funerals. When there was going to be a big fish fry or lodge dance they would fill a wagon up with a load of hay or they'd put some chairs in it. The brass band—some of them were five pieces—would climb up in that wagon and they would drive around town, stopping and playing at every street corner to drum up a crowd.[12]

From these local brass bands came some of the most prominent musicians of the early jazz era, including the legendary trumpeter Louis Armstrong, one of Bessie Smith's musical contemporaries. In the "little brass band" of the Colored Waif's Home for Boys in New Orleans, a twelve-year-old Armstrong perfected the basics of playing the bugle and paraded all over the streets of the city, years before he joined King Oliver's jazz ensemble.[13] As Armstrong's childhood band sprang from a New Orleans orphanage, community bands could give youths a sense of community and family in instances where these traditional structures did not exist, in addition to serving as positive social, educational, and employment outlets for young aspiring musicians.

One of the most popular musical genres at the end of the nineteenth century was black or "colored" minstrelsy.[14] The American minstrel genre began between 1815 and 1830 in the northeastern United States.[15] Initially, American minstrels were troupes of white males who performed comedic musical plays in blackface makeup for an audience of predominantly working-class white males.[16] Historians and cultural theorists have argued that the functions of the early white minstrel genre vary from sheer entertainment to a method for white entertainers to covertly criticize class injustices in American society to white males' unconscious desire to possess the supposed sexual power of black males.[17] Nonetheless, traditional minstrelsy contained numerous racist

elements, for white performers mimicked and often romanticized the ges-
tures, dialect, and daily life of enslaved blacks, of whom most of them had
little knowledge or understanding. White minstrelsy extracted humor from
a mythologized black experience by illustrating the supposed "combination
of simplicity and low cunning" attributed to African Americans.[18]

Minstrelsy became so popular in the latter half of the nineteenth century
that the 1890s music historian Charles Townsend contended that "there was
no form of entertainment capable of producing so much 'innocent' fun as a
good minstrel show."[19] The general format of a minstrel show usually consisted
of seventeen white actors selected for their skill in replicating the "carefree"
days of plantation slavery. These actors would apply burnt cork and such
theater makeup as "Mulatto" and "Indianola" to their faces (excepting the
lips) to achieve that authentic "nigger" look and then would perform a series
of small skits that included the songs and dances of the "jigging darkies" on
the plantation.[20] The most famous of these early minstrels include Daniel
Emmett and the Virginia Minstrels, who are credited with the creation of
"Dixie," a song that became an anthem of the Confederate South, and the
legendary Thomas D. Rice.[21] In 1828, Rice developed the infamous character
of "Jim Crow," a wizened, dilapidated, but ever jovial plantation laborer.[22]
The Rice character later became memorialized as the vernacular term for
legal segregation and a visual symbol for white supremacists' demand for
separate laws, transportation, and public accommodations for white and
African Americans.

"Colored" minstrelsy differed from the traditional genre in that the actors,
musicians, dancers, and singers were all African Americans. While some of
these black traveling shows remained true to American minstrel tradition
by including skits and songs that romanticized the plantation South and
glorified notions of a childlike, continuously happy, inferior African American, some attempted to move away from the buffoonery depicted in white
minstrel shows. An African American company such as George and Hart's
Georgia Minstrels included buck-and-wing dancing (a precursor to modern
tap dance) and a classical music overture in their evening's program, in addition to more familiar plantation songs like "My Old Kentucky Home" or
"Ring off Coon."[23]

Although African American minstrelsy's attempts to escape an emphasis
on plantation themes often proved unsuccessful, the colored minstrel show
did succeed in providing African Americans with an opportunity to enter
professional theater. W. C. Handy, one of the innovators of written or scored
blues music, began his career in the Frank Mahara minstrel show in the 1890s.

Handy later remarked that although black minstrel performers were often thought to be a "disreputable lot," many of the most talented African American "singers, musicians, speakers, and stage performers" rose to prominence on the minstrel stage.[24] Furthermore, as the historian Robert Toll maintains, minstrelsy was one of the few opportunities "for mobility—geographic, social, and economic" open to African Americans in the nineteenth century.[25] This mobility allowed for the transmission of early black theater culture and occasionally offered an alternative employment opportunity for youth who might otherwise have been confined to the limited service jobs available to impoverished African Americans.

Prominent black minstrel troupes of the 1890s and 1900s included Frank Mahara's Minstrels, Callendar's Georgia Minstrels, George and Hart's Up to Date Minstrels, and numerous others. Although most of these traveling shows had white managers, the overall popularity of the genre allowed for individual African American composers and performers such as James Bland, Billy Kersands, Sam Lucas, Bert Williams, George Walker, and Sissieretta Jones to rise to prominence on the American stage. A high profile performer could command from forty to eighty dollars and more weekly, an incredible sum when taken into account that the average laborer barely earned ten to twelve dollars a week.[26] As the 1900s advanced, troupe managers received constant requests from regional theaters "in favor of a colored company" as opposed to white troupes. Black minstrel revues traveled to such varied cities as Los Gatos, California; Mobile, Alabama; Kansas City, Missouri; Lincoln, Nebraska; Galveston, Texas; and hundreds of other cities in between.[27]

As minstrelsy thrived in American theaters, a new popular music craze was on the rise: ragtime. "Ragtime" referred to the "ragged" or syncopated rhythms that laced the instrumental music.[28] While the exact origins of ragtime are unknown, the popular ragtime player James P. Johnson contended that the upbeat ragged popular tunes sprang up in the African American "sporting houses and cabarets in the South—Baltimore, Norfolk, Charleston, Atlanta, and the Middle West—Pittsburgh, St. Louis, Memphis and other places" at the turn of the twentieth century.[29] Ragtime soon spread throughout the nation and was performed by the bands that accompanied traveling minstrel shows and more often by itinerant piano players who moved from saloon to saloon, eating house to eating house.[30] Ragtime was an instrumental and a vocal music that often accompanied the social dance, the cakewalk—the high-kicking, solid-upper-body dance created by enslaved African Americans mimicking the etiquette and behavior of their white masters. The cakewalk evolved from its antebellum roots to become one of the most popular social dances of the

1890s. The dance and its accompanying rags were featured on the minstrel stage as well as at dancing socials in cities as prominent as New York.[31]

By the onset of the twentieth century, particularly from the mid 1890s to the early 1900s, the ragtime craze was at its height. The compositions of Scott Joplin and James Scott, two of the most noted ragtime composers of the era, sprang up in musical venues throughout the nation.[32] Consumers purchased sheet music of such tunes as "Maple Leaf Rag" and piano rolls—the latest in technology that allowed player pianos to play compositions automatically— of "The Cascades" and other ragtime tunes. The popularity of ragtime can be attributed to the ever-growing presence of the piano, player pianos, and other keyboard instruments in middle-class and elite American homes. Music was an essential form of home entertainment in the era before the radio or the phonograph, and the piano might have been a home's central attraction. When traveling through the rural South, the educator Booker T. Washington saw the American fascination with keyboard instruments first-hand:

> I remember that on one occasion when I went into one of these cabins for dinner, when I sat down to the table for a meal with the four members of the family, I noticed that, while there were five of us at the table, there was but one fork for the five of us to use. Naturally there was an awkward pause on my part. In the opposite corner of that same cabin was an organ for which the people told me they were paying sixty dollars in monthly installments. One fork, and a sixty-dollar organ![33]

Although Washington maintained that the presence of an organ in a modest black cabin was a wasteful and detrimental material possession, supposedly "rarely used for want of a person to play it," the desire of the family to have such an instrument regardless of the cost illustrates the importance of recreation and music in their lives.[34] The prominence of music is further noted by the literary figure James Weldon Johnson, who argued that "it [ragtime] is music which possesses at least one strong element of greatness; it appeals universally; not only the American, but the English, the French, and even the German people find delight in it."[35] Before its popularity began to wane by 1917, the internationally popular music furthered the careers of the jazz pianists James P. Johnson, Willie "the Lion" Smith, Eubie Blake, Ferdinand "Jelly Roll" Morton, Lil Hardin, and Thomas "Fats" Waller,[36] each of whom began his or her professional career by experimenting with ragtime rhythms and composing "ragged" tunes.[37]

Ragtime rhythms also permeated turn-of-the-century African American vaudeville and musical theater. Black musical theater ascended from colored minstrelsy, and many of the entertainers who had corked up their faces to play plantation figures wiped off the makeup and developed musical comedies of their own in the early 1900s. While some of the "coon songs" that were featured in black musicals of the era still parodied the antics of supposedly jovial, slow-witted African Americans, black musicians and lyricists now began to write music with an African American audience in mind. These musicals differed from minstrel shows as they were not a collection of independent songs and skits but rather a continuous narrative with a cast of characters that could be followed throughout the story.[38] Some of these first black musicals included Bob Cole and Billy Johnson's *A Trip to Coontown* (1898), Will Marion Cook's *Clorindy* (1898), Bert Williams and George Walker's *In Dahomey* (1902), and S. H. Dudley's *The Smart Set* (1904).[39]

A transmission of black theater culture occurred when musical troupes lead by Cole, Johnson, Williams, and Walker began to travel throughout the nation performing the songs and skits they popularized in their off-Broadway musicals. White and African American patrons enjoyed black musical theater and songs from the latest Williams and Walker or Dudley show. The wide acceptance of black musicals also prompted many white artists to "cover" or reissue songs originally composed and performed by an African American artist in the form of "coon songs." These unfortunately labeled tunes were the vocal counterparts to instrumental ragtime pieces, often concerned the misadventures of black social life, and generally weaved the word "coon" into the title, chorus, or a verse of the song. As early as 1883, "coon" appeared in the title of J. S. Putnam's "New Coon in Town," and with the 1890 publication of the African American composer Ernest Hogan's "All Coons Look Alike to Me," these songs became a staple in American popular music.[40] Coon songs were composed and performed by white entertainers who were amused by the racist humor in the pieces and by black entertainers who observed the cultural conventions of the period and provided what many audiences enjoyed. In the early 1900s, the novelty reached its height, and white female performers who could perform coon songs with the phrasing, power, and dialect generally attributed to African American vocalists were known as "coon shouters."[41] Such performers, including May Irwin, Marie Cahill, and Sophie Tucker, popularized black songs for white American audiences.[42]

While songs composed by African Americans were a foundation of the popular music of the American masses at start of the twentieth century, the themes of early black musicals were not always flattering to black communities and could contain gross stereotypes with little understanding of the nuanced realities of black life. Nonetheless, the popularity of black musicals, like the popularity of colored minstrelsy, afforded African American entertainers an arena for their artistic creations to evolve and develop, as well as employment and a place on the circuit stage. By 1910, there were nearly eight thousand African Americans employed as actors, musicians, stagehands, carpenters, managers, and owners in everything from Broadway shows to circuses.[43] The amateur and professional varieties of African American musical entertainment wove their way into the tent shows, medicine shows, festivals, and regional theaters of the nation during the decade when an adolescent Bessie Smith found herself in the midst of the growing Chattanoogan recreational culture.

The Chattanooga Musical Landscape

AMATEUR MUSIC

Bessie Smith encountered much of the secular African American music of the city as she traveled the streets to and from her Blue Goose Hollow dwellings. She had likely been exposed to the hymns and worship songs of the African American church when she attended services with her family. However, after her parents' deaths in the early 1900s, Bessie began to listen to and later participate in black secular music culture.

Among the first elements of Chattanooga's musical culture one encountered were the sounds that emanated from the city's laborers—the community's worksongs. As a child surrounded by washerwomen, including her mother and her sister Viola, Bessie might have overheard the songs that laundresses used to lessen the monotony of their work. One Atlanta domestic, Ella Mae Hendrix, recalled that her mother would wash the family's laundry in the yard in front of their shotgun house while singing, "I'm on the battlefield; I'm on the battlefield for my Lord."[44] The black entertainer Tom Fletcher recounted that his first musical experiences included hearing his mother intone spirituals like "Nobody Knows the Trouble I See" on wash day.[45] According to the historian Lawrence Levine, African American worksongs "were characteristically marked by a realistic depiction of the worker's situation."[46] Hence, Hendrix's mother's choice of singing "I'm on the Battlefield" or Fletcher's mother's selection of "Nobody Knows" could represent how they and other laundresses felt about their work: it was a "battle" to complete the burdensome task of washing, and "nobody" understood their plight of trying to support families on the incomes earned through arduous manual labor. Bessie Smith could have heard snippets of church hymns or even the wordless humming from her mother, sister, and other neighboring washerwomen. These melodies offered some emotional escape from the taxing work at hand. While the "classic blues" format that Bessie and her counterparts would later popularize in the early 1920s was only emerging as the twentieth century began, she probably heard her first strains of the precursors to classic blues on the streets of her Blue Goose Hollow neighborhood in the form of washerwomen's worksongs.[47]

As Bessie traveled through the Ninth Street area, she would have encountered other worksongs and street cries from local laborers. One of the most noted figures in Chattanooga lore was Rev. Addison Cole, known as Big Wheel. As a pastor and general laborer, he could be heard on West Ninth Street prior to 1910 in any parade, sounding the cry, "Let Big Wheel roll on it," an adaptation of a worksong he chanted while working at a wheelbarrow-manufacturing company.[48] Although his antics were remembered by local residents as eccentric, his familiar chant would draw people to him, and perhaps they would remain to hear his street evangelizing. Other cries could be heard from street vendors or restaurant operators like Rhoda Jennings, "Aunt Roddy," who called attention to her fish-and-chicken shack with her lively personality and songs.[49] Jennings's eating house stood on West Ninth between Poplar and Pine Streets and was frequented by white and black customers.[50] Bessie Smith would have heard these and other songs that stemmed from labors of working citizens, which provided her with a foundation to build her musical stylings upon.

Another type of music that Bessie was exposed to were the popular tunes played at local rent parties or "chitlin struts." Gwendolyn Smith Bailey, Bessie's grandniece, maintained that rent parties, in which the resident of an apartment might charge ten cents for entry in exchange for an evening of music, dance, and food, were among of the most popular recreational outlets for the low-income black community, aside from the theater shows and saloon entertainment.[51] Thomas Dorsey, a young pianist and composer who later met Bessie Smith and Ma Rainey on the black vaudeville circuit, recalled that a rent party was

> "[a] little get-together, little functions, a few people give to sell their chitlins or sell their beans. . . . Those who had a piano could do that. And they wanted somebody to come and play it anyhow. You could [be the musician for the party], a piano player, there, if you could play any at all, they welcome you. "Come on, play my piano." . . . [Y]ou got all the food you could eat, all the liquor you could drink, and a good-looking woman to fan you."[52]

Dorsey was in his early teens when he played at rent parties in Georgia and was accepted by the slightly older crowd of partygoers because of his piano skills.[53] Although reports of an adolescent Bessie Smith performing at such parties in Chattanooga are not available, she undoubtedly heard the songs that came from the local gatherings in Blue Goose Hollow and the parties held in the attic and storefront residences along East Ninth Street. Smith's recordings would substitute for live piano players at many black house gatherings in the 1920s.[54]

PROFESSIONAL ENTERTAINMENT

While worksongs of the street and popular party tunes attracted Bessie Smith's attention, she would additionally have been mesmerized by the sights and sounds of the minstrel shows, circuses, and vaudeville acts that traveled through the city on a regular basis. The origins of the professional entertainment scene in the city can be traced to traveling revues like the Thayer and Noyes Great U.S. Circus, and mainstream minstrel shows like Bishop's Variety and Cumberland Minstrels had played in Chattanooga prior to the end of the Civil War. By the 1870s, colored minstrel acts like the Original Georgia Minstrels and Barlow, Wilson, Primrose, and West's Minstrels played the City Auditorium in the downtown sector.[55] By the close of the nineteenth and beginning of the twentieth centuries, African American shows came to Chattanooga frequently; the 1893 theater season hosted over nine minstrel and variety shows in the midst of several dozen mainstream and classical performances.[56]

Chattanooga's geographic location and involvement in railway manufacture furthered the city's entertainment industry and contributed to the frequency with which troupes were able to visit the midsized southern city. With two railway (Union and Terminal Stations) and as the terminus of ten railway lines, including the Nashville, Chattanooga, and St. Louis; Chattanooga Southern; Alabama Great Southern; Tennessee, Alabama, and Georgia; Cincinnati, New Orleans, and Texas; and Cincinnati Southern lines, Chattanooga was connected to most of the major cities in the nation.[57] Railway scheduling helped facilitate "layover" performances by musical troupes en route from Atlanta, New Orleans, Memphis, or even New York before moving on to a longer run in another city or state. Donald Clyde Runyan maintains that the city's New Opera Theater worked with rail lines to ensure that traveling acts could play the city "by occasionally timing trains to correspond within the hour of a performance."[58] Railroads further aided the city's entertainment because porters could transmit popular tunes from one city to another.[59] The latest songs from Memphis's Beale Street, Atlanta's Decatur Street, or New Orleans's Storyville district might be heard in a Ninth Street saloon if a porter brought the sheet music or personal knowledge of the new music with him from his layovers in other cities.[60]

The traveling black revues were generally advertised in the *Chattanooga Daily Times,* the African American newspaper *The Blade,* and on billboards throughout downtown, particularly near Union Station on Ninth Street. Traveling revues often sent handbills ahead of their performance to stoke the prospective audience's anticipation. For the 1901 season, George and Hart's Minstrel Extravaganza distributed a brightly colored handbill announcing that it was "En Route," "Grand in Its Own Magnifigence [*sic*]," had a "Stupendous Aggregation of Colored Artists," and possessed the "Strongest Novelty Parade of the Season."[61] Handbills such as these were passed out to several dozen people, and word of mouth would further promote news of the show throughout the rest of the city. By show day, eager crowds flocked to the theaters to see if a show's grandiose claims of magnificence were indeed true.

Once off the train and inside the city limits, African American shows performed in Chattanooga's segregated and exclusively black theaters as well as in outlying parks. The segregated New Opera Theater opened in October 1886 on Sixth and Market Street (renamed the Lyric in the early 1900s) and hosted dramatic, classical, and popular musical-comedy groups.[62] For fifty cents, African Americans could enter the "colored balcony" and view the latest the American stage had to offer.[63] As the 1900s progressed, African American theaters opened in the Ninth Street area. By May 1910, the Ivy opened at 329 East Ninth Street, and the Grand and Palace Theaters soon followed.[64] These black theaters primarily hosted African American variety acts and solo performers. Larger shows that did not fit in the city's theaters, like circuses and tent shows, often put up their mobile stages in public parks.[65]

At fifty cents a ticket, or even less for outdoor performances, Bessie Smith had the opportunity to watch some of the most popular African American entertainers of the era. Primrose and West's Minstrels played Chattanooga theaters several times during the theater season and was one of the few troupes that featured a "gigantic organization of whites and blacks" who "overcrowded houses" every night of their run.[66] The Al G. Fields Minstrels played the New Opera Theater frequently. Managed by Al "the Minstrel King" Fields, they often opened Chattanooga's theater season.[67] Other nationally recognized African American acts that played to full Chattanooga audiences included Pat Chapelle's *A Rabbit's Foot* and Sherman Dudley's *The Smart Set,* musical comedies that featured singers, dancers, and comedians.[68]

While these early minstrel shows typically featured predominantly male casts, Bessie Smith might have been able to see African American female performers take the stage when *Black Patti's Troubadours,* led by the soprano Sissieretta Jones, performed at the New Opera Theater in 1900, and when the restructured *Black Patti Musical Comedy Company* played the Lyric several years later.[69] The *Black Patti* shows were a mix of "coon songs, ragtime ballads, cake walks, and buck dancing blended with operatic melodies."[70] These were some of the few shows produced by women, and for more than twenty years they traveled nationally and internationally in Jamaica, Haiti, Surinam, and Panama, as well as England, Germany, and France.[71] Although much of the musical repertoire was classical, a *Black Patti* performance would have offered Bessie one of her first examples of African American women featured prominently on stage. The example would have been reinforced by other performers such as Ada Overton Walker, a member of *Black Patti Troubadours* and *The Smart Set,* and local performers like Alice Ramsey, Evelyn White, and Maude Browne.[72]

As a low-income black family, the Smiths probably did not have the disposable income to attend many theater performances. Even if her siblings could not afford to take Bessie to many professional performances she still would have witnessed the free large parades that preceded a minstrel or variety show, roaming the city in hopes of increasing the audience for that night's engagement. The actors, singers, and band members would advertise the show by marching up the most prominent street in the city, stopping at a central square, and playing medleys of classical and popular tunes from the show. They would then parade back to the theater, hopefully with hundreds of potential audience members in tow.[73] The trombone player Clyde Bernhardt describes seeing two of these preshow parades in his South Carolina hometown with awe:

> Colored people were all lined up along the curb. . . . [S]uddenly, from around the corner marched these colored men. Oh, they walked so tall and stiff. Bright buttons down the front of their uniforms, red caps on their heads with a round button right in front. As they came closer I saw them playing flashy, shiny instruments that bounced the bright sunshine right in my eyes. [H]orns all raised up high, blasting so very loud. . . . I never seen anything like this. The excitement was so great—the shining instruments, the music, real soldiers—I almost pulled my father's finger off asking fool questions.
>
> [A few months later.] It was heaven all over again, only better. The street parade was bigger, longer, and flashier. . . . In the last wagon I saw black-face comedians in huge spotted bow-ties and collars, wearing long coats and laughing like chickens. Playing banjos, buckdancing, making funny faces, just at me I thought.[74]

Bernhardt's exposure to the music and excitement of the parade spurred him to become a musician, and he later traveled on the same vaudeville

Black Patti ad. *Chatta-nooga Times*, February 1912.

Typical minstrel parade in theater ad from *Indianapolis Freeman*, 1909.

circuit as Bessie Smith and her musical contemporaries. Comparably, the spectacle of the Primrose and West Minstrels' parades or even the elaborate holiday parades staged for the May Festival, the Fourth of July, and Labor Day would have caught Bessie's attention as she traveled along Ninth Street. These spectacles would have offered her a glimpse of what the entertainment profession could be like and the favorable response she might receive from a welcoming crowd.[75]

Bessie Smith on Her Street Stage

With a variety of musical genres in her consciousness, a young Bessie decided to turn the streets that had been her playground into her stage, and between the ages of ten and twelve she began performing on the downtown avenues of Chattanooga.[76] To Bessie, entertaining would have appeared to be a far less strenuous alternative to helping her elder sister Viola with laundry work, and it brought some necessary supplemental income into the home. Through song and dance Bessie could escape the cast-iron wash pot, her crowded shotgun house, and a life of desolation in Blue Goose Hollow.

Bessie's interest in performing the music she had heard from others in the streets was prompted in part by her siblings' involvement in musical entertainment. Her brother Andrew, seventeen years her senior, had rudimentary skills on the guitar and was also a competent piano player.[77] Thus, Bessie would have been exposed to instrumental music on guitar in her home; Andrew became her chaperone and accompanist for her street-corner concerts.[78] Perhaps the sibling who had the greatest influence on Bessie's early street career was her brother Clarence. Seven years her senior, Clarence was also enthralled with popular black entertainment and seized the opportunity to leave Chattanooga for brief periods by joining a regional minstrel troupe in 1904 as a comedian.[79] Known for his ability to get "on stage and just tell lies [amusing stories]," Clarence's escape from a life of manual labor into the regional entertainment scene undoubtedly influenced young Bessie's interest in entertainment.[80] After she had witnessed Clarence's modest success, she took to the stages of the public street.

As a young preadolescent girl, it was not safe for Bessie to traverse Chattanooga's streets alone, so she and Andrew frequented downtown street corners in front of the shops, businesses, and eating houses that drew in the largest numbers of patrons. In 1902, there were nine saloons and eight eating houses between the 100 and 700 blocks of East Ninth Street alone.[81] Other key businesses like barbershops, tailors, grocery shops, and the City Auditorium, as well as private residences, were scattered among the saloons and eateries of Ninth Street—crowds would likely be present during the day.[82] Bessie and Andrew had several corners on which to set up their mobile show.

Bessie's show typically consisted of her dancing and singing popular tunes while Andrew played guitar. She placed something to receive money on the ground before her and took in whatever spare coins passersby threw her way. Yet street performing was not as simple as this basic description. The scholar Sally Harrison-Pepper contends that the success of a street performer is "partly measured by the ability to transform city 'space' into theater 'place'" and that the "noise surrounding the performance space, the proximity of other performers, the social as well as the atmospheric climates . . . are part of the street performer's daily, even minute to minute negotiations with a fluid and vital urban environment."[83] Bessie and Andrew had to make quick decisions about where to perform and what type of material would attract the most onlookers, while being mindful of other street performers around them. Businesses often relocated and others opened in their wake, which led Bessie and Andrew to move their act around accordingly.[84] Occasionally, when the Smiths preferred a more familiar and perhaps more receptive audience, Bessie and Andrew set up their traveling act in front of the White Elephant Saloon on the corner of Thirteenth and Elm, a few blocks from their Blue Goose Hollow neighborhood.[85] Fortunately, Bessie had an entertaining style that kept a crowd interested wherever she performed. One of Andrew's friends, Will Johnson, recounted that Bessie would often sing "Bill Bailey, Won't You Please Come Home," and while Johnson wasn't "impressed with her voice" in those early days, he recalled that "she sure knew how to shake money loose from a pocket."[86]

A mobile stage also mandated that Bessie negotiate "street politics," the unwritten rules of acceptable behavior in the public arena, as well as the task of creating a persona that appealed to the public. When Bessie and Andrew traveled the streets of Chattanooga in the 1900s, they entered an urban space that was regulated by racial, gender, and class conventions. The street was not an open forum where people could do whatever they wished but rather the "highly surveyed and scripted public arena of everyday life."[87] From the moment Bessie began her song and dance, she was on display as an African American female adolescent, an identity that may have complicated how the audience understood and received her performance. The African American theater scholar Harry Elam argues that when a black performer enters the stage, he or she "negotiates the spaces . . . between racial definitions and stereotypes."[88] Bessie was not free to traverse any street in downtown Chattanooga without race and gender affecting where and how she established her street stage. Like other urban southern areas, Chattanooga was organized by legal and social racial segregation, and even prior to the creation of "colored" and "white" racial markers, citizens were cognizant of a sense of "place" and the venues that serviced the needs of white customers and refused entrance to African Americans. Women and members of the working class were likewise well aware of establishments in which they could enter, how they should dress and speak, and how they should interact with others to gain social acceptance. Male saloon patrons might not have viewed a woman who publicly consumed alcohol and socialized inside the walls of the saloon as virtuous, and likewise a factory worker in work attire most likely would not have been served in an elite downtown restaurant. The sidewalks of Ninth Street were trafficked by a diverse multitude of people, but Bessie and Andrew would have had to note how the racial landscape shifted on Ninth from West to East and from a predominantly white to a predominantly black population. The same rules of racial deference in the presence of whites that Bessie learned as she traveled the streets to school would have been reemphasized in finding a suitable environment for her mobile show. Her song and dance might have been a welcome addition to the environment surrounding the White Elephant Saloon but perhaps not accepted on the sidewalks alongside the white-patronized Read Hotel. Bessie may have avoided being seen as a girl of "loose morals" and fended off unwanted sexual advances by performing with her elder brother, but street performing still was not the occupation of a "lady." Just how conscious Bessie or Andrew were of the gendered and racial responses of the street audience cannot be fully determined; yet we can identify the skills she had to acquire to become a successful street performer. As the embodiment of an entertainer, or one whose express goal was to earn income through antics that pleased the public, Bessie would have quickly learned that "the more pleasure is received by the public, the more money is made."[89] Hence, Bessie had to learn how to adopt a dance and song style that passersby would pay to watch and that did not affront their sensibilities about public street behavior.

The songs that Bessie performed as an amateur street entertainer in the early 1900s were not the "classic blues" she would become famous for in the 1920s, for the classic blues did not yet exist. She often performed a composite of popular songs, minstrel tunes, worksongs, and other genres that Andrew could play on the guitar. Popular songs of this pre-1910 period included "Rufus, Rastus Johnson Brown," "Nobody," "Under the Bamboo Tree," "All Coons Look Alike to Me," and "Oh, Didn't He Ramble."[90] Bessie and Andrew aided in the transmission of new popular music by performing highlights from the traveling shows that came into town, perhaps even before the sheet music or piano roll was available. Some of her typical fare is evidenced in the refrain to "Bill Bailey," written in 1902:

> Won't you come home, Bill Bailey,
> Won't you come home?
> She moans the whole day long.
> I'll do the cookin', darling,
> I'll pay the rent,
> I know I've done you wrong.
> 'Member that rainy eve that
> I threw you out
> With nothing but a fine tooth comb,
> I know I'm to blame
> Well ain't that a shame.
> Bill Bailey won't you please come home.[91]

"Bill Bailey" is not reminiscent of the blues format Bessie would sing in her many recordings, for it does not follow an AAB or AAA structure, but the song's themes are similar to those of more traditional blues. The noted music historian Daphne Duval Harrison maintains that the "essence of blues poetry, whether sung by women or men, is life itself—its aches, pains, grievances, pleasures, and brief moments of glory."[92] Bessie did address, albeit superficially, the pain of lost relationships in songs like "Bill Bailey" and perhaps touched on other blues themes in her early street fare while helping to make the latest songs in Chattanooga that much more popular.

A fundamental reason why Bessie performed blues-inflected but perhaps not traditional blues pieces in her street concerts was that classic blues were only coming into being in southern urban centers at the onset of the twentieth century. The "classic blues" that featured an AAB format, incorporated works-songs and field hollers, and focused on themes of love, sex, poverty, personal despair, and labor could be heard in rural areas of the South, particularly the Mississippi Delta and Texas, perhaps as early as the 1890s.[93] Nonetheless, the exact location and moment that blues was "created" is difficult to discern; as the musicologist Jeff Titon accurately maintains, "polygenesis is a likely possibility" when exploring the origins of blues music.[94] For example, Ma Rainey recalled hearing a young woman in 1902 at a Missouri tent show sing of how "her man" left her; she claimed that this was the first time she heard what would be later defined as the blues.[95] As the blues composer W. C. Handy waited at a train station in Tutwiler, Mississippi, in 1903, he witnessed "a lean, loose jointed Negro" who played the guitar as he sang "goin' where the Southern cross the Dog." This was the moment that Handy first heard "what we now call blues."[96] Hence, blues music did exist during Bessie's street performing years, and arguably she heard variations of it from other performers traveling through the city. The music historian Charles Wolfe remarks that at the onset of the twentieth century a "distinct musical climate was developing in Chattanooga, which because of its location, was even more of a crossroads for different musical styles, attracting not only artists from Tennessee but also musicians from north Georgia, Alabama, and Mississippi."[97] Blues music was a part of Bessie's musical foundation that she would expand upon as her own musical style evolved in her vaudeville years.

Bessie's musical experiences were also enhanced by the reality that she was not the only performer trained in Chattanooga; she was part of a tradition of local youth who honed their craft in the city before rising to a professional stage. Chattanooga's African American community produced musical performers as early as the 1860s. Three of the original members of the Fisk Jubilee Singers—Benjamin Holmes, Issac Dickerson, and Hinton D. Alexander—learned basic music skills in Chattanooga before refining them at Fisk.[98] Alexander resettled in Chattanooga after his Jubilee tours, and his musical success was praised in local African American history.[99] In the twentieth century, Chattanooga produced musical entertainers who later became Smith's contemporaries in blues and jazz music. Lovie Austin (neé Cora Calhoun), one of the few female jazz pianists on the black vaudeville circuit, was born in 1887 in Chattanooga and learned piano basics at home before training formally at Roger Williams University and Knoxville College.[100] Austin eventually became a fundamental part of the classic blues legacy as a composer of several blues hits, including Bessie Smith's first successful recording, "Downhearted Blues," which Austin arranged and cowrote with the blues vocalist Alberta Hunter in the early 1920s.[101] Additionally, Valaida Snow, one of the rare African American female trumpeters of the era, was born into a musical family in Chattanooga in 1900 and eventually went on to perform in Noble Sissle and Eubie Blake's *Chocolate Dandies* in 1924.[102] Snow's musical prowess also led her to travel through London, France, and Scandinavia in various jazz ensembles.[103]

What distinguishes Bessie from many of her Chattanooga predecessors and counterparts is that her essential training came from her performances on the street. Bessie's sound was not "refined" at a music conservatory, and it is probable that she never learned how to read or write music. In contrast, music educators formally trained all the other local performers thus far discussed once they reached their late adolescent years. The only other notable musician to rise to national prominence from his beginnings as a Chattanooga street performer was the classical tenor Roland Hayes. Prior to his formal training at Fisk University and in Boston, Hayes performed popular songs with his amateur Silver Toned Quartet on the "curbstones" and "railway stations" of Chattanooga.[104] Although formally trained in a different genre than Bessie, Hayes performed on Ninth Street's corners in the same years (1902–3) that she and Andrew began their mobile shows, and Hayes also pulled his "corner repertoire" from minstrel and variety performances.[105] Although information regarding other Chattanooga street performers who became professional entertainers is yet undiscovered, street-performing children were not a rarity in black communities.[106] Other female blues singers, such as Ethel Waters, began their early careers by street singing. When asked about her childhood performances, Waters recounted that at age twelve she started "right in jiggin', shimmyin', singin' any kind of songs I liked and everything like that" in the streets of Chester, Pennsylvania.[107]

Women's Spaces on the Big Nine

Although Bessie was not the only young woman to perform in the streets, the image of a young girl making her livelihood by dancing and singing for spare change is intriguing. What made it permissible for her to enter the streets of the 1900s, a stereotypically male domain? If, as the scholar Patricia Hill Collins argues, "male space included the streets, barbershops, and pool halls: female arenas consisted of households and churches," then where does Bessie, the Chattanooga street performer and eventually the nationally celebrated entertainer, belong?[108] The answers to these questions can be attributed in part to the increase in industrialization, the subsequent surge in African American migration to the urban environment in the 1880s and 1890s, and the evolving roles for women in public society. The growth of manufacturing industries in the urban South had attracted thousands of African Americans eager to leave the poverty and racial violence of the rural South. Just as rapid migration changed the racial landscape of Chattanooga by raising the black population to over 40 percent of the city's total residents, so too did migration alter the gender landscape of the city. There was not only an increase in the numbers of African American women among the black men in the city but a rise in the placement of women in the public environment—in retail and professional occupations.

The influx of migrants necessitated that more service industries began to cater to the migrants and paved the way for women to be employed in several of these service occupations. Migrants who relocated to the city needed shelter, food, and other provisions, and the segregated housing and commercial establishments did not suffice as the black community numbered over thirteen thousand by 1900 and nearly eighteen thousand by 1910.[109] Hence, many migrants who had arrived with the first surge of migration in the 1880s created entrepreneurial opportunities for themselves by saving wages from manufacturing or domestic labor jobs and opening their own barbershops, dry-goods stores, tailor shops, and other retail institutions.[110] African American women were a vital part of this population of small-businesses operators. Although many female migrants transferred directly from share-cropping in rural areas to domestic service in the urban arena, as the elder women in Bessie's family had, a select few accumulated a little capital from their domestic jobs and opened dressmaking shops, boarding homes, and eating establishments.

As the 1900s progressed, African American women in Chattanooga became increasingly visible as "petty entrepreneurs," according the historian Sarah Deutsch in her discussion of women in Boston.[111] Many of these petty entrepreneurs based their businesses in the Ninth Street area to attract as many customers and patrons as possible. Women such as Celia Good, a former slave, opened a boarding house at 221 West Ninth Street and was said by the local community "to be as wealthy as any colored citizen in the city."[112] Other women, such as Mrs. N. Morton and Rhoda Jennings, successfully operated grocery stores and eating houses on other blocks of the Ninth Street area.[113]

The overall increase of the black female presence on Ninth Street is evident in the compared demographics of Ninth Street in 1892, the year of Bessie's birth; in 1902, the year Smith likely considered entertaining in public; and in 1908, one of the last years of her street performances. In 1892, five female heads of household resided on East Ninth, while another four women operated eating houses, and an additional two ran dressmaking shops.[114] A decade later, a total of fifteen women headed households on East Ninth, yet only two operated eating houses.[115] By 1908, over thirty women headed households in the area, while five women operated eating houses, three managed boarding houses, two ran dressmaking and pressing shops, and two ran a hairdressing shop and a grocery store.[116] Although these numbers are not overwhelmingly large (there were only forty black women working and residing on East Ninth out of a total of 155 black residences and shops in 1908), they attest to the reality that the Ninth Street area was not solely a male space. In whatever way possible, as owners, managers, and customers, African American women converged on Ninth Street, and their presence made it more permissible for the young Bessie Smith to take her place among them.

The inclusion of black women in the residential and commercial life of Ninth Street was part of a larger evolution of American women's political, social, and economic roles in the late nineteenth and early twentieth centuries. Between the 1880s and the 1920s, American society gave rise to various articulations of the "New Woman"—a woman who strove for suffrage, educational advancement, employment opportunities, and a loosening of the rigid gender roles that kept women as the subordinates of men.[117] During this same period, African American women, many of whom were only a few generations removed from slavery, shared the same New Woman concerns of their white counterparts. These black female activists formed grassroots political and social organizations that evolved into a national black women's-club movement and the development of the National Association of Club Women in 1895.[118] With the dual identities of being African American and female, black club women targeted the stereotypes of black women as immoral and the effects of poverty, racial discrimination, and the continuing plight of racial violence in addition to the gender-inequity concerns of white middle-class activists. The actions of those club women thrust African American women, particularly those of the middle class, into public life as teachers, lecturers, and political activists. This activism at the onset of the twentieth century coincided with their new roles as entrepreneurs and consumers in the streets of black commercial districts like Ninth Street. As black women of the 1900s "slowly but surely made their way to the heights [of American society], wherever they could be scaled," conditions that created public performing opportunities for Bessie gradually arose.[119]

Another essential reason that Bessie was able to succeed in a predominantly male realm can be found in the gender shifts that occurred in the American entertainment industry near the close of the nineteenth century. Although some black performers ascended to the professional stage prior to emancipation, the roles for black women performers were severely restricted. The genres of sacred or classical music were deemed respectable for women to participate in, but rarely were women in the mid-nineteenth century permitted to perform in minstrel or variety shows.[120] Classically trained African American women such as Marie Selika Williams or Nellie Brown Mitchell could reach prominence and be praised as "prima donnas" on the concert stage, but performance opportunities for black women elsewhere were not often available.[121] Female dramatic and musical parts on the variety stage were generally played by men who performed their roles in falsetto voices.[122] Furthermore, all the instrumentalists who accompanied the shows were male, as were the featured "bawdy" comedians. Prior to the late nineteenth century, working-class men dominated the audiences of musical theater, and many men feared that theater material would injure the delicate consciousness of women.[123] In Chattanooga, some shows were criticized for being "so tainted with an immoral, irreligious conception of wit . . . that the audience had felt its refinement insulted and its sensibilities shocked to a sense of disgust."[124]

The gender shift in entertainment coincided with changes in labor practices more broadly. When wages increased and work hours decreased in the post–Civil War period, working-class Americans were able to participate more actively in the growing commercial market of leisure activities, including attending theater, music, and circus performances as well as sports functions.[125] With the close of the nineteenth century, working women secured some autonomy over their own finances and had the disposable income to spend on a theater ticket, an occurrence that coincided with more women becoming petty entrepreneurs. Realizing that there was a market for a female audience, show producers changed the nature of the shows themselves.[126] In 1900, African American shows like Mahara's Big Carnival Minstrels began to advertise themselves as "strictly an entertainment for *ladies* and *children,* replete with choice music and melody, strong singing features, magnificent choruses—not marred by loud mouthed comedians." This advertisement informed potential audiences that the performance would be an acceptable place for women and youth.[127] Black women entered the audience en masse a few years after they joined the choruses and primary casts of major theater shows. In 1890, Sam Jack's *Creole Show* bridged the gap between minstrelsy and black musical theater in its material and featured African American women in the chorus and in the typical lead minstrel role of the interlocutor.[128] By the turn of the twentieth century, theater troupes like Georgia-Up-to-Date Minstrels ran recruitment advertisements that read "Wanted: colored performers, comedians, singers, dancers, musicians, *ladies* and gentlemen."[129] As the shows of the twentieth century were no longer prohibited to women, Bessie was able to witness minstrel and variety performances that could have influenced her own decision to become an entertainer.

Objections to Popular African American Entertainment

Although the vibrant amateur and professional African American entertainment community opened its doors to include young black women in the

1900s, Bessie's choice of becoming a street performer and later a professional vocalist was not praised by all members of the Chattanooga African American community. While Bessie and her entertaining counterparts often found receptive audiences among the crowds of West Thirteenth or Ninth Streets, as evidenced by her continued performing efforts and modest profit, the recreational world patronized by low-income African Americans—the storefront theater, rent party, tent show, or saloon—was not seen as respectable by elite society at large. As Bessie pursued dancing and singing on the street corners of East Ninth, she would have encountered many people, especially practicing Christians and culturally conservative African Americans, who did not reward her with spare change but looked upon her with disdain.

Although African American Christians were far from a monolithic unit and were divided by denominational beliefs, class status, and regional differences, to many black Christian believers, singing, dancing, acting, and drinking—all actions Bessie either participated in or witnessed as she sang in front of institutions like the White Elephant Saloon—were not seen as acceptable and wholesome. Chattanooga's vibrant black churches had been fundamental to the African American community since the postemancipation era, and their influence extended beyond the Sunday worship service. In the 1900s, the strong influence of Baptists and Methodists in the realm of African American social activities is clearly evidenced by the news reports on Chattanooga that appeared in the national African American press. In the African American–produced *Indianapolis Freeman,* a newspaper noted for its inclusion of black entertainment news, black Chattanoogans generally announced news of Rev. G. W. Ward, who "preached an able sermon to the pleasure of a large congregation," praised the candidates for baptism at the Mount Parnam Baptist church, or noted the installation of a new pastor at Mount Calvary Baptist church.[130] Rarely, if ever, did the "Chattanooga Items" column mention any social or recreational activity that did not involve the local churches or benevolent institutions; the arrival of the latest black musical show simply did not warrant coverage as Chattanooga news. This exclusion of popular recreational entertainment stemmed from the bans that many denominations of the Christian church placed on unacceptable recreation.

Although Bessie may have been exposed to the power of music as a child in the African American church, that same institution also contended that only certain genres of music were "proper" for Christian listening. The Methodist Episcopal church only lifted their decree prohibiting members from "attending theaters, dances, races, circuses, or taking part in other forms of amusement" in 1924, and other Christian sects, including Baptists, Methodists, and Seventh Day Adventists, generally shared the same bans on any "sinful" activities that would compromise a member's focus on God.[131] For many Christians who believed in the inherently "sinful and lost condition of man" and contended that the "church must keep in its place as a spiritual institution, majoring in those things that are to redeem the world from sin," banning song and dance that might lead people to focus on the temporary body rather than the immortal soul was a righteous act.[132] These bans on popular amusement severely restricted the behavior of church members, particularly young women who, as "mothers in training," were supposed to be dedicated to the "the preservation of health and morals, through proper habits."[133] For the blues singer Lillie May "Big Mama" Glover, the daughter of a Pentecostal minister, singing popular music was "the worst thing in the world" to her family; "they [would have] liked to [have] killed" her once she became a young amateur performer and left the church.[134] The classical vocalist Roland Hayes remarked that once he was baptized and accepted by Chattanooga's New Monumental Baptist church, his "first act of renunciation was to give up buck and wing dancing" and to "refrain from street dancing and other low forms of minstrelsy."[135] Thus, as the daughter of a lay Baptist minister, Bessie fought against all the proscriptive Christian teachings she learned as a youth; crooning "Won't You Come Home, Bill Bailey," in front of alcohol-filled and crime-infested saloons for money was a far cry from singing for a Sunday morning service. As a young female street performer, Bessie would serve as an example to many practicing Christians of how wayward a child could become if she was not steeped in Christian discipline and morality.

Much of the black popular recreational landscape that Bessie aspired to become a part of was not only opposed for its sinful nature but was also viewed by conservative and upper-class African Americans as detrimental to the progress of the race as a whole. Since emancipation, African Americans had been concerned with elevating their political, economic, and social status in American society, and this desire manifested itself in the creation of a variety of movements and organizations dedicated to "racial uplift." According to the historian Kevin Gaines, "uplift . . . represented the struggle for a positive black identity in a deeply racist society, turning the pejorative designation of race into a source of dignity and self-affirmation through an ideology of class differentiation, self-help, and interdependence."[136] Yet the move for a "positive black identity" often prompted elite and conservative African Americans to scorn any activity that did not highlight blacks as honorable, dignified, and proper people, and the recreational activities of poorer blacks often fell into this category of scorn.

The popular musical landscape in which Bessie sang was criticized primarily because of where it was located and what institutions surrounded it. Crime was rampant in the Ninth Street area. As late as the 1890s, the city maintained a reputation as a "rough and ready place" where "saloons and all-night barrel houses" attracted visitors, African American and white alike.[137] Visitors could get off the train for a layover, be involved in a saloon brawl, and get back on the next train and escape repercussions. The eating houses, small theaters, and saloons that Bessie performed in front of were frequently plagued by arguments, drunkenness, and sometimes life-threatening violence. Saloons known by names like the Owl or the Shamrock were so full of life that they often made the annual police reports as the central sites of "general melee."[138] The variety or vaudeville theater could also attract a raucous crowd, and in some southern theaters, patrons were known to throw "sticks, bricks, spitballs, cigar butts, and peach pits" during a performance.[139] Prostitution houses lay near the outskirts of many of the recreational establishments on Ninth, particularly near Florence and Helen Streets, marked by "dark . . . stairways that led from the pavement to regions even darker . . . where human beings trafficked and traded with other human beings—sometimes colored and sometimes not."[140]

The crime, violence, and vice that surrounded black recreational establishments were all reasons that conservative African Americans looked upon these locations with distaste and why uplift advocates such as Fannie Barrier Williams believed, "The fact is that the colored race is not yet sufficiently aroused to its own social perils. The evils that menace the integrity of the home, the small vices that are too often mistaken for legitimate pleasures, give us too little concern."[141] As a prominent figure in the national black women's-club movement, Williams strongly denounced "small vices," which included the storefront theater or saloon environment, because of her larger belief that "there will never be an unchallenged vote, a respected political power, or an unquestioned claim to position of influence and importance, until the present stigma [of immorality and dishonor] is removed from the home and the women of its [colored] race."[142] Williams echoed the views of many African American reformers of the 1890s and 1900s who, as W. E. B. DuBois observed, "depreciated, belittled, and sneered at means of recreation" for African American youth "as time wasted and energy misspent."[143]

African American reformers' criticism of black amusement is understandable; they lived in an era in which much of white America denigrated the morality, intelligence, character, and basic humanity of African Americans. The stereotype that all black women, particularly those of the lower classes, were overbearing, sexually promiscuous, immoral, and lazy permeated much of American society. So prevalent were these stereotypes that the belief that there was no such "creation as a *virtuous* black woman" made its way into the mainstream white press.[144] It was imperative for uplift advocates to challenge the negative views of black people and attempt to foster the integrity of African American homes and womanhood. Many uplift advocates believed that if African Americans conformed to middle-class white values of propriety and respectability, they could overcome racial disparities and the shameful legacy of slavery. Yet, while uplift advocates and club women paved the way for black women to more fully occupy the public arena through political, social, and economic activism, their views of what constituted "respect," "honor," or "integrity" distanced many of these activists from the very people they hoped to "uplift."[145] As a young female street performer who sang popular black music, Bessie would have been exactly the type of young woman whom elite African Americans would have wanted to transform rather than celebrate for her musical creativity. Although many African Americans "wanted their men and women on the stage," they wanted them presented "in a decent and honorable way," and elite and conservative blacks held that bawdy ragtime- and blues-inflected tunes were neither decent nor honorable.[146]

African American Recreation as Alternative Resistance

In spite of the criticism of the popular black recreational environment from religious and uplift organizations, the storefront theaters, saloons, tent shows, and house parties served as a significant and distinct space for many poorer African Americans. In these spaces, impoverished African Americans could gather beyond the gaze of oppressive white society and the social confines of the "better class of negroes" to dance, listen to music, drink, and socialize.[147] Yet these were also locations where low-income African Americans carried out acts of economic, political, and social resistance against racial oppression and the rise of Jim Crow segregation.

African Americans had used recreational activities as forms of resistance as early as the colonial period. On the Middle Passage voyages that thousands of Africans were forced to make, imprisoned Africans used song and dance, often involuntarily to satisfy the whims of their captors, but also to stave off the utter depression that accompanied being shackled, kidnapped, and forced into slavery.[148] In Chattanooga and elsewhere in the South, enslaved Africans used fiddling to break up the monotony of corn shucking and songs of revival to spirit away from daily life, if only for a moment. Later, the clamor of brass bands alerted all that African Americans had joined the Union army and were agents in the destruction of slavery. In the post-Reconstruction South, blues, ragtime, and other black popular music replaced fiddling for the masters and the corn-shucking dances.

Black recreational environments are examples of economic resistance: vocalists, musicians, dancers, and the African American venue owners that showcased these entertainers were able to earn income outside of the demanding and often unjust manual- and domestic-labor arena. By becoming a street performer, Bessie Smith escaped much of the laundry work that her sister Viola was bound to perform to care for the family. Bessie and Andrew's meager earnings from their street concerts supplemented the family income and perhaps lessened Viola's burdens by allowing her to service fewer customers.[149] Similarly, Roland Hayes's street performances at Chattanooga's Union Station supplemented his income from his earnings at the Price and Evans Sashweight Factory and allowed him to send his younger brother, Robert, to public school. In turn, once Robert finished grammar school, Roland was allowed to attend school, bolstered by the savings from his supplemental entertaining job.[150]

The recreational environment also brought in income for the Chattanooga community as a whole, much like it did in other cities with a sizable African American entertainment culture such as Memphis, New Orleans, or Atlanta. The economic importance of the recreational environment was highlighted in an 1899 study on black businesses:

> The saloon, among these people, even more than among the Irish and other city groups, is a distinct social centre. In the country towns of the black belt, the field hands gather there to gossip, loaf, and joke. In the cities, a crowd of jolly fellows can be met there and in adjacent pool rooms. Consequently, the business has attracted Negroes with capital in spite of the fact that the Negro church distinctly frowns on the vocation, which means some social ostracism for the liquor dealer. Next to the saloons in importance come the traveling vaudeville shows. None of these are reported here, for having no permanent headquarters they are difficult to reach. . . . Most of them are compelled to have white managers in order to get entree into the theaters, but they are largely under Negro control and represent a considerable investment of Negro capital.[151]

Despite opposition from local churches, saloons, pool rooms, and small vaudeville theaters brought in revenue to black businesses in Chattanooga at a time when white-owned banks would not lend money to African American entrepreneurs.[152] John Lovell, the first African American saloon owner in Chattanooga, had amassed $6,500 in property by the late nineteenth century, property purchased with the capital he earned in the leisure business.[153] With his earnings, Lovell supported other African American businesses in the city, which aided in the development of the self-sufficient black community necessary with the advent of strict racial segregation. Lovell opened his saloon in the 1870s, and by 1902 there were ten African American–managed saloons in the city, including six in the Ninth Street area.[154]

The popular recreational environment also provided an arena for African Americans to plan small acts of political resistance against the rise of racial oppression in the city. The historian Robin D. G. Kelley maintains that black social spaces gave "Africans Americans a place to hide, a place to plan," and in select instances in southern cities this is exactly what occurred.[155] Admittedly, African Americans did not plan grand acts of revolution against white supremacy in between dancing to blues songs or shooting pool. Nonetheless, social spaces allowed people to gather together and discuss the most pressing issues of the day in private. W. C. Handy contended that on his travels as a minstrel-troupe bandleader in Mississippi, he would covertly sell copies of the *Chicago Defender, Indianapolis Freeman,* and *Voice of the Negro*, primary black periodicals of the era. Thus allowing African Americans to learn what their counterparts in other cities where doing was a subtle form of resistance because black newspapers "were looked upon with strong disfavor by certain local powers" in Mississippi.[156] Yet, as an entertainer, Handy was never suspected of such a political act.

Comparably, in Chattanooga, when Henry M. Turner and the International Emigration and Commercial Association of America met in 1902, the discussions of whether to migrate from the country would have extended from the convention meeting place into the city's social spaces, where African Americans could debate openly and frankly about their fate in the United States.[157] As racial violence escalated to horrifying heights with the lynching of the Chattanooga resident Ed Johnson, who was accused and convicted of raping a white woman in 1906, black saloons and eating houses became the locations where low-income African Americans planned a response. Many of the black churches had become the site where African Americans who feared for the overall safety of the black community vowed to search out the "vicious and degraded negro" that Ed Johnson was purported to be.[158] Thus, when many of the black factory laborers in the city went on strike the day after the lynching, on March 20, 1906, to demonstrate their outrage at the murder, the strike was undoubtedly planned in the social spaces of the city rather than at a church mass meeting.[159] So great was the fear of violent African Americans retaliation that the city's mayor "ordered all saloons frequented by black people to be closed" in the days following the lynching, while no restrictions were placed on similar white establishments.[160] Even the Chattanooga community at large recognized the potential power of black social spaces for fomenting political resistance.

One of the most significant functions of black social spaces was the opportunity they provided African Americans for spiritual renewal. At tent shows, saloon theaters, or house parties, blacks laughed, danced, sang, shed their communal worries, and bolstered themselves for the next workday. This ability for African Americans to have leisure time with each other is an example of covert resistance against a society that viewed black men and women primarily as laborers. At the house parties, women and men might have engaged in dances that were overtly sexual, such as the Slow Drag, the Eagle Rock, and the Buzzard Lope, all of which involved close physical contact between partners.[161] In dancing, African Americans reclaimed their bodies as their own, outside the tannery or a white employer's kitchen.[162] The author Ralph Ellison describes the function of blues music and its surrounding environment as "an impulse to keep the painful details and episodes of a brutal experience alive in one's aching conscience and to ultimately transcend it through near tragic, near comic lyricism."[163] In many of the recreational environments along Ninth Street, African American patrons attempted to "transcend" the constant pain of poverty, racism, and oppression by dancing it away, or, as the author Albert Murray refers to it, "stomping on the blues."[164]

Laboring African Americans viewed Ninth Street as a social center, a place to meet not only members of the local black community but surrounding black communities as well. The seamstress Tena Suggs recalled that she would leave her home on Lookout Mountain to attend vaudeville shows at the segregated Bijou Theater in downtown Chattanooga.[165] The city's saloons, theaters, and house parties attracted African Americans from Birmingham and Atlanta and afforded Chattanooga blacks the opportunity to congregate with other southern African Americans, undoubtedly forming lasting bonds before the work week forced them back to their respective jobs.[166] Ultimately, for many African Americans in Chattanooga, black social spaces were among the few veiled environments in which they could be truly human, and this renewal of their humanity occurred on the Big Nine, the home of Bessie Smith's first performances and "the sweetest street in the world."[167]

By the first decade of the twentieth century, Bessie Smith had started on her path to the world of professional African American entertainment. On

Chattanooga's social center of Ninth Street, Bessie encountered the music of laboring local residents combined with the tunes of minstrel and vaudeville shows. With her brother, she reformulated them into her own street-corner repertoire. As she delved into blues culture, she entered an arena that was only beginning to be occupied by African American women and that was still heavily criticized by many as sinful and uncivil. Yet, if there was any tragic element in Bessie's street performances, it was not that they challenged Christian virtues or black middle-class uplift strivings but that poverty was an impetus that forced the young adolescent Bessie into the streets to contribute to her family's income. Bessie entertained Ninth Street patrons despite the motivations for and criticisms of her street performances, and as the decade came to a close she would soon leave the emerging blues culture of Chattanooga to join African American entertainers on the professional stage. By the second decade of the twentieth century, an empress would be born in vaudeville.

AN EMPRESS IN VAUDEVILLE
BESSIE SMITH ON THE THEATER CIRCUIT

> Down in Atlanta, GA, under the viaduct every day
> Drinkin' corn and hollerin hooray, pianos playin' till
> the break of day.
> But as I turned my head I loudly said,
> Preach them blues, sing them blues, they certainly
> sound good to me,
> Moan them blues, holler them blues, let me convert
> your soul,
> Sing 'em, sing 'em, sing them blues, let me convert
> your soul.
>
> —BESSIE SMITH, "Preachin' the Blues"

The African American entertainment industry of the early twentieth century flourished with minstrel shows, vaudeville performances, and musical comedies. Inspired by performances in their small-town theaters, festivals, and carnivals, hundreds of young African Americans dreamed of joining the chorus of the Mahara Minstrels or the cast of a show like Bert Williams and George Walker's *Policy Players*.[1] Many black youth satisfied their desire to perform by joining their church choir or the local brass band ensemble, and they delighted audiences of relatives, friends, and neighbors. Yet other, perhaps more ambitious aspiring entertainers responded to handbills and advertisements in black newspapers that read:

WANTED
One Hundred Musicians
to Play Brass. For the New
GEORGE'S
NEGRO MINSTRELS
Also fifty Ladies, Singers, Dancers, and Drummers
Ladies' drum corps.[2]

A select few of those who responded to the advertisements earned positions as musicians, actors, vocalists, and dancers on a national level. These African American performers crisscrossed the nation and entertained audiences in large urban theaters and rural tent shows. They traveled by railway, car, and ship to entertain nobility in London, sharecroppers in Mississippi, and general laborers in Washington, D.C.[3] Entertainers endured the criticism of many morally conservative African Americans, as well as the racism and sexism inherent within the American entertainment industry, in their pursuit of a measure of fame and fortune.

By 1909, young Bessie Smith had joined this ensemble of performers and begun to refine her craft in the black theaters of the South, Midwest, and East Coast. Before she "preached them blues" to millions of Americans in her popular phonograph records in the 1920s, Smith enchanted thousands of African Americans in the regional theaters and tent shows of the black vaudeville circuit and completed the evolution from a Chattanooga street performer to a headlining star. Yet as Bessie Smith evolved into the "Empress of the Blues," she did not abandon her connections to the African American Chattanooga community.

The Initial Years on the Vaudeville Circuit

Bessie Smith was primarily an amateur performer until late 1908 or early 1909. She continued to refine her performing skills in her street-corner concerts with her brother Andrew until she had the opportunity to take her talent to a larger stage. Great confusion surrounds Bessie's early prerecording years, and there are several legends about her entrance into professional entertainment. Previous Smith biographers have posited that lauded blues singer Gertrude "Ma" Rainey kidnapped Bessie off the Chattanooga streets and made her a success, or that Bessie won a local talent contest and then rose to fame, or that she auditioned for the Moses Stokes Revue in 1912 at the suggestion of her brother, Clarence.[4] Speculation about the origins of Bessie's first forays onto the stage abounds because she gave no single account about her early vaudeville past, nor did she follow a linear progression from street performer in Chattanooga to national star. For example, Bessie's name might appear in theater ads as part of the chorus of an act in a Memphis theater in one part of the year and then later be listed as a dependent in her sister Viola's Chattanooga residence in another portion of the year.[5] The first mention of Bessie performing appeared in 1909 in the *Indianapolis Freeman*. In May of that year, she performed in the chorus of a show at the Arcade or Eighty-One Theater in Atlanta.[6]

The exact path that Bessie took from performing on Chattanooga's Ninth Street to relocating to the black theater district in Atlanta is difficult to discern. Several probable motives may have caused her to move by 1909. In the aftermath of their parents' deaths and the loss of their 100 Cross Street home, the remaining Smith family moved often throughout Chattanooga. Viola had moved with her daughter Laura, Bessie, and perhaps other siblings at least twice between 1907 and 1908, when she relocated from a boarding house at 1115 West Thirteenth Street to a small dwelling at 69 Pleasant Street.[7] Bessie's meager earnings from her amateur performances probably supplemented these moves and Viola's laundress income but would not have supplied enough to help Viola retain a more permanent residence. It is probable that Bessie grew weary of constantly relocating with Viola and hoped that her amateur income might increase to better support herself and her family once she entered professional theater. Perhaps one of the many ads from the widely circulated *Freeman* newspaper, or a general knowledge from her elder brother Clarence (who was already part of the vaudeville circuit) that Atlanta theaters were looking for new performers, prompted Bessie to audition for a vaudeville show. No matter what the impetus, she traveled across the state line into Georgia, presumably via the Nashville, Chattanooga, and St. Louis express railway route, and arrived in Atlanta's black entertainment district by mid 1909.

Once in Atlanta, Bessie joined a small crowd of other aspiring performers in the city's entertainment center on Decatur Street. In the first decade of the twentieth century, Atlanta was one of the largest cities in the South with a total of 89,872 residents in 1900 and 154,839 residents in 1910.[8] By this latter year African Americans comprised more than a third of the total population and numbered over fifty-one thousand. Although Atlanta's black population was nearly three times the size of Chattanooga's, Bessie would have found her surroundings vaguely familiar, as portions of Decatur Street were reminiscent of Chattanooga's East Ninth Street.[9] Atlanta residents claimed that among the great commercial and social districts in the nation, including Canal Street in New Orleans and Broadway in New York City, "there was not one of those whose romances matched that of Decatur Street, whose habitues were quainter or more original."[10] Like East Ninth Street, Decatur Street was the home of select African American–managed and -patronized restaurants, saloons, theaters, barbershops, boarding houses, and other commercial establishments.[11]

By Bessie's arrival in 1909, much of Decatur Street and black Atlanta in general had been recently reconstructed after violent white mobs demolished many of the "quaint" and "original" businesses during the horrifying racial massacre of September 1906.[12] Just as Chattanooga whites had done some months earlier in 1906, white residents in Atlanta tortured and killed African Americans and destroyed black social spaces ostensibly because they wanted to root out the sites of "Negro" crime, but arguably more because they wished to discourage African American prosperity, economic power, and resistance against white supremacy.[13] Fortunately, many Atlanta African Americans returned to the city and continued to frequent the street's restaurants and theaters—the same areas that Bessie and her counterparts would frequent while preparing for a night's performance at the Eighty-One.[14]

Bessie's early performing life at the Eighty-One and on similar southern theater stages was not a simple one. As the noted black theater critic Sylvester Russell commented,

> However sunny the smile may be, or however pleasant professional life to others may seem, the life of a showman is often provoking rather than always sweet, and the vicissitudes of life appear when least expected and without provocation. . . .
>
> The durability of a female performer most generally depends on her nerve and her constitution.[15]

For Bessie and her fellow soubrettes or chorus girls, success definitely depended on their willingness, ability, and "nerve" to perform songs, skits, and dances repeatedly with little formal training outside of show rehearsals and performances. In 1910, a cast hired for a typical show at the Eighty-One or Arcade Theater could expect a twelve-week engagement in which members performed for four weeks at the Arcade in Atlanta, four weeks at the Globe Theater in Jacksonville, Florida, and four weeks at the Belmont Street Theater in Pensacola, Florida, which shared the same management team at the time.[16] In the general minstrel and vaudeville companies that Bessie performed with in the 1910s, the cast would rehearse during the day for a nightly performance that occurred on Tuesday through Saturday nights, followed by a Sunday matinee. Often there was no sustained narrative or storyline that tied the performances together; performers offered audiences a variety of genres of entertainment. A ninety-minute "playlet" often featured several comedic skits, songs by chorus girls, a barbershop-type ensemble, and buck-and-wing dancers.[17] Bessie was not featured as a solo performer in these early Arcade shows and equally divided her attention between singing and dancing before the olio—the comedic-skit portion of a variety show, which often featured the headliner of the cast.[18] Bessie's fellow Eighty-One employee, the pianist

Thomas Dorsey, recalled that she and the other teenage cast members would practice in the backyard of the theater.[19] Blues music was not yet featured in these playlets, but Bessie earned between five and ten dollars a week, a tremendous increase from the collection of nickels and dimes she had amassed from her Ninth Street performances.[20]

Although some African American vaudeville shows were composed of stock companies of performers who based themselves at one theater such as the Eighty-One, many shows traveled to their audiences.[21] Bessie had the opportunity to be part of stock companies and a member of many traveling revues. The minstrel and vaudeville comedian Dewey "Pigmeat" Markham, one of Bessie's future castmates, recalled that in a traveling minstrel revue cast members "put up the show every day, and every night they would change towns."[22] According to Markham, a minstrel or vaudeville troupe played to different southern territories in a seasonal pattern and often performed in "Georgia in the peach crop time," "North Carolina in the cotton picking time," "West Virginia in her crop time," and ended a show's run in the "Mississippi Delta in September for the big cotton crop."[23] By following agricultural labor patterns, traveling revues hoped that they would arrive in a location at harvest time when laborers had just been paid and would be more likely to spend their money on the luxury of live professional entertainment. Laborers might also attend a professional show at harvest time in an effort to escape, if even for a moment, the exhausting tasks involved in readying a crop for market.

Traveling shows often broadened the recreational lives of agricultural workers and united various isolated communities from several different geographic locations. The vaudeville and blues musician Clyde Bernhardt recalled that in 1911 his father took him to nearly every minstrel or vaudeville show that set up a tent on the outskirts of his South Carolina hometown: "Papa kept taking me to all the weekend shows that came around. Silas Green Minstrels was in often. So was the Rabbit Foot Minstrels. And the Florida Blossom Minstrels. We didn't miss any. I once saw a minstrel trombone player take off his shoes and work his slide with his bare feet. It was the funniest thing I ever saw. And every time I heard a ragtime band with a blues singer, I went around the house the next day trying to act and sing like them."[24] Viewing traveling theater performances inspired Bernhardt to mimic what he had seen and led him to take formal music lessons and become a professional band musician himself. Without the seasonal travel pattern of black musical theater, Bernhardt would not have been able to witness such shows in his small coal-mining town of Gold Hill, South Carolina.[25]

As a chorus member in several mobile vaudeville shows, Bessie traveled from Atlanta to Memphis, Tennessee; Mobile, Alabama; Jacksonville, Florida; Jackson, Mississippi; and Bessemer, Alabama, in her first two years on the professional stage between 1909 and 1911.[26] Yet Bessie's frequent travel schedule did not completely isolate her from her family or the streets of Chattanooga. On the contrary, as shows often closed for eight-week periods to allow performers some vacation time, cast members were able to take up supplemental jobs in the last city where the show closed or return to their hometowns for several months.[27] Bessie returned to Chattanooga by April 1910 and took up residence with Viola for several months.[28] Bessie was able to continue her connection with her family, perhaps share any saved earnings with Viola, and a retain a sense of "home" despite the reality that she was evolving into a well-traveled entertainer.

Back in Chattanooga, Bessie could have kept abreast of several African American revues, for Chattanooga became even more of an integral part of the theater circuit with the opening of the Ivy Theater in May 1910.[29] At this time, many black theater professionals such as E. B. Dudley believed that Chattanooga could be a rising location for African American performers:

> Chattanooga Tenn. is going to be a theatrical center in a very few days as there are all kinds of progressive movements here for a bright future of the colored people, as they are getting together and making themselves useful. . . . At present Chattanooga has one of the finest colored drug stores seen in the South and will soon have a swell colored theater, which will be among the finest in the South.
>
> Let us hope that the white manager will give the theater-going people here some good acts, and not do as the average white manager of some of our Southern colored theaters . . . [A]s colored people we must demand from the white managers of some of these smaller houses good order and not so much vulgarity from the stage. Let us have good performers in this good house and we will have some good box receipts.[30]

Dudley definitely saw promise in the Ivy and black Chattanooga theaters but was equally concerned that the theater's white manager, J. H. Swords, would fail to hire quality entertainers and instead fill the stage with bawdy comedians, poor actors, or incompetent vocalists, dancers, and musicians. Dudley wanted to ensure that African Americans had some involvement in bringing the acts that they wanted to see to the city and not leave it all to the discretion of a white manager.[31] It is possible that Bessie took in some of the initial shows at the Ivy to keep up with and learn from any fledgling variety acts before continuing her contracts with Atlanta stock companies by late 1910.

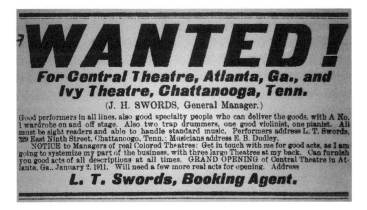

Ivy Theater ad from *Indianapolis Freeman,* 1912.

It was during the 1910 theater season that Bessie met and performed with an entertainer and composer who would decidedly influence her career— Gertrude Pridgett "Ma" Rainey. Born on April 26, 1886, in Columbus, Georgia, Rainey was one of the first African American women to perform blues music professionally, and for her efforts she was known as the "Mother of the Blues."[32] Like Smith, Rainey began her career during her adolescent years and performed in small venues in Columbus before joining the minstrel-show circuit after marrying her fellow entertainer William "Pa" Rainey in 1904. As an entertainment team, Ma and Pa Rainey traveled throughout the South and performed in the ensemble casts of minstrel shows and in programs designed specifically around Ma's vocal and Pa's comedic talents.

Although legend has it that Ma Rainey kidnapped Bessie Smith and forced her to perform the blues, this fascinating and dramatic tale is no more than a myth.[33] While it is unknown exactly when Bessie first witnessed Ma Rainey in performance, it is probable that the two first met when they performed together on the bill of Atlanta's Eighty-One Theater in the early 1900s. Ma Rainey's accompanist, the pianist and composer Thomas Dorsey, maintained that he first encountered Ma at the Atlanta venue during the same period in which Bessie Smith was rehearsing in the theater's backyard.[34] Bessie's sister-in-law, Maud Smith, further noted that "Bessie and Ma Rainey sat down and had a good laugh about how people was making up stories of Ma taking Bessie from her home, and Ma's mother used to get the biggest laugh out of the kidnapping story."[35] Furthermore, as Bessie had been performing publicly as early as the age of ten and had been in several shows before she even met Rainey, her initiation into the entertainment industry cannot be attributed to pressure from Ma Rainey. Nevertheless, Bessie undoubtedly noticed the skilled, seasoned performer's style when she and the Raineys shared the bill at the Eighty-One in 1910 and when they all later traveled together to Memphis's Pekin Theater in September of that same year.[36]

Myths aside, Bessie did include Ma Rainey in her list of the early influences upon her career and noted that when she first heard Rainey in performance, "she proceeded to cry all over the place."[37] Ma Rainey had incorporated blues music into her minstrel and vaudeville repertoire as early as 1902 and was praised in theater reviews for "setting the town wild with her singing."[38] Rainey's style can be seen as a bridge between the folk or country blues, originally performed by itinerant solo male performers who often accompanied themselves on guitar, and the classic or vaudeville blues performed primarily by women who were supported by instrumental ensembles onstage. Rainey performed folk blues songs with a "highly emotional manner and first-person point of view," but she also could incorporate blues into the scripted song-and-dance sketches of vaudeville theater.[39] Ma Rainey was a consummate entertainer whose performances prompted some spectators to comment that "she was all of what show business suppose [*sic*] to be . . . she *was* show business."[40] Her ability to connect with her audiences is eloquently captured in Sterling Brown's poem, "Ma Rainey":

> I talked to a fellow an' the fellow say,
> "She jes' catch hold of us, somekindaway.
> She sang Backwater Blues one day . . .
> An' den de folks, dey natchally bowed dey heads an' cried
> Bowed dey heavy heads, shet dey moufs up tight an' cried
> An' Ma lef' de stage, an' followed some de folks outside."
> Dere wasn't much more de fellow say:
> She jes' gits hold of us dataway.[41]

Brown clearly replicates the emotional atmosphere that was created by a Ma Rainey performance, an atmosphere that Bessie Smith experienced herself at her own initial Rainey show. Rainey at times held a spiritual connection with her audiences; according to Thomas Dorsey, "she possessed her listeners . . . they felt the blues with her."[42] As one of Rainey's castmates, Bessie would have absorbed much of Ma's ability to deliver a performance. It is probable that Bessie melded elements of Rainey's style into her own performances; theater notices do not mention Bessie Smith specifically as a blues performer until years after her early engagements and on-site training with the Raineys.[43]

From Chorus Girl to Blues Woman

Bessie spent her initial years on the vaudeville circuit as an ensemble cast member who supported the leading performer in the various shows with which she traveled. She eventually left her background status behind in 1912 when she slowly rose to prominence as part of the musical duo of Burton and Smith. Wayne Burton was an African American vaudevillian tap dancer whose skilled, frenzied-paced dancing earned him the label of Buzzin' Burton, "the boy with the insane feet."[44] Burton had been on the black theater circuit for a year when he and Bessie met on tour in a Birmingham theater in 1911.[45] By April 1912 they appeared in the *Freeman* theater routings schedule as Burton and Smith, a "sensational duo" who had performed in Philadelphia "with great success."[46] Wayne Burton and Bessie Smith performed as a duo throughout much of 1912 and early 1913. They developed such a following in this period that they received their own individual advertisement in the theater section of the *Indianapolis Freeman* that charted their routings and announced to African American theater patrons when "that boy and that girl" could be seen next.[47] Burton and Smith received generally favorable reviews and were lauded as "curtain raisers" who did a "good downhome act."[48] By the end of the 1912 season, Burton and Smith had renamed themselves Burton and Burton and joined the stock casts of the L. D. Joel Theater Companies in Atlanta, which included the Central, Dixie, and Joel theaters.[49]

Bessie's pairing with Wayne Burton proved significant, as it allowed her to step out of the chorus of vaudeville shows and prompted her to travel beyond the conventional routes of the southern theater circuit. Bessie played leading lady to Burton's leading man. As Burton was known for his dancing, Bessie became responsible for the vocal half of the team, and while she still acted out movements to her songs, she could leave the dancing chorus behind and concentrate on song delivery. As the season progressed, Burton and Smith garnered a small following of their own, and they often played on bills with more well-known headliners. Their small measure of success led them to Indianapolis, Philadelphia, Baltimore, Chicago, Cincinnati, Washington, D.C, and St. Louis. Burton and Smith's performances helped spread southern African American entertainment to midwestern and northern cities even prior to the advent of national black theater routes that opened in the 1920s.[50] Hence, through the vaudeville circuit, Bessie was able to share her talents with thousands of listeners across the eastern portion of the nation eleven years before her recordings introduced her to the nation at large. By the time that Burton and Smith dissolved their partnership in 1913, hundreds of African Americans had become well acquainted with Bessie Smith, "the girl with the ragtime voice," and Bessie continued on her path to becoming a blues woman.[51]

As Bessie Smith became as one of the featured entertainers on the black vaudeville stage, she began to refine her vocal style and entertaining skills. Spectators had already noted her ability to "sell" an audience during her street-performing years, and in her first years on the theater circuit, it was remarked that she was "quite a dancer" and that she "gets the hands in singing 'Southern Gal.'"[52] But it was in her years with Burton and Smith and thereafter that Bessie developed the blues sound she would become famous for in her recordings.

Achieving a distinctive sound was not an effortless process for Bessie. When the trumpeter Clyde Bernhardt witnessed an early Smith performance in Winston-Salem, North Carolina, he held that a "slender, dark . . . Bessie was moaning those blues and dancing up a storm," but "she was just another black woman singing the blues."[53] Bessie was not a formally trained vocalist, and some of her fellow musicians held that in her early years she did not have the "polish" or the pretty, refined sound of her contemporary Ethel Waters, nor the magnetism of Ma Rainey.[54] Yet the power, emotion, and force with which she infused her lyrics gave her a truly memorable voice. She was commended for her "strong" voice during her performances with Wayne Burton, and as a single act in 1914 she won praises from one theater reviewer for being "the best coon shouter" he had ever heard.[55] When Bessie joined the Florida Blossoms Company in 1915 and 1916, she was lauded for "singing the Blues as no one else can."[56] Her phrasing and power are clearly evidenced in the comments of her accompanist, the clarinetist Buster Bailey:

> Bessie Smith was kind of a roughish sort of woman . . . and she liked to sing her blues slow. She didn't want no fast stuff.
>
> She had a style of phrasing, what they used to call swing—she had a certain way she used to sing . . . she was clearly recognized among blues singers—a shouter, they called her. They all respected her because she had a powerful pair of lungs. There were no microphones in those days. She could fill up Carnegie Hall, Madison Square Garden, or a cabaret. She could fill it up from her muscle, and she could last all night. There was none of this whispering jive.[57]

As Bessie's career progressed, she crafted a sound that was improvisational, syncopated, and marked by a sustained slow rhythm that allowed the audience to feel every word of her song. She could omit a word and insert a hum or a moan to reveal even more emotion. Bessie's unique blues sound could transform a nonblues format song, as in her recording of "Nobody Loves You When You're Down and Out," into a memorable blues. For this ability to improvise and transform a song into her own, music critics have argued that Bessie was "not simply an exalted blues singer, but . . . one of the greatest of all jazz performers."[58]

The unique musical style that Bessie developed during this period often impressed critics, but her overall entertaining skills perhaps had an even more profound effect on her audiences. Bessie's constant touring allowed her to perfect a blues that, as the epigraph to this chapter suggests, could "convert the soul" of her listeners. She captured the imagination of female listeners with her memorable costumes, her "neat wardrobe on and off the stage" that had been commented on since her Burton and Smith years.[59] By 1918, an audience member remarked that Bessie was a "genuine song shouter with an excellent alto voice with power and is [also] a nobby looker."[60] Like many of her entertaining counterparts, Bessie exposed audiences to some of the glamor, humor, and adventure of vaudeville life. Yet she also related to her audience on their level. Her songs speak frankly about the hardships and joys of everyday life—a life that her listeners could comprehend and share. When she performed a song like W. C. Handy's "St. Louis Blues," which she sang as early as 1916 as a Florida Blossoms company member,[61] she could convey emotion with the lyrics:

I hate to see de evenin' sun go down,
hate to see de evenin' sun go down,
'Cause my baby, he done lef dis town.

Feelin' tomorrow lak Ah feel today,
Feelin' tomorrow lak Ah feel today,
I'll pack my trunk, make ma get away.

St. Louis woman, wid her diamond rings,
Pulls dat man roun' by her apron strings,
Twan't for powder, an' for store-bought hair
De Man I love would not gone nowhere.

Got the St. Louis Blues, jes' as blues as Ah can be.
Dat man got a heart lak a rock cast in the sea
Or else he wouldn't gone so far from me.

Bessie's female listeners could relate to losing a man to the wiles of that "St. Louis Woman," with her overly madeup face and "store-bought hair." Men and women could empathize with Bessie as she expressed her need to pack up her trunk and make her getaway, for many of them also desired to escape loneliness and hardship. By speaking from an individual perspective that was similar to the lives of many in her audiences, Bessie and her music captured the hearts of African Americans throughout much of the South and Midwest.

Migration and Its Influence on African American Entertainment Culture

One of the fundamental reasons that Bessie's audiences, particularly in northern and midwestern cities, generally felt so connected to her music was because of their status as migrants. African Americans had exercised their freedom of geographic mobility immediately after the Civil War, yet a significantly larger number of them traveled from the South to northern metropolitan areas during the period known as the Great Migration, approximately between 1916 and 1930.[62] Between these years, the South experienced a dramatic loss of African American residents, while cities such as Chicago, New York, Pittsburgh, and Detroit suddenly saw a tremendous surge in their black populations. Between 1910 and 1920, an estimated 454,000 African Americans left the South, while between 1920 and 1930, an estimated 749,000 left the region.[63] Consequently, by 1920 black populations in New York had increased 66.3 percent, while Chicago and Detroit experienced black population increases of 148.2 percent and 611.3 percent, respectively.[64] As thousands of African Americans left the South behind, they brought with them their southern heritage, which for many included a fondness for the music and dance found in southern tent shows, vaudeville theaters, and house parties. The historian Darlene Clark Hine maintains that an overall "cultural transference" from black southern communities can be seen in the food preferences, musical tastes, religious practices, and speech patterns of black northern communities.[65] Hence, a welcoming appreciation of the music of Bessie Smith and other southern African American entertainers was part of this cultural transference.

For many migrants to the North and Midwest, witnessing a Bessie Smith performance was similar to seeing a familiar face from home. Thus, when the shows in which she performed reached the Monogram Theater in Chicago, the Washington Theater in Indianapolis, or the Gilmor Theater in Baltimore in 1918, Bessie danced and sang before a welcoming audience for whom she represented a piece of their Mississippi, Alabama, Georgia, or Tennessee origins.[66] As a product of the South, Bessie belted out songs to other southerners about despair, confusion, and frustration but also about joy, a need for amusement and escape, and sexual desire—all emotions that might be intensified for southern migrants in their new homes of the urban North. Ralph Ellison remarked that Bessie might have been merely an entertainer or a "blues queen to society at large," but "within the tighter Negro community where the blues were a part of a total way of life . . . she was a priestess, a celebrant who affirmed the values of the group and man's ability to deal with chaos."[67] Ellison's comments are further illuminated by Bessie's contemporary, the guitarist Danny Barker:

> "Bessie Smith was a fabulous deal to watch. She was a pretty large woman and she could sing the blues. She had a church deal mixed up in it. She dominated a stage. You didn't turn your head when she went on. You just watched Bessie. You didn't read any newspapers in a night club when she went on. She just upset you. . . . When you went to see Bessie and she came out, that was it. If you had any church background, like people who came from the South as I did, you would recognize a similarity between what she was doing and what those preachers and evangelists from there did, and how they moved people. The South had fabulous preachers and evangelists. Some would stand on corners and move the crowds from there. Bessie did the same thing on stage . . . she could bring about mass hypnotism."[68]

Bessie's ability to connect with her audience on this "hypnotic" and spiritual level was probably influenced by her travels with Ma Rainey at the beginning of her professional career and her childhood experiences with congregations who were moved by Christian hymns. For many migrants, Bessie's performances mirrored the healing and transcendence achieved in a church service because the emotions her songs evoked took her listeners on a spiritual journey. Hence, when African Americans in Atlanta, Chattanooga, Philadelphia, or Chicago attended her shows and later "formed a line twice around the block" to buy her most recent recording, they wanted to hear someone who understood their woes and who could lead them on that journey.[69]

The spiritual quality that some audience members, like Barker, attributed to a Bessie Smith performance was a result of the fusion of the sacred and the secular in her delivery and in the function of a blues performance itself. The power, sustained phrasing, and wordless improvisations characterized Bessie's blues songs reflected the dynamics heard in the sacred congregational songs or hymns she would have witnessed in her childhood church services, while blues lyrics revealed the joys and tribulations of the secular world. The author Albert Murray explains that "the elements of blues music seem to have been derived from the downhome church" because a blues musician, particularly from the South, was likely to have "been conditioned by church music from infancy."[70] While the details of a blues song that chronicle how "my man got a heart like a rock in the sea" might seem distant from a traditional hymn praising God, both genres allowed the performer and the audience to express their woes in song and to reaffirm their humanity.[71] Consequently, blues performers were often influenced by spirituals, and the gospel music that emerged in the urban North after the migration era often reflected a blues sound of its early musicians and vocalists.[72] For example, Thomas Dorsey, one of the leading figures in the urban gospel music movement, transferred the piano skills he had learned accompanying Ma Rainey and Bessie Smith to composing gospel standards like "Precious Lord."[73] As black migrants made lives for themselves in the urban sector, they turned to blues and gospel music to make sense of the injustices and confusion of city life, and a Bessie Smith performance that bridged the gap between the sacred and the secular could aid in the migration transition.

The Theater Owners Booking Association and Life on Stage

The spread of black southern culture that was a by-product of the Great Migration also contributed to the establishment of the Theater Owners Booking Association (TOBA), a national theater circuit that bolstered the careers of black entertainers like Bessie Smith. Formally founded in Chattanooga in 1920, TOBA consisted of black- and white-managed theaters that contracted various African American entertainers and organized them into a systematic route of performances.[74] The predecessors of TOBA date back to 1909 and the emergence of the Afro American Vaudeville Booking Association, the Tri-State Circuit, and the Dudley Circuit. While each of these organizations attempted to link black entertainment venues together, the African American theater professional Sherman H. Dudley's circuit truly illuminated how systematically organized theater chains could successfully function.[75] Dudley began to manage his first chain of theaters in 1910, and by 1912 the circuit included African American theaters in Washington, D.C.; Norfolk, Virginia; Wilmington, North Carolina; Indianapolis, Indiana; Cleveland, Ohio; Memphis, Tennessee; and Philadelphia, Pennsylvania.[76] Dudley hoped to establish "colored theaters in every important city of the country" and maintained that "a strong circuit will bring colored performers up to a higher standard."[77] His circuit functioned in various capacities until he was forced to sell theaters during the Depression in the late 1920s.[78]

Ten years after the emergence of the Dudley Circuit, TOBA opened with similar goals. Yet TOBA covered a larger geographic span and gave the opportunity to any theater owner, regardless of race, to own part of the association by purchasing three shares of company stock.[79] The executive board of TOBA consisted of the white theater professionals Sam Reevin, Milton Starr, and J. J Miller, while the regional managers were the African American theater owners S. H. Dudley, John T. Gibson, and Charles Turpin.[80] By the mid 1920s, TOBA included over eighty theaters and extended into such states as Oklahoma, Missouri, Ohio, Illinois, Arkansas, and Louisiana.[81] It was the training ground for many young African American performers and featured singers (Alberta Hunter, Ethel Waters, Clara Smith, Sara Martin, Lovie Austin, Ma Rainey, and the Whitman Sisters), comedians (Butterbeans and Susie, Whitney and Tutt, and Dewey "Pigmeat" Markham), and numerous other variety acts.[82] When Markham reflected on his days in TOBA, he commented, "[T]he TOBA was more of a school. . . . [Y]ou joined that circuit and you learned your craft," for "everybody would help you, they [more established performers] brought you right along and molded you."[83]

While TOBA offered opportunities for African American entertainers to learn from each other and be steadily employed throughout a theater season, the actual daily operations of the association were highly flawed and revealed the racism, sexism, and other detriments that could accompany life as a professional entertainer. The same battles that African Americans had to fight on a daily basis in the nation as a whole extended to the stage. Even prior to the establishment of TOBA, black entertainers traveled to various cities and successfully performed for thousands, yet often they encountered virulently racist white communities and could not find establishments that would house and feed them. W. C. Handy recalled that during his travels in the late nineteenth and early twentieth centuries, a white mob in Missouri lynched a member of his traveling revue for a supposed incident of "impudence," white supremacists fired bullets at the train carrying the black performers as it passed through some towns in Texas, and the entire group of entertainers stocked up on arms for self-protection and food in the event that eating establishments refused them service.[84]

Entertainers who worked the TOBA circuit generally did not fare as poorly as Handy did in the early twentieth century, but there were problems. Alternatively known as "Tough on Black Artists" among performers, life on the TOBA circuit could be extremely demanding.[85] African American entertainers criticized white TOBA managers for doing exactly what E. B. Dudley feared would occur at Chattanooga's Ivy Theater—contracting poor-quality shows with the belief that "anything at all was good enough for the patrons of Negro houses."[86] Conflicts often occurred when white theater owners believed that they knew what was "best" for their African American performers and adopted a dictatorial attitude. Such was the case with Charles P. Bailey, the 1920s manager of Atlanta's Eighty-One Theater. Bailey attempted to control where black entertainers slept and ate and other details of their offstage lives.[87] As TOBA was such a large circuit, with different theater managers in every city, performers encountered theaters that were not as well managed as others. Dressing rooms could be cold and damp, overheated and poorly ventilated, or simply nonexistent. Additionally, booking problems resulted in performers who were "never sure of the next date until they had reached the place booked and the curtain went up on their first performance."[88] Furthermore, for entertainers who were not headliners, a TOBA contract generally benefited the theater manager as opposed to the performer, as it greatly restricted when and where an entertainer could perform.[89]

For female performers, theater life was riddled with additional obstacles. As many "so-called society people regarded the stage as a place to be ashamed of," African American female entertainers often had to defend their chosen profession to people who disparaged them as promiscuous or immoral.[90] The theater critic Sylvester Russell argued that "the life of a woman who is a great performer in any line is the hardest life that any woman, outside of a woman in poverty, who has to do drudgery, can follow."[91] Many women had to fend off the sexual advances of eager audience members or fellow performers. A vaudevillian woman lived her life in the public eye and had to be on guard, for any mistake she made in personal or professional life would be judged by a wide audience. Within the confines of the theater arena, African American women also had to negotiate racist and sexist standards of beauty that valued light skin, svelte figures, and long-flowing hair, which prevented some darker-skinned women from getting quality employment.[92] While male performers might be hired for their talent as dancers, singers, or musicians, there was little opportunity for a skilled, dark-skinned female entertainer to succeed in a group such as the Seven Florida Creole Girls, known for "their beauty of face and figure."[93] Furthermore, a female performer might be asked to perform in skits in which the humor was vulgar and the costumes were scant, whereas male performers would rarely, if ever, be required to be scantily clad to "sell" a song or skit.

In her early years on the theater circuit, Bessie Smith encountered many of the difficulties of theater life. She rapidly moved from city to city with various theater troupes and undoubtedly changed in inadequate dressing rooms and spent much of her day in shoddy theaters. She initially earned low to moderate wages, and her fellow vaudeville performer Leigh Whipper recalled when Bessie "only made ten dollars a week, but people would throw money on the stage, and the stage hands would pick up about three or four dollars" to add to her earnings.[94] Additionally, Bessie endured the skin-color and body-type discrimination that was often leveled at African American female performers. The theatrical producer Irvin C. Miller denied Bessie a role in his show's chorus, for he "stressed beauty in the chorus line and Bessie did not meet his standards as far as looks were concerned." Bessie's future record producer, Frank Walker, described his initial impression of Bessie as "tall, fat and scared to death—just awful."[95] Bessie triumphed over the impediments associated with theater life because of the power and efficacy of her voice and her large popularity with her audiences. Yet she was not unaffected by the downside of show life and arguably developed a persistent and aggressive nature in her pursuit of survival in the vaudeville arena. Bessie fostered a reputation for being a "very rough" woman with "raucous and loud voice," a woman who "could be plenty tough" and could "handle her own."[96] Perhaps these qualities did not make her a refined or genteel black woman, but they did help propel Bessie Smith into becoming one of the most popular entertainers on the African American vaudeville circuit.

Family and Community Connections

Although Bessie Smith was a featured headliner in several TOBA shows as the 1920s approached, she continued to foster the connection with her Chattanooga hometown that she had exhibited during her initial years in vaudeville. As evidenced by her routing schedule, Bessie made efforts to perform in Chattanooga when the opportunity arose. She played the city's Queen Theater from the 1915 to the 1918 season; in 1915 the theater's "SRO [Standing Room Only] sign was out all week," and she met "with great success."[97] Bessie continued to perform in Chattanooga once TOBA headquartered itself in the city and was a featured headliner at TOBA's Liberty Theater at 312 East Ninth Street.[98]

Bessie's return to the streets where she had performed for pennies must have been personally gratifying, but perhaps more significantly, it allowed her the opportunity to reconnect with her large family. She visited with the rest of the Smiths during the off-season of the vaudeville circuit and always funneled money from her earnings back to her siblings to supplement what they earned from their various occupations as domestic and general laborers.[99] Bessie's continued contact with her siblings prompted her to try and help them also escape the impoverished sectors of Chattanooga. This desire would become a reality once Bessie acquired a recording contract that raised her visibility, popularity, and income.

Bessie would become instrumental in leading a "migration chain" of the Smith family, particularly its female members, to Philadelphia by the mid 1920s. The term "migration chain" refers to the patterns black southerners followed as they relocated to northern cities. An individual family member might move North first, secure employment, and then send money for remaining family members to relocate. Darlene Clark Hine suggests that women were critical links in the migration chain, for they were instrumental in convincing family members and friends to make the move North.[100] Once Bessie and her future husband, Jack Gee, relocated to Philadelphia in the 1920s, Bessie sent for her sisters, Viola, Tinnie, Lulu, and their respective children and grandchildren, and purchased homes for them in the downtown district.[101] Additionally, she gave her sisters an opportunity to support themselves by helping them establish a restaurant, Viola's Place, on Philadelphia's South Street.[102] Her elder brother, Clarence, had relocated to the urban North with his own family some years earlier. Clarence eventually became the featured comedian in Bessie's shows and helped in the daily management of her revues.[103] By the late 1920s, only Andrew, the eldest living Smith sibling, and his family remained in Chattanooga.

Not only did Bessie remain linked to her Chattanooga family, she continued her connection to working-class African American communities in general. Her involvement in black communities extended beyond the "downhome" feeling she shared with them through her music. In her initial years on the circuit, Bessie was a resident in many of these communities, working as a laundress to support herself during the off-season in Atlanta and later in Birmingham.[104] She made no separation between herself and other working people because she was still doing the same demanding labor that she had aided with as a child, before returning to the stage when the next show resumed its course.

As Bessie's career advanced, particularly in the 1920s, she performed in theaters that were not on the TOBA circuit and included white patrons in the audience.[105] Yet she continued to perform for black audiences in primarily African American venues. When not performing, she spent much of her leisure time in establishments frequented by the same African Americans who shared in her music. When she played in Chattanooga, she often stayed and socialized with her Andrew's family near her old Blue Goose Hollow neighborhood, instead of in a hotel.[106] In Washington, D.C, Bessie reportedly often spent time with black residents in the impoverished alley dwellings and perhaps attended the same "chitlin' struts" as her listeners.[107] On the road, Bessie was known to socialize with fellow performers in "back alley cafes" or private house parties.[108] Her slowly evolving fame did not cause her to lose sight of who she was as a southern African American woman who grew up in poverty. Although her income was on the rise, when possible she did not separate herself from the people and communities who had allowed her to earn that income.

The "Discovery" of Bessie Smith

It was Bessie's connection to common African American communities, physically and through the music of her vaudeville shows, that eventually prompted the fledgling "race record" industry to take notice. African American popular music, such as blues and jazz, had been recorded in the early twentieth century; yet it was performed by white musicians and vocalists, as racism prevented African American entertainers from entering the studios themselves. White vaudevillians, including Sophie Tucker and Marion Harris, had recorded blues-inflected pieces in the 1910s, while the white Original Dixieland Jazz Band made the first jazz recording with Victor Records in 1917.[109] Yet only a select few African Americans had been recorded prior to the 1920s (including the vaudevillian comedian Bert Williams and the noted Fisk Jubilee Singers).[110] At this time, African American women soloists were not recording artists, and W. C. Handy recounted that white recording managers held that "their [black women] voices were not suitable, their diction was different from white girls."[111] This dislike for African American female recording artists was only altered once the black vaudevillian Mamie Smith (no relation to Bessie) recorded "That Thing Called Love" and "You Can't Keep a Good Man Down" in February 1920 on General Phonographs' Okeh records. When Mamie Smith's "Crazy Blues," released in August 1920, sold several thousand copies to a primarily African American market, the race-record boom began.[112]

When the recording industry realized that there was a vast number of African Americans and some whites who would be willing to pay to hear black voices on record, a number of companies developed catalogs of African American songs recorded by black vocalists and musicians. By 1922, several black women, including Ethel Waters, Trixie Smith, and Lucille Heagmin, followed in Mamie Smith's footsteps and earned contracts at Paramount, Columbia, Okeh, and the black-owned Harry Pace company, Black Swan Records.[113] Bessie Smith made attempts to enter the recording industry as early as 1921, when she tested for Black Swan Records. In the middle of the demonstration recording, Bessie reportedly told the sound engineers, "Hold on, let me spit."[114] Because of her blunt behavior and "rough" sound, Pace decided that Bessie was not right for Black Swan and never released the record nor gave her a contract. Instead, Pace selected the "smoother"-sounding Ethel Waters, later referred to as a "shining example for the youth who must follow," as his initial blues artist.[115] In the next year, Bessie also recorded "I Wish I Could Shimmy Like My Sister Kate" for Okeh and Columbia Records, but neither recording was released. Okeh believed that Smith was just another blues singer among the many, and Columbia held that she was "course and loud," and they "didn't want any part" of the recording.[116] These three record companies maintained that Bessie Smith's sound, which mesmerized listeners on stage, was too harsh to record and likely feared that her folk sound would not be marketable to urban African Americans nor "crossover" to a white audience.

By 1923, the Black Swan recording artist Trixie Smith had been billed as the "World's Greatest Blues Singer," and Ethel Waters was advertised as "the Queen of the Blues," while Bessie Smith continued as a praised headliner on the black vaudeville circuit.[117] In that same year, the Columbia executive Frank Walker, entranced by the frenzy and profit that race records garnered, looked for his own blues queen to place on Columbia. He recalled seeing Bessie Smith on the southern vaudeville circuit in the 1910s and asked one of his employees, the pianist Clarence Williams, to "find her and bring her back up here."[118] Williams retrieved Walker's "discovery," Bessie Smith, and brought her to New York City and Columbia Records to record her brand of blues. In February 1923, Bessie signed a contract that promised her $125.00 a side (individual song) and no royalties.[119] Bessie's first Columbia side, "Downhearted Blues," sold over 780,000 copies, and Bessie Smith became Columbia's "Empress."[120]

Bessie Smith's "overnight" success in reality encompassed fourteen years of performances in tent shows, amusement parks, and vaudeville theaters and several other years of street-corner performances on Chattanooga's Ninth Street. She had performed in Atlanta, Birmingham, Mobile, Chicago, St. Louis, Washington, D.C., and numerous other cities, "preaching the blues" to her audiences. She endured the detriments of theater life, and her hardened personality was a manifestation of this endurance. Bessie had eased the pains of many migrant listeners, and as a migrant herself she relocated to Philadelphia, yet did not lose sight of her southern African American identity or

1920s Bessie Smith sheet music. Samuel DeVincent Illustrated Sheet Music Collection, Archives Center, National Museum of American History, Smithsonian Institution.

Empress of the Blues. Warshaw Collection of Business Americana, Archives Center, National Museum of American History, Smithsonian Institution.

the functions her music served. "Overnight," the talent that a young girl had honed with her siblings, Ma Rainey, and various other African American musicians, dancers, and vocalists was carved into wax audio reproductions for the nation and generations of music listeners to hear and learn from. Although Bessie Smith never forgot her Chattanooga roots, the general public often forgot her origins as a street performer and became mesmerized by the image of the vaudeville headliner and the recording artist. Bessie Smith, the southern woman, and the social function of blues music, would become obscured by the stories of alcohol-filled nights, wild parties, violent confrontations, and other legends surrounding the Empress of the Blues.

EPILOGUE
A BLUES WOMAN'S LEGACY

I'm a young woman and ain't done runnin' 'round,
I'm a young woman and ain't done runnin' 'round.

Some people call me a hobo, some call me a bum,
Nobody knows my name, nobody knows what I've done.

I'm as good as any woman in your town,
I ain't no high yella, I'm a deep killer brown.

I ain't gonna marry, ain't gon' settle down,
I'm gon' drink good moonshine and run these
    browns down.

See that long, lonesome road, Lord, you know it's
    gotta end,
And I'm a good woman and I can get plenty men.

—BESSIE SMITH, "Young Woman's Blues"

Bessie Smith lived much of her career and the remainder of her life in the manner that she sang about in "Young Woman's Blues." She was a relatively young woman of thirty-one when she earned her first Columbia recording contract, and the "runnin' 'round" that she had done as a popular vaudeville artist only increased. Although by the mid 1920s Bessie was based in Philadelphia, her recordings greatly enhanced her popularity, and she spent the pinnacle of her career traveling the nation in her own stylized revue. The stage was her home, and Bessie could have been criticized for being the "hobo" she sang about. The stories of her many complex love affairs and her problems with alcohol reveal that she did imbibe that "good moonshine" and "ran those browns down."[1] Bessie's "long lonesome road" ended on September 26, 1937, when she perished in a car crash in Clarksdale, Mississippi. Yet so much happened in her life and career that when she died there was still a feeling in the larger community that "nobody *really* knew her name, nobody knew *all* what she'd done." This study has been an effort to probe Bessie Smith's life and early environment to help illuminate the complexities of who she was as a southern African American woman and how her music functioned in the black communities where she perfected her craft.

Bessie Smith's legacy as an entertainment icon, the "Empress of the Blues," lives on in American social history and popular culture to the present day. The popular images of Bessie adorned in a glamorous gown, a feathered head-dress, and wide smile have been reproduced on postcards, t-shirts, coloring books, posters, and a postage stamp. Her image was used to market Dewar White Label scotch in the 1970s, and the lyrics of "Young Woman's Blues" can be found in select greeting cards today.[2] Smith's life has been the subject of dramatic productions such as Edward Albee's *The Death of Bessie Smith* (1960) as well as musical productions such as 1977's *Me and Bessie*.[3] More recently, the author Terry McMillan has been referred to as "a literary Bessie Smith" for the frank attitudes of her characters in the novel *A Day Late and a Dollar Short,* and entertainment-industry rumors abound about the pos-sibility of a contemporary movie musical of Smith's life starring the actress and hip-hop entertainer Queen Latifah in the title role.[4] Smith's Chattanooga heritage is commemorated by the Bessie Smith Hall in Chattanooga.

Much has changed in Chattanooga since Bessie left its downtown street corners. Cameron Hill—and Bessie's Blue Goose Hollow neighborhood, which laid at its base—was leveled as part of urban-renewal efforts in the 1950s. Ninth Street, like many African American commercial districts, has been renamed Martin Luther King Jr. Boulevard and does not entirely re-flect the vibrancy that characterized it in years past. However, on the corner of King Boulevard and Lindsay Street, right across from where the TOBA Liberty Theater once stood, stands Bessie Smith Hall and its counterpart, the Chattanooga African American Museum. Discussed as early as 1977 and formally conceived in 1985, Bessie Smith Hall opened on February 10, 1996.[5] Chattanooga city officials and the hall's three founding groups—the M. L. King Development Corporation, the Bessie Smith Hall Board, and the Chattanooga African American Museum Board—generally hoped that the hall would bring white and black people together to socialize and "put some jive back into the languishing black district" on King Boulevard.[6] However, a search for funds, construction difficulties, and a series of conflicts among the organizing entities stalled the opening for over ten years and totaled a cost of over four million dollars.[7]

One of the main conflicts concerned the mission of the hall itself. Tourism officials wanted the hall to increase city dollars; Bessie Smith Hall represented a "golden opportunity" to "cash in on the name of a famed blues performer."[8] Black city leaders were equally hopeful that the hall would revitalize black businesses and draw more tourists to the historic Ninth Street area. Yet a former chairperson of the Bessie Smith Hall Board, LaFonde McGee, also maintained that blues education should be a fundamental component of the hall's mission and that it should be instrumental in taking blues "out to the schools and the community."[9] Finally, the Chattanooga African American Museum wanted to take the concept of education a step further and combine Bessie's legacy with Chattanooga's black history.

Among these conflicting missions also came concerns from some in the larger Chattanooga community as to whether "minority-oriented organizations" could actually carry out the development of the hall. As progress stalled and costs rose, some wondered if predominantly African American organizations could bring Bessie Smith Hall to fruition without the leadership of white city officials.[10] Furthermore, city leaders feared that the completed hall would evolve into a "cabaret" and did not want alcohol to be served at the establishment. City officials did not want yet another black social space that could invite lower-class African Americans to the downtown district and tarnish the family-friendly image of downtown Chattanooga they were attempting to create. The mayor, Gene Roberts, further maintained that he would pull city funds from the project if it were to evolve into a dreaded "cabaret."[11] The promised presence of alcohol also caused some African American community members to question the appropriateness of naming an institution after Bessie Smith, a noted heavy drinker.[12] Was Bessie Smith even deserving of a monument that emphasized the debaucherous elements of her behavior like alcohol consumption? Debate about Smith's character resulted in commentary like the following: "Why is it so easy to be enamored of Billie Holiday (who was beset by drug addiction), but we dogmatically critique Bessie Smith? Maybe because Ms. Holiday was not from Chattanooga. Bessie was one of our own and even native Chattanoogans say they devour their own."[13]

Chattanoogans continued to "devour their own," and the negative press surrounding the hall persisted until it opened in 1996 with a celebration that featured the modern blues singer Koko Taylor, local musical groups, and interactive instructional musical workshops.[14] Bessie Smith Hall continues to host visiting performers and local talent, serves alcohol at selected events, shares a building with the Chattanooga African American Museum, and educates the surrounding community about the historical significance of blues music. The hall is one of key sites listed in vistor's guides to the city and attracts many patrons, particularly as tourists stream into the city in June, the month of the Bessie Smith Strut, an annual music festival that also honors Chattanooga's Empress.[15]

The prolonged dilemmas surrounding the establishment of Bessie Smith Hall embody many of the larger issues raised in this study, including African American southern community development, intra-racial class tensions, African American community responses to racist actions, the various functions of recreational space in black communities, conservative criticism of black social space, and the roles of women in developing social spaces and transmitting African American entertainment culture. As the Chattanooga black community attempted to revitalize its commercial district through the creation of the hall, many of the internal divisions and external pressures that the community had known since the inception of black Chattanooga in the post-Reconstruction era resurfaced. The questions of respectability that surrounded Bessie Smith's street performances on Ninth Street pervaded the issue of how her legacy should be honored on that same street.

In his biography of Bessie Smith, Chris Albertson notes that from the moment Smith became a Columbia recording artist, her life story "loses much of its vagueness and some of its mythical embroidery. People find it much easier to remember the famous, and Bessie was about to achieve that status."[16] With this work, I have desired to clear up some of the "vagueness" and unravel the "mythical embroidery" by searching out Bessie Smith's origins and the historical context of the music and environment that created her fame. The questions and concerns that posed difficulties for a young Bessie Smith as she strove to escape poverty and join the professional stage still arise today and are vividly evidenced in the path to the opening of Bessie Smith Hall in 1996. Part of Smith's legacy is that her image still evokes questions of morality, racism, and judgments of women's "place." Yet the other part of her legacy is the boldness and artistry she brought to blues music and the various outlets that blues and black music more generally provide for African American communities. Bessie's recordings brought her international fame and allowed generations of musicians, vocalists, critics, and music listeners to explore her music. However, the music and its environment affected the lives of hundreds of other working-class African Americans during the period when Bessie was still a Chattanooga street performer, just a young woman singing her blues.

NOTES

Introduction

1. I use the terms "African American" and "black" interchangeably throughout the text; when I examine the era of slavery, I will use "enslaved laborer" or "black slave" to reflect the noncitizen status of black people.

2. This vignette of downtown Chattanooga is a composite of the descriptions of businesses in White, *Biography and Achievements;* and Crawford, "Business Negroes."

3. Van Vechten, "Negro Blues," 67, 106.

4. There is much confusion over the year of Smith's birth. Because no record of a birth certificate has been found, by the time of her death she was rumored to be everything from forty-three to fifty years old. Most recently, biographers have placed her birth date as April 15, 1894—the date she listed on her 1923 marriage license. This date can be verified using the 1910 Chattanooga census, which lists Smith's age as sixteen. However, the 1900 Chattanooga census lists her birth year as 1892. I will use the 1892 date because it was most likely reported by Smith's mother, who is also included in the census entry. See Department of Commerce and Labor, *Thirteenth Census.* While entertainers, particularly women, have been known to raise or lower their age according the conventions of their occupation, Smith's mother would have had little reason to alter her daughter's age for a census taker.

5. Much of mainstream America was enamored with black blues music. To capitalize on the growing interest in this "authentic" music by and for blacks, record companies, including Columbia and Okeh, created a separate "Race Record" labeling system. For more on how blues prompted this system, see Collier, *Making of Jazz,* 110–22; Harrison, *Black Pearls,* 44–61.

6. Billy Rowe, "Moanin' Blues Voice of Bessie Smith, Who Made $60,000 a Year, Will Never Be Stilled by Death," *Pittsburgh Courier,* October 9, 1937.

7. Olmstead, *Hidden Tennessee,* 151–54; Bradley, *Tennessee Handbook,* 218–40.

8. Russell asserts that Smith's lyrics voice the unwritten histories of African American women. See Russell, "Slave Codes." Carby argues that through song, blueswomen were able to celebrate and reclaim their sexuality in spite of the patriarchal order. See Carby, "It Just Be's Dat Way." Harrison discusses the role of blueswomen in the creation, development, and performance of the blues. See Harrison, *Black Pearls.* Collins uses Smith's and other blues singers' lyrics to argue that African American women have the power of self-definition despite the existence of sexual inequality. See Collins, *Black Feminist Thought.* Davis explores how the recordings of Ma Rainey, Bessie Smith, and Billie Holiday reflect a working-class black feminist consciousness and examines how their recordings often challenged stereotypical definitions of political power, spirituality, and women's roles. See Davis, *Blues Legacies.*

9. Kelley, *Race Rebels,* 53.

10. Hunter, *To 'Joy My Freedom,* 176.

11. Williams, "Club Movement," 101.

12. For more on the significance of black recreational environments, see Kelley, *Race Rebels,* 35–54.

13. See Kyriakoudes, *Social Origins;* Berkeley, *Like a Plague.* For discussions of southern-to-northern and -western migration, see Lemke-Santagelo, *Abiding Courage;* Adero, *Up South;* Trotter, *The Great Migration;* Grossman, *Land of Hope;* Johnson and Campbell, *Black Migration.*

14. Govan and Livingood, *Chattanooga Country,* 277.

15. Ibid., 405.

Chapter 1: Beyond the Contraband Camps

Note on the epigraph: This is an excerpt of a spiritual that was first heard among former slaves in the Fortress Monroe contraband camp in 1861 and quickly spread to contraband camps throughout the South. The song exemplifies the sentiment of many black people as they experienced the Civil War and awaited emancipation. See Epstein, *Sinful Tunes,* 363.

1. Berlin, et al.,*Freedom,* vol. 2, 369, 376.

2. "The Refugees," *Chattanooga Daily Gazette,* November 26, 1864, 2.

3. Livingood, *Hamilton County,* 13.

4. Notes from the National Urban League Collection, series 6, box 22, Manuscript Division, Library of Congress; Starkey, *Cherokee Nation,* 18. Chattanooga came into being as a thriving Tennessee town only because of the forcible removal of the remaining members of the Cherokee nation in 1838. Between May and June 1838, over two thousand federal troops drove off 3,500 Cherokees at Ross's Landing (named for Cherokee Chief John Ross). Cherokee involuntary emigration from Ross's Landing marked the beginning of the infamous Trail of Tears and paved the way for white encroachment into Tennessee and the upper South. In preparation for Removal, thou-

sands of soldiers were dispatched to the holding camps that contained the Cherokees at Ross's Landing. Along with the soldiers' arrival came the development of new businesses to cater to the rapidly growing population. The new settlers and expanding businesses remained long after the Removal, and Ross's Landing was incorporated as Chattanooga on December 20, 1839—a direct result of the destruction of the Cherokee Nation. See King, "Cherokee Removal," 11–24; Govan and Livingood, *Chattanooga Country*, 104–9.

5. Livingood, *Hamilton County*, 472.

6. Department of the Interior, *Eighth Census: 1860–Agriculture*, 134–35.

7. Federal Writers Project, *Tennessee*, 104.

8. By 1860 there were only 1,419 slaves and 275 slaveholders in Hamilton County. The majority (202) of these slaveholders owned between one and five slaves, while fewer than two dozen slaveholders owned between ten and fifteen slaves each. Department of the Interior, *Eighth Census: 1860–Agriculture*, 238.

9. Qtd. in Bailey, "Tennessee's Antebellum Common Folk," 84.

10. Rawick, *American Slave*, 230.

11. Although slavery did not exist in Chattanooga specifically during the seventeenth and eighteenth centuries, the contact the enslaved had with their masters during the antebellum era was reminiscent of the labor environment of the initial colonial era. Before becoming its own territory and state, Tennessee was a part of the Carolinas until 1790, and thus Tennessee slavery had its origins in North Carolina statutes and traditions. In the early 1700s slaves worked alongside their masters on small farms and aided with livestock, gardened, hunted, and fished. The nature of slavery changed on the Carolina coastline with the development of rice and indigo production. More labor was needed for the production of these crops, and hence a plantation system developed in which slaves worked the land and many planters became "absentee masters" and moved inland to towns. Once Tennessee separated from North Carolina, the geographic features of the land prompted slaveholders in East Tennessee to return to the early labor relationships of colonial-era master/slave contact. See Mooney, *Slavery in Tennessee*, 7–8; Berlin, "Time, Space, and the Evolution."

12. Rawick, *American Slave*, 214–15.

13. Epstein, *Sinful Tunes*, 65.

14. Ibid., 63–67.

15. Southern, *Music of Black Americans*, 43–44.

16. Wolfe, Liner notes.

17. Epstein, *Sinful Tunes*, 69–74; Southern, *Music of Black Americans*, 46–47.

18. Bailey, "Tennessee's Antebellum Common Folk," 91.

19. Hartman, *Scenes of Subjection*, 43.

20. Furman, *Slavery in Clover Bottoms*, 22.

21. Southern, *Music of Black Americans*, 162.

22. Mary Sharpe Jones to Rev. and Mrs. C. C. Jones, Marietta, October 20, 1855, in Myers, *Children of Pride*, 163–64.

23. Department of the Interior, *Eighth Census: Population,* 459, 463.

24. Govan and Livingood, *Chattanooga Country,* 161.

25. *Chattanooga Daily Rebel,* September 12, 1862. Ironically, the location of Johnstons' slave-trading center would later become the center of the black commercial district of the early 1900s, transforming the hub of trade in African American lives into the hub of trade in African American–manufactured and –distributed material goods.

26. Mooney, *Slavery in Tennessee,* 29.

27. T. J. Campell, "Romance of River Travel on the Tennessee," *Chattanooga Times,* September 18, 1938, 5–A.

28. Connor, *Historical Guide,* 72; Govan and Livingood, *Chattanooga Country,* 130–31.

29. Department of the Interior, *Eighth Census: Manufacturers,* 565.

30. Livingood, *Hamilton County,* 136–37; Livingood *Chattanooga,* 58.

31. Robert Mallard to Mrs. Mary S. Mallard, Chattanooga, May 18, 1859, in Myers, *Children of Pride,* 483. Mallard praises the black female servants of the Crutchfield House, the most prominent hotel of the city, as "some of the most obliging" he had ever met.

32. Blassingame, *Slave Testimony,* 618–19.

33. Jasper T. Duncan, "From Slavery: Negroes' Progress," *Chattanooga Times,* September 18, 1938, 11–A.

34. It was relatively easy for a Tennessee owner to free his slaves until the early 1830s, and there was actually an abolitionist presence in East Tennessee in the mid 1830s. In December 1831, the Tennessee legislature enacted a law that made it "not lawful . . . for any court or any owner or owners of slaves to emancipate any slave or slaves, except on the express condition that such slaves be immediately removed from the state." See *Godspeed's General History,* 756.

35. Livingood, *Hamilton County,* 139.

36. Govan and Livingood, *Chattanooga Country,* 161.

37. In the 1850s, Chattanooga had an ordinance that stated, "[I]f any free person of color or mulatto shall entertain or permit any slave to visit or remain in his or her home during the Sabbath day, or between sunset and sunrise, without permission from the employer or owner of said slave, he shall for such and every offense forfeit and pay the sum of five dollars." This was likely meant to restrict any private time that free blacks and slaves might have shared and to limit their interactions to labor activities. Additionally, the city patrol could "disperse all gatherings of slaves and were authorized to inflict punishment of from five to ten lashes for any violation." See Livingood, *Hamilton County,* 131. These laws may have arisen as a result the onslaught of prohibitive regulations that came about after the Nat Turner Rebellion of 1831. After Turner and his followers, free and enslaved African Americans, fought the institution of slavery by slaughtering over sixty white people in Virginia, several states enacted laws that prevented free and enslaved blacks or any large group of blacks from

gathering. These restrictions were meant to prevent the planning of future rebellions and to quell resistance among African Americans. For a brief discussion of the Nat Turner Rebellion and its repercussions, see Turner, "I Should Arise," 150–53.

38. Epstein, *Sinful Tunes*, 164–5.

39. Southern, *Music of Black Americans*, 148.

40. Epstein, *Sinful Tunes*, 168. For further information on antebellum worksongs, see Epstein, *Sinful Tunes*, 161–83.

41. Southern, *Music of Black Americans*, 150.

42. Rev R. Q. Mallard to Mrs. Mary S. Mallard, Chattanooga, May 18, 1859, in Myers, *Children of Pride*, 483.

43. Floyd, *Power of Black Music*, 62, 19–22.

44. Livingood, *Hamilton County*, 139.

45. Temple, *East Tennessee*, 199.

46. Livingood, *Chattanooga*, 59–61.

47. Cimprich, *Slavery's End*, 17; Govan and Livingood, *Chattanooga Country*, 191–92.

48. Livingood, *Chattanooga*, 69–70; Berlin et al., *Freedom*, vol. 2, 376; Berlin et al., *Freedom*, vol. 1, 263.

49. The term "contraband," as devised by a Union officer, Benjamin Butler, initially referred to the runaway slaves who followed Union camps. Butler deemed these fugitive slaves as "contrabands of war," or smuggled goods that could be used to benefit the Union effort by draining Confederate labor resources and working on Union military fortifications. As the war progressed, all runaway slaves in Union lines came to be known as "contrabands" and were eventually organized into a formal labor force for the Union army. See Tindall, *America*, 640–41.

50. "The Refugees," *Chattanooga Daily Gazette*, November 26, 1864; Govan and Livingood, *Chattanooga Country*, 277.

51. Qtd. in in Livingood, *Chattanooga Country*, 500.

52. Govan and Livingood, *Chattanooga Country*, 277; Cimprich, *Slavery's End*, 52.

53. Cimprich, *Slavery's End*, 31.

54. Berlin et al., *Freedom*, vol. 2, 370; Cimprich, *Slavery's End*, 52.

55. Harrison, "Recollections," 177.

56. Cimprich, *Slavery's End*, 54.

57. Berlin et al., *Freedom*, vol. 2, 420 (emphasis mine).

58. Berlin et al., *Freedom*, vol. 1, 278.

59. Berlin et al., *Freedom*, vol. 2, 461.

60. Berlin et al., *Freedom*, vol. 1, 263–65.

61. Klebenow, *Two Hundred Years*, 154.

62. Berlin et al., *Freedom*, vol. 2, 377.

63. The Emancipation Proclamation mandated that "as of January 1, 1863, all persons held as slaves within any state or designated part of a state the people whereof

shall be in rebellion against the United States shall be then thenceforward and forever free." As the Union occupied much of Tennessee by late 1862, Tennessee was longer "in rebellion against the United States" and hence did not fall under the jurisdiction of the proclamation. The proclamation in effect legally freed no slaves because Lincoln had no legal control over the Confederate states during wartime, and the proclamation said nothing about slaves in states that had been loyal to the Union. See "All Persons Held as Slaves within Said Designated States," in Wright, *African American Archive*, 327–30.

64. Ibid., 392. For further information on how this decision was arrived at, see the exchange of letters in Berlin et al., *Freedom*, vol. 2, 408–20.

65. Berlin et al., *Freedom*, vol. 2, 408.

66. Irwin was a washerwoman for several Union surgeons, and she petitioned the military to request back pay for her and her companions' services. The Abernathys were farmers from middle Tennessee who agreed to plant and harvest subsistence crops for a wage they never received. They wrote the Union forces requesting action and noted the terms of the original agreement they had made with their former master, Thomas Abernathy, to produce five acres of corn in exchange for fifteen dollars a month. See ibid., 466–69.

67. Ibid., 384.

68. Cimprich, *Slavery's End*, 21.

69. Berlin et al., *Freedom*, vol. 2, 390.

70. Furman, *Slavery in Clover Bottoms*, 79–80 (for an in-depth discussion of the daily activites of a black Union soldier and laborer in the greater Chattanooga area, see esp. 51–105).

71. Berlin et al., *Freedom*, vol. 2, 391.

72. This very situation occurred in Memphis at the close of the war. In 1865, a dispute between militia men and white police officers erupted into the Memphis Riot in which a reported forty-six African American men, women, and children were murdered, and several African American women testified that white officers had molested and raped them. See excerpts of this testimony in Lerner, *Black Women*, 173–79.

73. Berlin et al., *Freedom*, vol. 2, 466–67.

74. New black entrepreneurs also forged small businesses in Tennessee contraband settlements in Memphis, Pulaski, and Nashville. See Cimprich, *Slavery's End*, 56; Lovett and Wynn, *Profiles of African-Americans*, xxv–xxvii.

75. Furman, *Slavery in Clover Bottoms*, 75.

76. Livingood, *Chattanooga Country*, 501.

77. Cimprich, *Slavery's End*, 71.

78. American Missionary Association, *Nineteenth Annual Report*, 8.

79. Ibid.

80. The Freedmen's Bureau and the AMA were also known for their paternalistic behavior towards those who received their aid. See Richardson, *Christian Reconstruction*, 187–211, 235–57.

81. Southern, *Music of Black Americans,* 165. "Poor Rosy" continued to be a popular worksong into the twentieth century; one of the most recent versions was "Rosie," performed by inmates of the Parchman Farm Penitentiary in 1947 and recorded by the folklorist Alan Lomax. See O'Meally, Liner notes, 3.

82. Furman, *Slavery in Clover Bottoms,* 75.

83. Ibid.

84. Epstein, *Sinful Tunes,* 246, 276–77 (see esp. the epigraph that introduces an excerpt of the lyrics to "Let My People Go").

85. Southern, *Music of Black Americans,* 210–11.

86. Harrison, "Recollections," 185–86.

87. Cimprich, *Slavery's End,* 72.

88. Ibid., 73.

89. Qtd. in Fleming, *Documentary History,* vol. 1, 310–11.

90. Cartwright, *Triumph of Jim Crow,* 7.

91. Ibid., 6; Cimprich, *Slavery's End,* 118.

92. Taylor, *Negro in Tennessee,* 12.

93. Govan and Livingood, *Chattanooga Country,* 283.

94. Qtd. in McKenzie, *One South or Many?,* 126.

95. Qtd. in Fleming, *Documentary History,* vol. 1, 81.

96. U.S. Congress, *Report of the Joint Committee on Reconstruction,* 112, 117, 121.

97. McKenzie, *One South or Many?,* 130.

98. Harrison, "Recollections," 187.

99. *United States Census Reports,* 102, 109. The white population also increased during this period from 2,088 in 1860 to 3,812 in 1870.

100. Lamon, *Blacks in Tennessee,* 30.

101. Fuller, *History of Negro Baptists,* 90; Notes, National Urban League Collection, series 6, box 21, Manuscript Division, Library of Congress; *109th Anniversary of First Baptist Church,* Program, October 12, 1975, 2, Chattanooga African American Collection, Chattanooga African American Museum.

102. Notes, National Urban League Collection, series 6, box 21, Manuscript Division, Library of Congress.

103. The AME Zion denomination of Methodism was founded by African Americans in New York City in 1796 and operated primarily in northern states until emancipation. Nonetheless, the AME influence could be found in southern states even prior to the Civil War through their extensive missionary efforts. In the antebellum era, AME churches existed in Baltimore, Charleston, and New Orleans, and AME Zion churches appeared in the southern United States as the Civil War came to a close. Raboteau, *Slave Religion,* 204; DuBois, *Negro Church,* 47–48.

104. American Missionary Association, *Twenty-First Annual Report,* 13, 47. The AMA as a whole was even more patronizing in their treatment of freedmen. AMA white missionary motivations for uplift and "civilization" of African Americans were often fueled by the following sentiments expressed by Rev. J. Blanchard:

The Freedman now believes us his friends. Long crushed and kept down by the mighty power of this great nation, the whole United States have done to them, what the miserable faction of slaveholders never could, namely, we have crushed these people into complete subjection to authority; and the means of drunkenness and infidelity, bad books and worse lectures, have been kept from them by their condition. Such is the freedman of today, *gentle, docile, mild*; his submission to his owner may be transformed into submission to Christ.

See American Missionary Association, *Seventeenth Annual Report,* 120.

105. Fuller, *History of Negro Baptists,* 26.

106. Rabinowitz, *Race Relations,* 198–99.

107. Preparation Notes, *A Study of the Economic and Cultural Activities of the Negro Population of Chattanooga, Tennessee,* 1947, National Urban League Collection, series 6, box 22, Manuscript Division, Library of Congress.

108. First Congregational and First Baptist were especially helpful to their black congregations in times of great need such as the disastrous flood of 1867, which devastated much of the city. Reverend Tade wrote many of his counterparts throughout the South pleading for food, clothing, and even seedlings for the next growing season. See E. O.Tade to Rev. E. P. Smith, March 23, 1867, American Missionary Association Archives, Microfilm Reels, Manuscripts Division, Library of Congress.

109. American Missionary Association, *Twenty-Fourth Annual Report; African American Presence in Chattanooga,* p. 4, Chattanooga African American Collection, Chattanooga African American Museum.

110. *African American Presence in Chattanooga,* p. 4. It is unclear whether Howard was specifically a secondary school or a common school for all African Americans when it became public in the late 1870s. James D. Anderson notes that there were supposedly no black students enrolled in public high school in Tennessee by 1890, thus, perhaps Howard did not evolve into a secondary school until the 1890s. See Anderson, *Education of Blacks,* 188–89.

111. American Missionary Association, *Twenty-Second Annual Report,* 54–55; American Missionary Association, *Thirty-First Annual Report.*

112. E. O. Tade to E. P. Smith, November 16, 1868, American Missionary Association Archives, Microfilm Reels, Manuscripts Division, Library of Congress.

113. *Chattanooga City Directory 1880,* 29.

114. E. O. Tade to E. P. Smith, July 23, 1869, American Missionary Association Archives, Microfilm Reels, Manuscripts Division, Library of Congress.

115. Ibid.

116. *Chattanooga City Directory and Business Gazetteer,* 65–81.

117. Govan and Livingood, *Chattanooga Country,* 344.

118. *Chattanooga City Directory and Business Gazetteer,* 65–81.

119. Jasper T. Duncan, "From Slavery: Negroes' Progress," *Chattanooga Times,* September 18, 1938, 11–A; Taylor, *Negro in Tennessee,* 169.

120. It is doubtful that the clientele of these prominent black establishments, particularly Heggie's and Henderson's shop, were actually other African Americans. Many whites patronized African American barbershops, and the Read House was one of the exclusive white-only hotels in the city. When racial hostility escalated in the city near the close of the nineteenth century, the only African Americans to enter the Read House were employees. See McGehee, "E. O. Tade," 387.

121. "First City Directory Was Compiled in 1871," *Chattanooga Times*, September 18, 1938, 14–A; *Chattanooga City Directory and Business Gazetteer*, 69, 78; Taylor, *Negro in Tennessee*, 160.

122. American Missionary Association, *Twenty-First Annual Report*, 48.

123. *Chattanooga City Directory and Business Gazetteer*, 125–26.

124. Taylor, *Negro in Tennessee*, 236.

125. *Chattanooga City Directory and Business Gazetteer*, 92.

126. E. O. Tade to John Ogden, April 6, 1968, American Missionary Association Archives, Microfilm Reels, Manuscripts Division, Library of Congress.

127. Ward, *Dark Midnight*, 22–23. Holmes and Dickerson were among the original Fisk Jubilee Singers, while Alexander joined the ensemble in 1873.

Chapter 2: "The Freest Town on the Map"

1. Chattanooga's population doubled from 6,093 in 1870 to 12,892 in 1880. See Waring, *Report on the Social Statistics*, 135.

2. Advertisement, *Chattanooga Republican*, December 8, 1868, Livingood, *Chattanooga*, 85.

3. The Fourteenth Amendment (adopted in 1868) provides that "all persons born or naturalized on the United States and subject to the jurisdiction thereof are citizens of the United States and of the State wherein they reside," thus overturning rulings like that of the Dred Scott case and ensuring that native-born African Americans were citizens. The Fifteenth Amendment (adopted 1870) ensures the that "right of citizens of the United States to vote shall not be denied . . . on account of race, color, or previous condition of servitude."

4. Klebenow, *Two Hundred Years*, 193. For further information on Ochs's times in Chattanooga, see Tifft and Jones, *The Trust*, 13–31.

5. Waring, *Report on the Social Statistics*, 136; Connor, *Historical Guide*, 15; Livingood, *Chattanooga*, 90–95.

6. Woodward, *Origins*, ix, 147.

7. Rabinowitz, *First New South, 1865–1920*, 2.

8. For studies that examine the fundamental ideologies of the antebellum South and its social hierarchies, see Cash, *Mind of the South*; Williamson, *Rage for Order*. Both discuss how white southerners were bound by a sense of kinship that stemmed from the reality that they all were related (often directly) to the families who established the southern colonies. Many white members of the Old South also shared a

love of romanticism, hedonism, honor, and tradition, which unified them. Although there was a distinct hierarchy between planters and common whites, the possibility of conflict was lessened by *noblesse oblige,* or the belief that the planter had an honor-bound obligation to the weak and powerless (Cash 74). Most importantly, the antebellum South avoided class conflict through the institution of slavery. As long as enslaved African Americans were thought of as subhuman, planters and common whites could unite in the belief of white supremacy. Cash's text further explores how a sense of southern nationalism developed in the face of the Civil War and what many southerners perceived to be "northern aggression."

9. According to Waring, *Report on the Social Statistics,* which highlighted the most populated United States cities of 1880, Memphis and Nashville were the other two prominent Tennessee urban centers. Doyle, *New Men,* 16.

10. Waring, *Report on the Social Statistics,* 136.

11. Qtd. in Livingood, *Chattanooga Country,* 644. Chattanooga publicly rejected the terrorist activities of the Klan soon after the organization had been founded and several years before the federal government took action against violent white supremacist groups with the passage of the Ku Klux Klan acts, or "Force Acts," in April 1871. The violent chaos the Klan could have inflicted would have destroyed the image that city leaders like John T. Wilder perpetuated: that "Chattanooga is not a Southern nor a Northern city" and is tolerant of a regional, religious, and racial mix of citizens. See Livingood, *Chattanooga,* 85.

12. McCallie and Crutchfield were members of two of the most prominent families in antebellum Chattanooga. As a leading spiritual figure, McCallie would be called on to keep the peace between hostile white Chattanoogans and the African American community in the early 1900s. See Curriden and Phillips, *Contempt of Court.* Crutchfield owned Crutchfield House, one of the premier hotels that hired African American slaves in the antebellum era.

13. Livingood, *Chattanooga,* 84–87.

14. Qtd. in *Reconstruction and Industrialization,* 589.

15. *Chattanooga City Directory 1880,* 34; *Chattanooga City Directory 1881,* 31.

16. *Report on Population of the United States,* 656.

17. *United States Census Reports,* 102, 109; Waring, *Report on the Social Statistics,* 135.

18. *United States Census Reports,* 102, 109; Waring, *Report on the Social Statistics,* 135. Between 1870 and 1880, 2,864 blacks moved to the city, while between 1880 and 1890, the number of black migrants totaled 7,478.

19. Ayers, *Promise of the New South,* 55.

20. *Report on Population of the United States,* 481. Chattanooga's total population was 29,100, of which 16,525 were white and 12,563 were black. There were also ten Chinese, one Japanese, and one Indian resident in the city. Hamilton County's entire population totaled 53,482, of which 35,747 were white and 17,717 were black.

21. Johnson and Campbell, *Black Migration,* 62.

22. Tena Thomas Suggs and Sadie Thomas Mickle, "The Black Community: An Integral Part of Lookout Mountain's History and Growth," p. 2, Chattanooga African American Collection; Interview with Tena Suggs by Chattanooga African American Museum Staff, August 1994, Chattanooga African American Museum.

23. Tena Thomas Suggs and Sadie Thomas Mickle, "The Black Community: An Integral Part of Lookout Mountain's History and Growth," pp. 1, 3, Chattanooga African American Collection, Chattanooga African American Museum.

24. White, *Biography and Achievements*, 21.

25. Ibid., 22, 48.

26. "African American Presence in Chattanooga, 1900–1940," Chattanooga African American Collection, Chattanooga African American Museum; Author's interview with Vilma S. Fields, November 9, 2000.

27. The exact year of the Smith family's relocation is unconfirmed. The city directory for 1892, the year of Bessie's birth, lists the Smith family living on 11 Evans and Cross Streets near Charles Street in West Chattanooga. See *Directory of Chattanooga* (1892), 772. The Smith family will be discussed in greater depth in the following chapter.

28. Johnson, *Honorable Titan*, 78.

29. Connor, *Historical Guide*, 59.

30. *Points of Interest*, 2–3.

31. Connor, *Historical Guide*, 59–61.

32. Livingood, *Hamilton County*, 256; Klebenow, *Two Hundred Years*, 210.

33. *Directory of Chattanooga* (1892), 52, 54, 118, 119. By "substantial number," I refer to the fourteen African American blacksmiths listed out of a city total of thirty, the thirty-four black shoemakers out of sixty-one, and thirty-nine black barbers out of a city total of forty-four.

34. Connor, *Historical Guide*, 19–21; *Points of Interest*, 6.

35. Doyle, *New Men*, xiv.

36. In general, "class" in the black Chattanooga community was not solely defined by income bracket but rather by a level of community-prescribed social status and customs. For example, a teacher might be revered as a black professional by his or her peers for his or her type of occupation and the community respect attached to the position, despite a relatively low income. Likewise, a person could have a working-class job such as a domestic servant but earn and save enough money to live a middle-class lifestyle in terms of material possessions and social status. These subtle distinctions about class terminology in the Chattanooga community were derived through personal discussions with Vilma S. Fields and Leroy Henderson, November 9, 2000.

37. Author's interview with Vilma S. Fields, November 9, 2000.

38. For a discussion of the longevity of these initial black firms in Chattanooga and East Tennessee, see Kenzer, "Black Businessmen."

39. White, *Biography and Achievements*, 23, 58.

40. See Cartwright, *Triumph of Jim Crow*, for a comparative discussion of the demise of the Republican party in each of these Tennessee cities.

41. Ezzell, "Yankees in Dixie," 146.

42. Ibid., 162; Jasper T. Duncan, "From Slavery: Negroes' Progress," *Chattanooga Times*, September 18, 1938, 11–A.

43. White, *Biography and Achievements*, 21, 32; Cartwright, *Triumph of Jim Crow*, 154–55.

44. White, *Biography and Achievements*, 22, 24, 46, 58, 63, 72; Jasper T. Duncan, "From Slavery: Negroes' Progress," *Chattanooga Times*, September 18, 1938, 11–A.

45. White, *Biography and Achievements*, 58.

46. Kenzer, "Black Businessmen," 63–66.

47. White, *Biography and Achievements*, 48, 57, 81, 88.

48. *City Directory of Chattanooga*, 839.

49. An example of this type of neighborhood overlap can be seen in the detailed outline of West Tenth Street in 1910. The Fannie Johnson household, which consisted of a mother and her four grown children from Alabama, lived in the middle of a block in the midst of the Freidman, Kaplan, and Siskin families, all Jewish immigrants from Russia. See Department of Commerce and Labor, *Thirteenth Census*, Hamilton County, Chattanooga City, 1910.

50. *Report on Population of the United States*, 481. In 1890, Ward 4 housed 2,444 blacks and 1,162 whites, while Ward 7 housed 3,352 blacks and 2,161 whites.

51. *G. M. Connelley and Co.'s Alphabetical Directory* (1903), 712–16.

52. *City Directory of Chattanooga*, pages at end of directory listing suburbs.

53. Qtd. in Wilson, *Chattanooga's Story*, 220.

54. Coulter, "Negroes of Chattanooga," 22–28.

55. Doyle, *New Men*, 13.

56. Livingood, *Hamilton County*, 270–74, 304–6. Only 559 blacks relocated to the city between 1890 and 1900, while 7,478 blacks migrated between 1880 and 1890. See *Report on Population of the United States*, 475, 520, 556.

57. Jasper T. Duncan, "From Slavery: Negroes' Progress," *Chattanooga Times*, September 18, 1938, 11–A; White, *Biography and Achievements*, 13, 22, 39.

58. Coulter, "Negroes of Chattanooga," 57; *Directory of Chattanooga* (1892), 13; *City Directory of Chattanooga*, 15; "African American Presence in Chattanooga, 1900–1940," p. 6.

59. Author's interview with James Bowles, November 9, 2000.

60. McGehee, "E. O. Tade," 386.

61. In 1890 there were a total of 4,451 students, of which 2,573 were white and 1,963 were black. There were seventy-four teachers, of which forty-five were white and twenty-nine were black. See Livingood, *Hamilton County*, 239–40.

62. *City Directory of Chattanooga*, 17–20; White, *Biography and Achievements*, 35, 43–44, 75–76; Notes, National Urban League Collection, series 6, box 21, Manuscript Division, Library of Congress.

63. Fuller, *History of Negro Baptists*, 162–72.

64. "Local Notes" and "Christmas Entertainment," *Justice*, December 24, 1887, 4.

65. White, *Biography and Achievements,* 14, 49; Directory of Lodges, *Justice,* December 24, 1887, 4.

66. See advertisement for the Phoenix lodge opening festival in *Justice,* December 24, 1887, 1.

67. *City Directory of Chattanooga,* 110–11.

68. McGehee, "E. O. Tade," 383.

69. Cartwright, *Triumph of Jim Crow,* 255.

70. Qtd. in Ezzell, "Yankees in Dixie," 146–47.

71. Qtd. in ibid.; qtd. in Cartwright, *Triumph of Jim Crow,* 149.

72. Cartwright, *Triumph of Jim Crow,* 150.

73. Ibid., 152–53.

74. Ibid., 158; Lamon, *Black Tennesseans,* 40. The poll tax was a significant deterrent to black suffrage; one dollar often represented one or two days' salary for African American workers.

75. The local police force remained entirely white from 1883 until 1948. However, some Chattanooga African Americans retained political office even after redistricting. Hiram Tyree was an alderman in the Fourth Ward through 1904, while Charles Grigsby was a member of the city council during the same period. See Centurion Committee, *Centurion,* 41–42, 99–100; White, *Biography and Achievements,* 32, 48.

76. Lamon, *Black Tennesseans,* 2.

77. Connor, *Historical Guide,* 16 (emphasis mine). Ironically, Connor made this comment in 1889, immediately before the greatest surge in African American migration in the 1890s.

78. McGehee, "E. O. Tade," 387.

79. Ayers, *Promise of the New South,* 138.

80. Lamon, *Black Tennesseeans,* 4.

81. Ibid., 7–8.

82. Author's interview with Vilma Fields, November 9, 2000; author's interview with Tommy Mauldin, November 9, 2000; "African American Presence in Chattanooga, 1900–1940," p. 5.

83. Lamon, *Black Tennesseans,* 29–31.

84. Interview with George A. Key by Chattanooga African American Museum Staff, August 1994. When asked about segregation in the city, Key remarked that although all public facilities, like drinking fountains and streetcars, were segregated, he never desired to use white-only facilities for he could obtain almost everything he needed within the black commercial center.

85. Crawford, "Business Negroes," 534, 537.

86. "African American Presence in Chattanooga, 1900–1940," pp. 1–3.

87. White, *Biography and Achievements,* 78, 80, 84; Crawford, "Business Negroes," 536.

88. "African American Presence in Chattanooga, 1900–1940," pp. 4–5; *Justice,* December 24, 1887, 1.

89. *Justice,* December 24, 1887, 3; Lamon, *Black Tennesseans,* 29–30; "African American Presence in Chattanooga, 1900–1940," p. 5.

90. Qtd. in Lamon, *Black Tennesseans,* 31.

Chapter 3: The Empress's Playground

1. I use the 1892 birth date in accordance with the data reported in the 1900 Hamilton County manuscript census. The 1900 census quotes July 1892 as Smith's birth date, while most other sources note April as Smith's birth month. Laura Smith's age as well as the Smiths' state of origin as Alabama were as derived from the 1900 census. Department of Commerce and Labor, *Twelfth Census: Population,* roll 1574, book 2, 69a.

2. Calculating the exact year of the Smith family's arrival is difficult because of the absence of personal records on the family, such as a diary or family interviews, that recount the trip from Alabama in to Chattanooga. I have arrived at this time span because the 1900 manuscript census lists the birth date of Clarence, the youngest of the Smith children to be born in Alabama, as October 1885. See Department of Commerce and Labor, *Twelfth Census: Population.*

3. Livingood, *Chattanooga,* 94.

4. Ibid., 98; Connor, *Historical Guide,* 27–29.

5. *Chattanooga Map.*

6. Connor, *Historical Guide,* 22.

7. Tifft and Jones, *The Trust,* 18.

8. Out of the sixteen families who had households on Evans Street, where the Smith family made their home at the time of Bessie's birth, five were white. See *Directory of Chattanooga* (1892), 772.

9. Gwendolyn Smith Bailey, interviewed by George Ricks and Suzanne Marcus, March 3, 1987, Chattanooga African American Collection, Chattanooga African American Museum.

10. Author's interview with Vilma Fields, November 9, 2000.

11. Qtd. in Jenkins, "1890's Tour," 245.

12. Although there is no formal record of William Smith's birth date, Laura Smith and her children's birth dates are given in the 1900 manuscript census. See Department of Commerce and Labor, *Twelfth Census: Population.*

13. See Albertson, *Bessie,* 7–8; Moore, *Somebody's Angel Child,* 3. Few clergymen earned enough income to only have one occupation, and Smith's bivocational status would have been typical. See Flynt, *Alabama Baptists,* 158–60.

14. If William was the same age as Laura Smith (b. 1850) or older, he spent at least fifteen years in slavery, most likely performing some type of agricultural work. His birth state of Alabama was determined from the 1900 and 1910 census under the category "Place of birth of the Father of said person." See Department of Commerce and Labor, *Twelfth Census: Population.*

15. Connor, *Historical Guide,* 60; *Norwood's Directory,* 346.

16. See Chattanooga city directories, 1887–98; *Directory of Chattanooga* (1898), 639.

17. Industrial jobs offered considerably higher wages than farm labor. In 1899, a farm laborer in the Southeast on average earned $10.72 a month, while a construction worker in 1900 could earn $11.43 a week. See "Farm Laborers—Average Monthly Earnings with Board, by Geographic Divisions," in *Historical Statistics,* 162. The "rise through the ranks" scenario, in which agricultural workers became factory laborers and then entrepreneurs, is one of the most common labor patterns found in the biographies of Chattanooga's rising black entrepreneurs of the early 1900s. See White, *Biography and Achievements.*

18. Qtd. in Helm, *Angel Mo' and Her Son,* 68 (emphasis mine).

19. Ibid., 75.

20. Ibid., 67; Lamon, *Black Tennesseans,* 136.

21. U.S. Bureau of the Census, "Annual Earnings by Occupation," in *Historical Statistics,* 166.

22. Lamon, *Black Tennesseans,* 136.

23. Qtd. in Schneider, *African American History in the Press,* 1185.

24. Ibid., 1184.

25. For a brief discussion of the depression of the 1890s, see Ayers, *Promise of the New South,* 252–54, 283–82. For a further explanation of how the depression affected Chattanooga specifically, see Ezzell, "Yankees in Dixie," 278–85.

26. Schneider, *African American History in the Press,* 1185. The *New York Times* reported that over seven hundred African Americans fled the city in November 1892 alone. There are no reports that the company Smith worked for that year, Montague and Company, shut down or let workers go for any period.

27. "They Quit Work: Fifty Negro Laborers Object to Compulsory Insurance," *Chattanooga Daily Times,* February 1, 1898.

28. Ibid.

29. Like his birth date, William Smith's exact date of death is not known but can be placed within these ranges because he was still listed as living on Cross Street in the 1899 directory, published in November of that year, while Laura Smith was noted as a widow by the June publication of the 1900 federal census.

30. Grimes, *Backwater Blues,* 134. Although many of the assertions that result from Grimes's attempt to trace the Smith family back to their Alabama roots have not been verified (including the claim that the Rev. William Smith of Lawrence County was indeed Bessie Smith's father), I will use Grimes's assertions for the purposes of this chapter, for she delves back further into research on the Smith family than any other Bessie Smith biographer.

31. *Directory of Chattanooga* (1892), 18.

32. Fuller, *History of Negro Baptists,* 91.

33. Qtd. in Helm, *Angel Mo' and Her Son,* 70.

34. "Church History," accessed September 27, 2005, <www.angelfire.com/tn/fbaptist/indexdirect.html>.

35. "An In-Depth Account of Second Missionary Baptist Church," accessed October 1, 2005, <www.smbchurch.org/history2.html>.

36. *Directory of Chattanooga* (1892), 18; Connor, *Historical Guide*, 1889 map insert.

37. "An In-Depth Account of Second Missionary Baptist Church."

38. H. L. Walker, A.R. "The Influence of Women," in Carter, *Biographical Sketches*, 86.

39. DuBois, "Of the Faith of Fathers," 327–28.

40. Ibid.

41. Fuller, *History of Negro Baptists*, 204.

42. Carter, *Biographical Sketches*, 116–17; Flynt, *Alabama Baptists*, 182–83.

43. Flynt, *Alabama Baptists*, 155, 237–38.

44. Carter, *Biographical Sketches*, 165–68.

45. Lincoln and Mamiya, "Performed Word," 47; Southern, *Music of Black Americans*, 44.

46. Work, "Negro Spiritual," 19.

47. Lincoln and Mamiya, "Performed Word," 47.

48. For the lyrics of some of these early African American worship songs, see Allen, Ware, and Garrison, *Slave Songs of the United States*. For further information on the lining out process and the collection of hymns, see Southern, *Music of Black Americans*, 262–63, 454–56. Also see Floyd, *Power of Black Music*, 58–61.

49. Fellowship services that received unusually high attendance from different denominations or even races often made the society pages of black newspapers. Such was the case in March 1901, when the Warren AME church hosted white and black pastors from the Presbyterian, Methodist Episcopal, and Baptist churches. "Chattanooga News," *Indianapolis Freeman*, March 9, 1901.

50. In 1899, there was an even number of black Baptist and black Methodist churches, each having fourteen established congregations in the city. *City Directory of Chattanooga*, 17, 19–20.

51. Southern, *Music of Black Americans*, 76, 81; Southern, "Hymnals of the Black Church," 143.

52. Payne and Smith, *Recollections of Seventy Years*, 237–38, 254; Maultsby, "Use and Performance of Hymnody," 87.

53. "Chattanooga News," *Indianapolis Freeman*, June 20, 1903.

54. Although Smith's later antics of bawdy behavior and a quick temper are legendary, these traits apparently coexisted with the Christian virtues of generosity and kindness, which she particularly bestowed on her loved ones. Such acts could be an example of how she transferred the traditional Christian teachings of her youth into her own life. After Smith's death, the drummer Zutty Singleton commented that she appeared to be "real close to God, very religious" in her personality and that she always called upon "the Lord's name." See Singleton, "I Remember the Queen."

55. Brown, "Black Religion," 257.

56. Ibid., 259.

57. For brief discussions of African American women and sharecropping, see Jones, *Labor of Love*, 81–95; Hine and Thompson, *Shining Thread of Hope*, 152–53.

58. Qtd. in Helm, *Angel Mo' and Her Son*, 66.

59. Waring, *Report on the Social Statistics*, 137–39.

60. Ibid., 138.

61. Albertson, *Bessie*, 8.

62. Cowan, *More Work for Mother*, 162.

63. Ibid., 56–57, 162–63; Green, *Uncertainty of Everyday Life*, 96–100.

64. Livingood, *Hamilton County*, 273.

65. Department of Commerce and Labor, *Twelfth Census: Population*, sheet 12.

66. Born in 1850, Laura would have been a little over fifteen years old by the end of the Civil War and the demise of slavery, an age by which many enslaved women had already experienced voluntary or involuntary sexual activity and pregnancy. For more on women, health, and childhood during slavery, see Steckel, "Women, Work, and Health"; King, "'Suffer with Them till Death.'"

67. Jones, *Labor of Love*, 123.

68. Ayers, *Promise of the New South*, 185.

69. In the aftermath of slavery, many African Americans understandably wanted African American women to forgo working in white homes so that they could care for their own children and loved ones and escape the sexual advances and violent abuses of their white employers, rights that could not be enjoyed under the institution of slavery. See Hine and Thompson, *Shining Thread of Hope*, 152–53; Hunter, *To 'Joy My Freedom*, 51.

70. Data gathered from the 1900 federal census indicates that a native-born white woman with native parentage would sometimes perform wage labor until she was of marriageable age but then "gives up that occupation when she marries, or soon thereafter, and devotes herself to the duties of domestic life." In contrast, many immigrant and African American women contributed significantly to the financial stability of the household, even after marriage. The census notes that in 1900, out of the over two million African American women aged sixteen and up, over 40 percent were engaged in "breadwinning" or gainful occupations. See Department of Commerce and Labor, *Statistics of Women at Work*, 9–11.

71. Schweninger, *Black Property Owners*, 179–80.

72. Ibid., 180.

73. Jones, *Labor of Love*, 114.

74. At the time of William's death, the Smith family included Laura, her sons Bud, Andrew, and Clarence, and her daughters Viola, Tennie, Lulu, and Bessie. Andrew's young wife Cora was also a resident in the household. Although Andrew and Viola were gainfully employed—Andrew was listed as a boilermaker, and Viola was listed as a cook in the 1900 manuscript census—neither of them carried the financial responsi-

bility of leading the Smith household. On the contrary, Laura was officially designated "head of household," and the 100 Cross Street house was apparently mortgaged in her name. See Department of Commerce and Labor, *Twelfth Census: Population.*

75. For more on how black religious and benevolent institutions aided after a community member's death, see Brown, "Black Religion," 256–60; Rabinowitz, *Race Relations,* 210–12.

76. For brief sketches of African American female professionals in the city, see White, *Biography and Achievements;* Jasper T. Duncan, "From Slavery: Negroes' Progress," *Chattanooga Times,* September 18, 1938, 11–A.

77. Tucker, *Telling Memories,* 84.

78. Classifieds, *Chattanooga Daily Times,* August 3, 1912, September 2, 1912.

79. Department of Commerce and Labor, *Statistics of Women at Work,* 57.

80. Interview with Viola Lomax by Dr. Elizabeth Clake Lewis, March 6, 1993, "My Soul Looks Back and Wonders: A Dialogue with Women on the Ways of Work," Program in African American Culture Collection, National Museum of American History, Smithsonian Institution.

81. Qtd. in Lerner, *Black Women,* 227–28.

82. For a discussion of married women performing day domestic labor, see Katzman, *Seven Days a Week,* 86–91.

83. Joseph E, Smith, "The Care of Neglected Children," in "Social and Physical Conditions of Negroes in Cities," *Atlanta University Publications No. 2,* May 25, 1897, 41–42.

84. Ibid., 42.

85. For more on the social function of the service pan, see Hunter, *To 'Joy My Freedom,* 60–61; Jones, *Labor of Lover,* 128–29; Tucker, *Telling Memories,* 87, 176, 208; Nelson and Clark-Lewis, *Freedom Bags.*

86. Qtd. in Lerner, *Black Women,* 157. During the height of racial violence in the South, a number of men and women were lynched for defending themselves and loved ones or even addressing the crime of rape at the hands of white men. See Lerner, *Black Women,* 161–63.

87. Qtd. in ibid., 157–58.

88. Spencer Williams, "Washerwoman's Blues," Bessie Smith, Columbia 14384–D. The "Gold Dust Twins" refers to a caricature of two naked African American infants, a common advertising icon of the era for Fairbanks Gold Dust Washing Powder. See the Afro-Americana file in the Warshaw Collection of Business Americana, Archives Center, National Museum of American History, Smithsonian Institution.

89. Tucker, *Telling Memories,* 90–92.

90. Ibid., 199; Biola, "Black Washerwoman," 24–25.

91. Tucker, *Telling Memories,* 84.

92. Hunter, *To 'Joy My Freedom,* 62.

93. For a discussion of Atlanta's "washing amazons," the washerwoman's organization, see ibid., 88–101.

94. Department of Commerce and Labor, *Occupations*, 432–33.

95. "How Negro Washerwomen Have Fine Cars Is Told," *Chattanooga News*, February 17, 1925.

96. Ibid.

97. *G. M. Connelley and Co.'s Alphabetical Directory* (1907), 590. The directory notes Viola's occupation as a laundress.

98. Ibid. (1909), 623.

99.. Hampton and Haskins, *Hamp*, 25.

100. Laura Smith died sometime in 1902. There is no formal record of her death, but some of the most recently written articles on Bessie Smith contend that she died shortly before Bessie was ten, which would have been in 1902. See "Bessie Sang for Coins along City's 'Big Nine,'" *Chattanooga Free Press*, April 10, 1994, A5. William and Laura Smith both died from undisclosed illness. Perhaps their deaths can be attributed to the high rate of disease that swept across the Chattanooga black communities due to inadequate living conditions. The small shotgun houses that bordered Chattanooga's industrial district often had little sanitation or ventilation, and infectious diseases could rampantly spread throughout such a neighborhood. As early as 1897, African American doctors complained about the high rates of tuberculosis in the impoverished black sectors, and by 1916 a Chattanooga health report commented that "tuberculosis, organic heart disease, pneumonia and pellagra . . . were rapidly decreasing the negro race in this city." See A. J. Love, M.D., "Causes of Consumption and Practical Methods of Preventing It" and "Social and Physical Conditions of Negroes in Cities," *Atlanta University Publications No. 2*, May 25, 1897, 46–50; Lamon, *Black Tennesseans*, 137–38.

101. Viola Smith was born in May 1877. See Department of Commerce and Labor, *Twelfth Census: Population*, roll 1574, book 2, 69.

102. A. J. Love, M.D., "Social and Physical Conditions of Negroes in Cities," *Atlanta University Publications No. 2*, May 25, 1897, 41.

103. By late 1902 the home was occupied by John Massengale. See *G. M Connelley and Co.'s Alphabetical Directory* (1903).

104. Between 1908 and 1910, Viola boarded at 69 Pleasant Street (1908), at 153 Charles Street (1909), rented a home with her daughter Laura and Bessie at 14 School Street (1910), and boarded at 175 Charles Street (1910). Andrew and Cora established their own household in the same West Chattanooga neighborhood where Bessie was born and in 1910 rented a home on 30 Charles Street. See *G. M. Connelley and Co.'s Alphabetical Directory* (1908, 1909, 1910); Department of Commerce and Labor, *Thirteenth Census: Population*, roll 1502, book 3, 164 b, and roll 1503, book 1, 67 b.

105. "Annual Baccalaureate Sermon: Chattanooga School Graduates a Large Class of Students—Interesting Program Rendered," *Indianapolis Freeman*, May 28, 1904.

106. "Bessie Sang for Coins along City's 'Big Nine,'" *Chattanooga Free Press*, April 10, 1994, A5.

107. Anderson, *Education of Blacks*, 199.

108. Lindenmeyer, "Adolescence."

109. Department of Commerce and Labor, *Occupations,* cclxiv.

110. An example of the young age of women wage earners can be seen in the statistics gathered from the 1900 federal census, which report that there were gainfully employed women as young as ten. See Department of Commerce and Labor, *Statistics of Women at Work,* 13, 58.

111. See Department of Commerce and Labor, *Twelfth Census: Population;* Department of Commerce and Labor, *Thirteenth Census: Population,* roll 1503, book 1, 67 b. The 1900 census notes that Lulu, age sixteen, and Clarence, age fourteen, had spent six months and nine months, respectively, in school the past year and that they were both literate. Interestingly, the 1910 census notes that Viola had acquired some reading and writing skills since the 1900 census and that Bessie, approximately age sixteen, was also literate.

112. White, *Biography and Achievements,* 73.

113. See "History of the Phyllis Wheatley Branch of the YWCA," p. 1, in National Urban League Collection, series 6, box 22, Manuscript Division, Library of Congress; Jasper T. Duncan, "From Slavery: Negroes' Progress," *Chattanooga Times,* September 18, 1938, 11–A.

114. Jones, *Recreation and Amusement,* 101.

115. Ibid., 91; Department of Commerce and Labor, *Thirteenth Census: Population.*

116. Interview with George A. Key by Chattanooga African American Museum Staff, August 1994.

117. Allan McMillan, "New York Sees Bessie Smith; Wonders Where She's Been," *Chicago Defender,* March 28, 1936.

118. "Local Notes, *Justice,* December 24, 1887; "For Thirty Days," *Chattanooga Daily Times,* February 1, 1898; "In Criminal Court," *Chattanooga Daily Times,* January 24, 1906.

119. "Exciting Reencounter: Dr. Love, a Colored Physician, Gets in Trouble at Anderson's Drug Store," *Chattanooga Daily Times,* March 18, 1898.

120. "Saloon Tragedy: Martin Hackett the Well Known Fireman, in Trouble," *Chattanooga Daily Times,* March 4, 1898.

121. For an in-depth discussion of Johnson's trial, his lynching, and its importance in legal history, see Curriden and Phillips, *Contempt of Court.* Many in the white and African American communities sought to stop violence before it began, but for different reasons. Much of the white community called for Johnson's death for his alleged crime, but they wanted him to be legally executed after a trial. One of the city's most prominent white citizens, Reverend McCallie, publicly maintained that mob violence was "contagious and would lead to other atrocities." See Curriden and Phillips, *Contempt of Court,* 67. Hence, many white residents, particularly the elite, did not want the economic and social productivity of the city to come to a halt in the midst of chaos. The elite in the black community were careful to denounce whoever

raped the young white woman as a "vicious and degraded negro" and called for his capture. This condemnation of the rape was an attempt to prevent the white citizens from assaulting and destroying African Americans at will. See "Better Class of Negroes Vigorously Condemn Crime," *Chattanooga Daily Times,* January 26, 1906.

123. For more on how African American children learned the "rules of segregation" and how to survive in the racist southern environment, see Litwack, *Trouble in Mind,* 3–52.

Chapter 4: Life on "Big Ninth" Street

1. "Ninth Street in New Gown: Famous Thoroughfare Has Reformed," *Chattanooga Times,* September 2, 1917, 13.

2. *G. M. Connelley and Co.'s Alphabetical Directory* (1908), 903.

3. "History of the East Ninth Street Area," n.d., p. 1, Chattanooga African American Collection, Chattanooga African American Museum.

4. The East Ninth Area includes the central street itself, the surrounding cross streets, and Gilmer Street (now East Eighth).

5. Interview with George A. Key by Chattanooga African American Museum Staff, August 1994; interview with Ted Bryant by Paul Moss, June 9–10, 2000; author's interview with Leroy Henderson, November 11, 2000. Beale Street became the hub of black life in Memphis when the prominent and wealthy black resident Robert Reed Church Sr. purchased land formerly ravaged by yellow fever and developed Church's Park, a black recreational center, in 1899 After the 1910s, Beale Street became home to churches, shops, saloons, and theaters patronized by African Americans. As a hub of black musical and recreational activity and the area where W. C. Handy resided when he first popularized written blues music, Beale Street became known to many as the street "where blues began" and a "Main Street of Negro America." See Lee, *Beale Street;* McKee and Chisenhall, *Beale Street Black and Blue,* 5–81.

6. "History of the East Ninth Street Area," p. 2; Travis Wolfe, "M. L. King Business Area Named to Historic Register," *Chattanooga Times,* April 24, 1984, B2.

7. See Southern, *Music of Black Americans,* 224–27, for further information on the use of worksongs in the late nineteenth and early twentieth centuries.

8. Hazen and Hazen, *Music Men,* 43; Newsom, "American Brass Band."

9. Hazen and Hazen, *Music Men,* 41–67.

10. Hennessey, *From Jazz To Swing,* 17.

11. *Make It Funky;* Stewart et al., "The Origins of Jazz—Pre-1895."

12. Jackson, *Movin' on Up.*

13. Armstrong, *Satchmo,* 40–51.

14. African American troupes often referred to themselves as "colored" minstrels, while white revues called themselves "negro" or "nigger" minstrels. See Toll, *Blacking Up,* 199.

15. Nathan, *Dan Emmet,* 32.

16. Butcsch, *Making of American Audiences*, 89–92.

17. For a discussion of the functions of minstrelsy and its racist and arguably antiracist platforms, see Lhamon, *Raising Cain;* Lott, *Love and Theft.*

18. Townsend, *Negro Minstrels*, iv.

19. Ibid., 5.

20. Powell, *World's Best Book*, 55.

21. While Emmett is traditionally credited with writing "Dixie," the Snowdens, a family of black Ohio minstrels who were Emmett's contemporaries, may have originated the tune that Emmett "borrowed" and made famous. See Sacks and Sacks, *Way Up North in Dixie.*

22. Nathan, *Dan Emmet,* 50.

23. George and Hart's Georgia Minstrels, *Opera House Program,* Great Bend, Kansas, January 29, 1901, in George and Hart's Up to Date Georgia Minstrels Scrapbook, Archives Center, National Museum of American History, Smithsonian Institution.

24. Handy, *Father of the Blues,* 33.

25. Toll, *Blacking Up,* 223.

26. Ibid., 223; Handy, *Father of the Blues,* 62.

27. Frank Melville to J. Ledlie Hees, New York, March 23, 1904, in Music File, Warshaw Collection of Business Americana, Archives Center, National Museum of American History, Smithsonian Institution; Billings-Merriam Family Vaudeville Scrapbooks, Archives Center, National Museum of American History, Smithsonian Institution; "The Stage," *Indianapolis Freeman,* 1900.

28. Hasse, "Ragtime: From the Top," 6. For a brief, nonspecialist explanation of syncopation, see Sales, *Jazz,* 26–34.

29. Davin, "Conservations with James P. Johnson," 169.

30. Hasse "Ragtime: From the Top," 9.

31. Malone, *Steppin' on the Blues,* 71–72.

32. Southern, *Music of Black Americans,* 322–25.

33. Washington, *Up from Slavery,* 89.

34. Ibid.

35. Johnson, *Autobiography of an Ex-Colored Man,* 448.

36. Southern, *Music of Black Americans,* 326–31; Davin, "Conversations with James P. Johnson," 175–77.

37. Fletcher, *One Hundred Years,* 154, 167–70.

38. Sampson, *Blacks in Blackface,* 9.

39. Ibid., 23–25.

40. Fletcher, *One Hundred,* 135–48; Jansen and Jones, *Spreadin' Rhythm Around,* 23–24.

41. Fletcher, *One Hundred,* 137; Jansen and Jones, *Spreadin' Rhythm Around,* 24.

42. Sampson, *Blacks in Blackface,* 71.

43. Ibid., 9.

44. Biola, "Black Washerwoman," 25.

45. Fletcher, *One Hundred*, 214.

46. Levine, *Black Culture*, 214.

47. The classic blues format sung by Bessie Smith, Ma Rainey, Mamie Smith, Alberta Hunter, and other vocalists had a twelve- or sixteen-bar format, an AAB lyric structure, and was usually accompanied by a rhythm section of piano, drums, and brass instruments. For further information on the technical structure of the blues, see Southern, *Music of Black Americans*, 333–38; Sales, *Jazz*, 16–22.

48. "Looking Backward," *Chattanooga Daily Times*, July 1, 1952.

49. Ibid.; *G. M. Connelley and Co.'s Alphabetical Directory* (1908), 906.

50. "Looking Backward," *Chattanooga Daily Times*, July 1, 1952.

51. Interview with Gwendolyn Smith Bailey by James Hardy, October 16, 1986, Chattanooga African American Museum; Interview with Gwendolyn Smith Bailey by George Ricks and Suzanne Marcus, March 3, 1987, Chattanooga African American Museum.

52. Qtd. in Harris, *Rise of Gospel Blues*, 38–39.

53. Ibid.

54. Jackson, "Singing of Good Tidings," 447.

55. Runyan, "Influence of Joseph O. Cadek," 140.

56. Ibid., 153–55; "Amusements," *Chattanooga Daily Times*, 1893.

57. *Directory of Chattanooga* (1897), 20; Nashville, Chattanooga, and St. Louis schedule, 1886, Railroad File, Warshaw Collection of Business Americana, Archives Center, National Museum of American History, Smithsonian Institution; "Railway Time Table," *Chattanooga Daily Times*, February 4, 1912.

58. Runyan, "Influence of Joseph O. Cadek," 19.

59. For further information on railroad porters and the transmission of culture, see Perata, *Those Pullman Blues*.

60. Like Beale Street, Decatur Street and Storyville were centers of low-income black entertainment in their respective cities. Decatur was home to popular black vaudeville theaters like the Eighty-One Theater and the Ninety-One Theater, while Storyville was a legendary red-light district in New Orleans in which several young jazz musicians got their starts in brothels and house parties. See Harris, *Rise of Gospel Blues*, 30–31; Collier, *Making of Jazz*, 64–65.

61. Handbill, George and Hart's Up to Date Georgia Minstrels Scrapbook, Archives Center, National Museum of American History, Smithsonian Institution.

62. Livingood, *Hamilton County*, 316–17; Wilson, *Chattanooga's Story*, 315–17.

63. New Opera House advertisement, *Chattanooga Daily Times*, March 3, 1898.

64. "The Stage," *Indianapolis Freeman*, May 14, 1910; *Chattanooga Daily Times*, January 28, 1912, and September 29, 1912.

65. Runyan, "Influence of Joseph A. Cadek," 28.

66. "Primose and West Minstrels," *Chattanooga Daily Times*, January 8, 1898.

67. *Chattanooga Daily Times* September 2, 1912; Runyan, "Influence of Joseph A. Cadek," 150–56; Sweeley, *Minstrel King March*.

68. *Indianapolis Freeman,* Theater notices, June 6, 1909; *Chattanooga Daily Times,* Theater advertisements, February 18, 1912.

69. "May Festival," *Indianapolis Freeman,* May 5, 1900; *Chattanooga Daily Times,* Theater advertisements, February 14, 1912. Jones was referred to as "Black Patti" by music critics who contended that his voice was similar to that of the European vocalist Adelina Patti.

70. *Indianapolis Freeman,* Theater advertisements, April 28, 1900.

71. Sampson, *Blacks in Blackface,* 383–88; Daughtry, "Sisseretta Jones," 40, 48.

72. Sampson, *Blacks in Blackface,* 438–39; "Ivy Theater Chattanooga," *Indianapolis Freeman,* December 24, 1910; White, *Biography and Achievements,* 24.

73. Handy, *Father of the Blues,* 34–36.

74. Bernhardt and Harris, *I Remember,* 7–8.

75. *Chattanooga Daily Times,* January 16, 1898; "Chattanooga Items," *Indianapolis Freeman,* September 19, 1903; "May Festival," *Indianapolis Freeman,* May 5, 1900.

76. Smith's age at the time she began street performing, like her birth year, is an issue of debate. Newspaper articles have reported that she was anywhere between seven and nine when she began her career. Chris Albertson, Smith's most referenced biographer, contends that she became a street performer sometime after her mother's death, "between the ages of eight and nine." Mabel Chew, "Singer Began at Seven," *Baltimore Afro-American,* March 27, 1926; Allan McMillan, "New York Sees Bessie Smith; Wonders Where She's Been," *Chicago Defender,* March 28, 1936; Albertson, *Bessie,* 8. There is little evidence to suggest that Smith began performing before her mother's death sometime in 1902, when Smith was ten years old. Bessie's interest in performing and need to supplement the household income escalated as she watched her brother leave home for the traveling stage in 1904, when Bessie was twelve years old. Smith most likely began her street performances during this window of time.

77. Andrew was reportedly born in February 1875. Department of Commerce and Labor, *Twelfth Census: Population;* Albertson, Liner notes, 8; Interview with Gwendolyn Smith Bailey by George Ricks and Suzanne Marcus, March 3, 1987, Chattanooga African American History Museum.

78. Albertson, Liner notes, 8.

79. Ibid.

80. Interview with Gwendolyn Smith Bailey by George Ricks and Suzanne Marcus, March 3, 1987, Chattanooga African American History Museum.

81. *G. M. Connelley and Co.'s Alphabetical Directory* (1902), 940–44.

82. Ibid. 940.

83. Harrison-Pepper, *Drawing a Circle,* xv.

84. How the commercial geography of a block changed is exemplified by the 600 block of East Ninth. In 1902, the block featured a black barbershop, an eating house, and ten African American residences divided by a stockyard, coal distributor, and white residences. By 1908, the same block was entirely composed of African American residences and businesses, except for a white grocery store managed by W. M.

Warren, the Lookout Transfer Company, and the G. R. Phillips saloon. See *Directory of Chattanooga* (1902), 940; *Directory of Chattanooga* (1908), 904.

85. "Bessie Sang for Coins along City's 'Big Nine,'" *Chattanooga Free Press*, April 10, 1994, A5; Albertson, Liner notes, 8.

86. Albertson, Liner notes, 8; Albertson, *Bessie*, 8.

87. Domosh, "Those 'Gorgeous Incongruities,'" 211.

88. Elam, "Black Performer," 289.

89. Mason, *Street Theater*, 28–30.

90. Jansen and Jones, *Spreadin' Rhythm Around*, 105–6; Fletcher, *One Hundred*, 137–43.

91. Hughie Cannon, "Won't You Come Home, Bill Bailey" (1902), *Parlor Song: Popular Sheet Music from the 1800s to the 1920s*, n.d., accessed March 18, 2002 <http://www.parlorsongs.com/issues/2002-1/thismonth/featureb.asp>.

92. Harrison, *Black Pearls*, 6.

93. Southern, *Music of Black Americans*, 332; Titon, *Early Downhome Blues*, 29–30; Oakley, *Devil's Music*, 42–43.

94. Titon, *Early Downhome Blues*, 29.

95. Lieb, *Mother of the Blues*, 3.

96. Handy, *Father of the Blues*, 74–75.

97. Qtd. in Bastin, *Red River Blues*, 38.

98. Ward, *Dark Midnight*, 22–23, 27, 300, 398.

99. Ibid., 398; "Negro Pioneers in Chattanooga in the 1800s," *Chattanooga Times*, July 1, 1928.

100. Handy, *Black Women in American Bands*; Santelli, *Big Book of Blues*, 16.

101. Harrison, *Black Pearls*, 204.

102. Charles, "The Age of a Jazzwoman," 183, 185; Sampson, *Blacks in Blackface*, 181.

103. Charles, "Age of a Jazzwoman," 188.

104. Helm, *Angel Mo' and Her Son*, 72, 97–99.

105. Ibid., 70–80; "Ticket Sale for Hayes Concert Today Forces Use of Larger Memorial Hall," *Chattanooga Times*, February 9, 1947.

106. Dall, *Wild Women Don' t Have the Blues*; Marvin, "Children of Legba," 144–45.

107. Waters, Price, and Blackburn, *To Me It's Wonderful*, 17.

108. Collins, *Black Feminist Thought*, 55.

109. National Urban League, "Table II: Population by Race Per Cent Negro 1870–1946," in *A Study of the Economic and Cultural Activities of the Negro Population of Chattanooga, Tennessee*, 1947, National Urban League Papers, series 6, box 22, Manuscripts Division, Library of Congress.

110. See the biographical sketches in White, *Biography and Achievements*, esp. 23, 58.

111. Deutsch, *Women and the City*, 115.

112. Crawford, "Business Negroes of Chattanooga," 536–37.

113. White, *Biography and Achievements,* 58; "Looking Backward," *Chattanooga Daily Times,* July 1, 1952.

114. *Directory of Chattanooga* (1892), 813–15.

115. *Directory of Chattanooga* (1902), 940–44.

116. *Directory of Chattanooga* (1908), 902–6.

117. Matthews, *Rise of the New Woman,* 19.

118. Hine and Thompson, *Shining Thread of Hope,* 180.

119. Terrell, "Progress of Colored Women," 294.

120. Marvin, "Children of Legba," 93–94.

121. Southern, *Music of Black Americans,* 244–48.

122. Ibid., 236.

123. Butsch, *Making of American Audiences,* 92.

124. "A Ringing Protest," *Chattanooga Daily Times,* January 28, 1898.

125. Butsch, *For Fun and Profit,* 14.

126. Butsch, *Making of American Audiences,* 112.

127. *Indianapolis Freeman,* January 13, 1900.

128. Marvin, "Children of Legba," 95; Sampson, *Blacks in Blackface,* 6–7.

129. *Indianapolis Freeman,* February 10, 1900 (emphasis mine).

130. "Interesting Items," *Indianapolis Freeman,* June 12, 1903; "Chattanooga Items," *Indianapolis Freeman,* May 14, 1904; "A Condensed Publication of Many Important Happenings of the Past Few Days," *Indianapolis Freeman,* June 25, 1904.

131. "Church Bans on Amusements," *New York Age,* June 14, 1924.

132. Fuller, *History of Negro Baptists,* 205, 300.

133. Ibid., 161.

134. McKee and Chisenhall, *Beale Street Black and Blue,* 146.

135. Helm, *Angel 'Mo and Her Son,* 72–73.

136. Gaines, *Uplifting the Race,* 3.

137. Centurion Committee, *Centurion,* 48.

138. Bureau of Police, *Seventh Annual Report,* 25.

139. Butsch, *Making of American Audiences,* 119.

140. Ezzell, "Yankees in Dixie," 56; "Ninth Street in New Gown: Famous Thoroughfare Has Reformed," *Chattanooga Times,* September 2, 1917, 13.

141. Williams, "Club Movement," 101. For a detailed overview of the black woman's-club movement, see Giddings, *When and Where I Enter,* 95–119.

142. Williams, "Club Movement," 102.

143. DuBois, "Problem of Amusement," 181.

144. Qtd. in Williams, "Social Status of the Negro Women," 298.

145. Hine and Thompson, *Shining Thread of Hope,* 183.

146. "Ragtime Music," *Indianapolis Freeman,* March 16, 1901.

147. The phrase "better class of negroes" stems from an article concerning the Ed Johnson lynching of 1906 in which many African Americans affiliated with religious

institutions condemned the supposed violent acts committed by Johnson. See "Better Class of Negroes Viciously Condemn Crime," *Chattanooga Daily Times,* January 26, 1906.

148. Kubik, *Africa and the Blues,* 6–8.

149. Viola was not completely supportive of her youngest sister performing on Ninth Street, but according to Bessie's niece by marriage, Ruby Walker Smith, "she [Viola] liked the money, though." See Albertson, Liner notes, 8.

150. Helm, *Angel 'Mo and Her Son,* 72–76.

151. "The Negro in Business" May 30–31, 1899, p. 15, in Atlanta University Press, *Atlanta University Publications, Nos. 1, 2, 4, 8, 9, 11, 13, 14, 15, 16, 17, 18.*

152. Author's interview with Vilma Fields, November 9, 2000; Interview with Theodore Bryant by Paul Moss, June 9–10, 2000, Chattanooga African American Musem.

153. Kenzer, "Black Businessmen," 75.

154. *Directory of Chattanooga* (1902), 940–44.

155. Kelley, *Race Rebels,* 51.

156. Handy, *Father of the Blues,* 79–80.

157. *Indianapolis Freeman,* June 14, 1902.

158. "Better Class of Negroes Viciously Condemn Crime," *Chattanooga Daily Times,* January 26, 1906.

159. Curriden and Phillips, *Contempt of Court,* 218.

160. Ibid., 220.

161. Hazzard-Gordon, *Jookin',* 88 (see esp. 84–119 for more on the function of the jook-joint, honky-tonk, and rent party).

162. Hunter, *To 'Joy My Freedom,* 180–83.

163. Ellison, "Richard Wright's Blues," 78.

164. For more on the function of dance and the blues environment, see Murray, *Stomping the Blues.*

165. Interview with Tena Suggs by Chattanooga African American Museum Staff, August 1994.

166. Author's interview with Vilma Fields, November 9, 2000; Author's interview with James Bowles, November 9, 2000.

167. Interview with Theodore Bryant by Paul Moss, June 9–10, 2000, Chattanooga African American History Museum.

Chapter 5: An Empress in Vaudeville

1. Theater Advertisements, *Indianapolis Freeman,* February 10, 1900.

2. Theater Advertisement, *Indianapolis Freeman* April 5, 1902.

3. Aida Overton Walker, "Aida Overton Walker: Says the Profession Has Improved with the Progression of Time," *Indianapolis Freeman,* December 28, 1912; "Seven Florida Creole Girls Minstrel," *Indianapolis Freeman,* January 3, 1903; "The New Howard Theatre, Washington, D.C.," *Indianapolis Freeman,* September 3, 1909.

4. Moore, *Somebody's Angel Child*, 18–25; Stewart-Baxter, *Ma Rainey*, 44, 47; Albertson, *Bessie*, 14–15.

5. "Pekin Theater, Memphis, Tenn.," *Indianapolis Freeman*, September 3, 1910; Department of Commerce and Labor, *Thirteenth Census: Population*, Hamilton County, Chattanooga City. Bessie is listed as part the chorus of a William and Gertrude ("Ma and Pa") Rainey Revue at the Pekin. She later returned to Chattanooga to live at 14 School Street with her sister Viola and niece Laura by April 1910.

6. "The Stage," *Indianapolis Freeman*, May 8, 1909. A key document that led me to further explore notices in the *Freeman* is Lynn Abbott and Doug Seroff, "Bessie Smith: The Early Years," in *The Ascendancy of Blues and Jazz in Minstrelsy and Vaudeville, 1910–1920*, Bessie Smith File, Chattanooga African American Museum.

7. *G. M. Connelley and Co.'s Alphabetical Directory* (1907) 590; *G. M. Connelley and Co.'s Alphabetical Directory* (1908), 610.

8. Pomerantz, *Where Peachtree*, 88; Department of Commerce, *Thirteenth Census: Population*, vol 2, 400.

9. In 1910 the Chattanooga black population totaled 17,942, while Atlanta's black population totaled 51,902. African Americans comprised a greater percentage of the total Chattanooga population than the Atlanta population (40.2 percent of Chattanooga's population and 33.5 percent of Atlanta's), yet by 1910, in the aftermath of Jim Crow segregation, substantial numerical presence did not necessarily translate into political power as it could in the late nineteenth century. See Department of Commerce, *Thirteenth Census: Population*, vol. 2, 400, and vol. 3, 762.

10. Qtd. in Harris, *Rise of Gospel Blues*, 280 n.13.

11. While Decatur Street did house some African American businesses, particularly places of amusement between the 80 and 100 blocks, it was far from the most African American–populated street in the downtown sector. One of the streets that housed more African American residents and establishments was Auburn Avenue, later known as "Sweet Auburn" by black Atlantans. In terms of commercial variety, Auburn Avenue was more similar to Chattanooga's Ninth Street than Decatur Street. See *Atlanta City Directory*, 36–38, 98–101; Pomerantz, *Where Peachtree*, 123–25.

12. The Atlanta Riot resulted in the death of twenty-five African Americans, the injury of hundreds more, and the flight of over a thousand from the city. Fueled by reports of black attacks against white women, thousands of white Atlanta residents terrorized and lynched members of the black community and destroyed black businesses, particularly the "dives" or saloons that they believed to be the "'breeding ground of Negro lust and crime'" (qtd. in Crowe, "Racial Massacres," 153). Many white Atlanta residents used the well-publicized Ed Johnson lynching in Chattanooga, which resulted in a Supreme Court trial, as a model of how white men should defend white womanhood. For further information, see Crowe "Racial Massacres."

13. See chapters 3 and 4 of this volume for a discussion of the Ed Johnson lynching in Chattanooga in March 1906. For more on the motives and results of the Atlanta Riot, see Litwack, *Trouble in Mind*, 315–19.

14. Harris, *Rise of Gospel Blues*, 42.

15. Sylvester Russell, "The Strenuous Life of a Showman," *Indianapolis Freeman*, May 29, 1909.

16. Arcade Theater advertisement, *Indianapolis Freeman*, September 24, 1910.

17. "Luna Park, Atlanta, GA," *Indianapolis Freeman*, August 13, 1910. In this Luna Park show, Bessie, along with Rosa Brannon and Nellie Nelson, were the chorus girls, while Walter Broadgedale was the comedian, and Wiggins and Wiggins were both the barbershop ensemble and the buck-and-wing dancers.

18. McKee and Chisenhall, *Beale Street Black and Blue*, 147–48. For a typical program listing for such a show, see "W. M. Benbow's Alabama Chocolate Drops," *Indianapolis Freeman*, December 24, 1910.

19. Harris, *Rise of Gospel Blues*, 42–43.

20. Mabel Chew, "Singer Began at Seven Years Old," *Baltimore Afro-American*, March 26, 1927.

21. For more on the evolution of African American stock companies, see Sampson, *Blacks in Blackface*, 10–14.

22. Bruno, "Dewey 'Pigmeat' Markham," 154.

23. Ibid.

24. Bernhardt and Harris, *I Remember*, 11.

25. Ibid., 10.

26. Abbott and Seroff, "Bessie Smith," pp. 1–2; "The Stage" *Indianapolis Freeman*, August 1909–October 1911.

27. Bruno, "Dewey 'Pigmeat' Markham," 155.

28. *Thirteenth Census: Population*, roll 1503, book 1, 67 b.

29. *Indianapolis Freeman*, May 14, 1910.

30. E. B. Dudley, "Chattanooga Show Talk," *Indianapolis Freeman*, May 21, 1910.

31. Swords proposed to "systemize" his business and was in the midst of developing four other black theaters across the Southeast in addition to the Ivy. As Swords's music manager, Dudley wanted to insure that his theaters attracted skilled African American performers "who could deliver the goods" and that African American audiences would have a hand in deciding who those performers would be. See Advertisement Section, *Indianapolis Freeman*, December 24, 1910.

32. Lieb, *Mother of the Blues*, 2, 24; *The Paramount Book of Blues*, n.d., p. 9, in Blues Women Folios, Samuel DeVincent Illustrated Sheet Music Collection, Archives Center, National Museum of American History, Smithsonian Institution.

33. Moore, *Somebody's Angel Child*, 18–25; Oliver, *Bessie Smith*, 5–6.

34. Harris, *I Remember*, 30.

35. Qtd. in Albertson, *Bessie*, 14.

36. "Pekin Theater, Memphis, Tenn.," *Indianapolis Freeman*, September 3, 1910. The entire cast included William and Gertrude Rainey, Bess [*sic*] Smith, Webb and Webb, and Gomez Lee.

37. Chew, "Singer Began at Seven Years Old," *Baltimore Afro American*, March 26, 1927.

38. "Pekin Theater, Memphis, Tenn.," *Indianapolis Freeman*, September 3, 1910.

39. Lieb, *Mother of the Blues,* 58. For further differentiation between folk or traditional blues and classic or vaudeville blues, see Titon, *Early Downhome Blues,* xv–xvii. Although there were distinct differences between traditional and vaudeville blues performers, the boundaries were not always so rigid that a traditional blues player could not perform before a paying theater audience or a vaudeville performer would not perform in the intimate juke joints or parties generally serviced by the solo traditional blues musician. Although labeled a classic blues performer, Bessie Smith was able to perform both styles.

40. Bernhardt and Harris, *I Remember,* 26.

41. Sterling Brown, "Ma Rainey," in Gates and McKay, *Norton Anthology,* 1221.

42. Qtd. in Bernhardt and Harris, *I Remember,* 89.

43. "The Stage," *Indianapolis Freeman,* November 8, 1913. Earlier reviews mention Smith as a "Tennessee coon shouter" (*Indianapolis Freeman,* September 3, 1910), but this 1913 review mentions specifically that "Bessie Smith set the house crazy singing 'I Got the Blues and Mean to Cry.'" See Abbott and Seroff, "Bessie Smith," p. 3. Bessie continued to perform alongside Ma Rainey as her career evolved, and in Smith's recording years, she and Ma Rainey wrote two songs together, "Don't Fish in My Sea" (1928) and "Weepin' Woman Blues" (1928). See Lieb, *Mother of the Blues,* 194, 196.

44. Theater Advertisements, *Indianapolis Freeman,* July 5, 1912.

45. Abbott and Seroff, "Bessie Smith," p. 2; *Indianapolis Freeman,* December 1, 1911.

46. "The Stage," *Indianapolis Freeman,* April 20, 1912.

47. Theater Advertisements, *Indianapolis Freeman,* July 5, 1912.

48. Theater Advertisements, *Indianapolis Freeman,* July 5, 1912; "The Stage," *Indianapolis Freeman,* June 24, 1912.

49. "Joel Theaters Advertisement," *Indianapolis Freeman,* December 28, 1912. The reason behind the name switch is unknown, but it does not convey that Smith and Burton married. Burton married Ebbie Forceman in early 1913. See Abbott and Seroff, "Bessie Smith," 2.

50. Abbott and Seroff, "Bessie Smith," 2; *Indianapolis Freeman,* June 1, 1912; *Indianapolis Freeman,* June 15, 1912; *Indianapolis Freeman,* July 5, 1912. The Theater Owners Booking Association was the primary black theater circuit of the 1920s; it will be discussed in detail below.

51. *Indianapolis Freeman,* July 5, 1912. Although they did not resume as a musical team, Smith continued to include Wayne Burton in her own variety shows up until his death in 1925. See W. R. Arnold, "Bessie at Bijou," *Chicago Defender,* February 28, 1925; "Obituaries," *Chicago Defender,* August 29, 1925.

52. Albertson, Liner notes, 8; "Savoy Theater," *Indianapolis Freeman,* October 22, 1910; *Indianapolis Freeman,* December 11, 1912.

53. Bernhardt and Harris, *I Remember,* 27.

54. Shapiro and Hentoff, *Hear Me Talkin' to Ya,* 152; Bernhardt and Harris, *I Remember,* 27.

55. Abbott and Seroff, "Bessie Smith," 2–3; *Indianapolis Freeman*, August 2, 1914. For more on "coon songs" and "coon shouting," see Southern, *Music of Black Americans*, 316–19.

56. Abbott and Seroff, "Bessie Smith," 4; "Notes from the Florida Blossoms Co.," *Indianapolis Freeman*, December 18, 1915.

57. Shapiro and Hentoff, *Hear Me Talkin' to Ya*, 241.

58. Lyttelton, "Bessie Smith," 931–32 (for an example of how a music theorist would describe the evolution of Bessie's sound, see 925–32, particularly Lyttelton's reading of "Nobody Knows You When You're Down and Out"). Although Bessie Smith will not be discussed as a preeminent jazz vocalist in this study, see Schuller, "Bessie Smith," 231–41, for a full treatment of the issue.

59. Theater Advertisements, *Indianapolis Freeman*, July 5, 1912.

60. Qtd. in Abbott and Seroff, "Bessie Smith," 4.

61. "Florida Blossoms Company," *Indianapolis Freeman*, July 29, 1916.

62. The dates of the Great Migration have been a source of contention among scholars. Some identify the period from 1916–19, during the onslaught of mass movement, as the "Migration." See Johnson and Campbell. *Black Migration.* Yet many African Americans fled southern rural areas during the Reconstruction era, left the south crn region in droves from World War I to the Depression, and continued to move to northern cities until the end of World War II in 1945. Hence, for the purposes of this study, 1916 to 1930 will be included under the term "Great Migration," for this period reflects the largest population shift in the South and had the most influence on the early reception of vaudeville blues in the North and Midwest. For more on migration periodization, see Marks, *Farewell*, 1–2.

63. Marks, *Farewell*, 2.

64. Ibid., 122. By 1920, a total of 60,758 African Americans had relocated to New York City, 65,355 to Chicago, and 35,097 to Detroit.

65. Hine, "Black Migration to the Urban Midwest," 134.

66. Abbott and Seroff, "Bessie Smith," 4; Theater Advertisements, *Baltimore Afro-American*, September 13, 1918.

67. Ellison, "Blues People," 257.

68. Sharpiro and Hentoff, *Hear Me Talkin' to Ya*, 240.

69. Stearns, *Story of Jazz*, 167–68.

70. Murray, *Stomping the Blues*, 27.

71. Cone, *Spirituals and the Blues*, 117.

72. Best, *Passionately Human*, 108–10.

73. Harris, *Rise of Gospel Blues*, 209–40.

74. Sampson, *Blacks in Blackface*, 14.

75. The Afro American Vaudeville Booking Association opened on January 22, 1910, and its circuit of theaters is unknown. Founded by F. A. Barrasso in October 1910, the Tri-State circuit attempted to contract black performers in Memphis, Tennessee; Jackson, Mississippi; and Vicksburgh and Greenville, Mississippi. "The Stage,"

Indianapolis Freeman, January 22, 1910; "The Stage," *Indianapolis Freeman,* October 4, 1910.

76. "S. H. Dudley to Become Theatrical Manager," *Indianapolis Freeman,* January 15, 1910; "Dudley's Enterprise!" *Indianapolis Freeman,* December 28, 1912.

77. "Dudley's Enterprise!" *Indianapolis Freeman,* December 28, 1912.

78. Sampson, *Blacks in Blackface,* 49; Southern, *Music of Black Americans,* 298.

79. Sampson, *Blacks in Blackface,* 14–16.

80. Ibid., 16, 30; Southern, *Music of Black Americans,* 298.

81. Southern, *Music of Black Americans,* 298; W. R. Arnold, "TOBA News," *Chicago Defender,* February 25, 1925.

82. W. R. Arnold, "TOBA News," *Chicago Defender,* February, 25, 1925; Sampson, *Blacks in Blackface,* 17.

83. Bruno, "Dewey 'Pigmeat' Markham," 155–56.

84. Handy, *Father of the Blues,* 43–54.

85. Ibid., 155.

86. Qtd. in Sampson, *Blacks in Blackface,* 19.

87. Harrison, *Black Pearls,* 26–27.

88. Salem Tutt Whitney, "The TOBA," *Chicago Defender,* February 6, 1926.

89. Sampson, *Blacks in Blackface,* 455.

90. Aida Overton Walker, "Aida Overton Walker: Says the Profession Has Improved with the Progression of Time," *Indianapolis Freeman,* December 28, 1912.

91. Sylvester Russell, "The Strenuous Life of a Showman," *Indianapolis Freeman,* May 29, 1909.

92. Harrison, *Black Pearls,* 32–33.

93. "Seven Florida Creole Girls," *Indianapolis Freeman,* January 3, 1903.

94. Qtd. in Albertson, *Bessie,* 14.

95. Ibid.; Shapiro and Hentoff, *Hear Me Talkin' to Ya,* 236.

96. Shapiro and Hentoff, *Hear Me Talkin' to Ya,* 239, 244; Bechet, *Treat It Gentle,* 185.

97. "Chattanooga, Tenn.—Queen Theater," *Indianapolis Freeman,* March 20, 1915.

98. W. R. Arnold, "TOBA News," *Chicago Defender,* February 25, 1925; G. M. Connelley and Co.'s *Alphabetical Directory* (1921), 856.

99. Albertson, *Bessie,* 45–46.

100. Hine, "Black Migration to the Urban Midwest," 133.

101. Albertson, *Bessie,* 126.

102. Bernhardt and Harris, *I Remember,* 42.

103. Interview with Gwendolyn Smith Bailey by George Ricks and Suzanne Marcus, March 3, 1987, Chattanooga African American Museum.

104. Hampton and Haskins, *Hamp,* 25; *Atlanta City Directory,* 224.

105. Once Bessie's recordings became popular, white patrons began to attend her shows more frequently at her northern venues. The white author and cultural critic Carl Van Vechten describes one of these northern performances in "Negro Blues."

106. Interview with Gwendolyn Smith Bailey by George Ricks and Suzanne Marcus, March 3, 1987, Chattanooga African American Museum.

107. Interview with Mary Jefferson by Berniece Johnson Reagon, December 22, 1984, Program in African American Culture Collection, Archives Center, National Museum of American History, Smithsonian Institution.

108. McKee and Chisenhall, *Beale Street Black and Blue,* 149; Hampton and Haskins, *Hamp,* 25.

109. Collier, *Making of Jazz,* 72; Harrison, *Black Pearls,* 44; Handy, *Father of the Blues,* 199–200.

110. Harrison, *Black Pearls,* 44.

111. Handy, *Father of the Blues,* 200.

112. Collier, *Making of Jazz,* 113; Harrison, *Black Pearls,* 45–46; Handy, *Father of the Blues,* 200–201.

113. Harrison, *Black Pearls,* 49–50; Handy, *Father of the Blues,* 202.

114. W. C. Handy, Press Release Letter, Handy Brother Music Co. Inc., 1948, in W. C. Handy Collection, Archives Center, National Museum of American History, Smithsonian Institution.

115. Ibid.

116. Bechet, *Treat It Gentle,* 136; Shapiro and Hentoff, *Hear Me Talkin' to Ya,* 237–38.

117. Theater Advertisements, *Chicago Defender,* December 22, 1922; Theater Advertisement, *Chicago Defender,* April 14, 1923.

118. Shapiro and Hentoff, *Hear Me Talkin' to Ya,* 236.

119. Albertson, *Bessie,* 37. The injustice in this contract, as with many contracts for African American entertainers of the period, is that with no promise of royalties, Columbia could make a continuous profit from Smith recordings and never share any of it with the Smith family or Smith estate. In the late 1970s, forty years after Bessie's death, Jack Gee Jr., Bessie's adopted son, filed suit against CBS and Columbia Records to "challenge the validity" of these early contracts. It is not clear what became of these suits, but the recordings have been reissued several times under the Columbia label and Sony Music Entertainment, Inc. See "Smith Family Sues," *Cablelines,* January–February 1977, 4; "Bessie Smith Heirs Sue," *New York Post,* November 29, 1976.

120. Shapiro and Hentoff, *Hear Me Talkin' to Ya,* 243.

Epilogue

1. Many of these stories are documented in Albertson, *Bessie,* and in Albertson's interviews with Ruby Walker Smith found on *Bessie Smith: The Final Chapter, the Complete Recordings, Vol. 5* (Columbia Records, Sony Music Entertainment, 1996).

2. Nelson George, "The Ghost of Bessie Smith Would Be a Millionaire," *New York Amsterdam News,* January 15, 1977.

3. Ibid.

4 McMillen, *Day Late and a Dollar Short,* inside cover; Alec Cawthrone, "Queen Latifah on 'Chicago,'" BBC News,

January 6, 2003, accessed December 16, 2005, <http://www.bbc.co.uk/films/2003/01/06/queen_latifah_chicago_interview.shtml>.

5. Steve Bornfeld, "Rehearsals Over, Hall Ripe to Perform," *Chattanooga Times,* February 5, 1996, A1.

6. John Wilson, "Merchants Hope Bessie Smith Hall Will Put Life Back in King Blvd.," *Chattanooga Free Press,* April 11, 1994, B1.

7. Steve Bornfeld, "Rehearsals Over, Hall Ripe to Perform," *Chattanooga Times,* February 5, 1996, A1.

8. John Wilson, "Idle Hall Would Make Bessie Smith Sing Blues," *Chattanooga Free Press,* April 11, 1994, A1.

9. John Wilson, "Unclear Mission Has Hurt Bessie Smith Hall Progress," *Chattanooga Free Press,* April 14, 1994, B1.

10. John Wilson, "New Community Effort Urged to Open Blues Hall," *Chattanooga Free Press,* April 15, 1994, B2.

11. John Wilson, "Unclear Mission Has Hurt Bessie Smith Hall Progress," *Chattanooga Free Press,* April 14, 1994, B2.

12. Author's interview with Vilma Fields, November 9, 2000.

13. Letter to the Editor, *Chattanooga Times,* July 19, 1996.

14. Noble Sprayberry, "It's Not the Outside, but What's Inside That Counts," *Chattanooga Times,* February 10, 1996, B3.

15. Bradley, *Tennessee Handbook,* 234; *Riverbend Festival,* "Bessie Smith Strut," accessed December 13, 2005, <http://www.riverbendfestival.com/artists_strut.html>.

16. Albertson, *Bessie,* 31–32.

BIBLIOGRAPHY

Manuscripts

American Missionary Association Archives, Microfilm Reels, Manuscripts Division, Library of Congress.

American Variety Stage: Vaudeville and Popular Entertainment Collection, 1870–1920. Library of Congress.

Bessie Smith Clippings File. Schomburg Center for Research in Black Culture, New York Public Library.

Bessie Smith Collection. Chattanooga African American Museum.

Bessie Smith File. New York Public Library.

Billings-Merriam Family Vaudeville Scrapbooks. Archives Center, National Museum of American History, Smithsonian Institution.

Black Women's Oral History Project. Schlesinger Library, Radcliffe College, Harvard University.

Carl Van Vechten Papers. Beinecke Library, Yale University.

Chattanooga African American Collection. Chattanooga African American Museum.

Chattanooga Music Club. Chattanooga–Hamilton County Bicentennial Library.

Ernie Smith Jazz Film Collection. Archives Center, National Museum of American History, Smithsonian Institution.

Frank Schiffman Apollo Theater Collection. Archives Center, National Museum of American History, Smithsonian Institution.

George and Hart's Up to Date Georgia Minstrels Scrapbook. Archives Center, National Museum of American History, Smithsonian Institution.

Howard High School Collection. Chattanooga–Hamilton County Bicentennial Library.

National Urban League Papers. Manuscripts Division, Library of Congress.

Program in African American Culture Collection. Archives Center, National Museum of American History, Smithsonian Institution.

Samuel DeVincent Illustrated Sheet Music Collection. Archives Center, National Museum of American History, Smithsonian Institution.

Warshaw Collection of Business Americana. Archives Center, National Museum of American History, Smithsonian Institution.

W. C. Handy Collection. Archives Center, National Museum of American History, Smithsonian Institution.

Government and City Documents

Atlanta City Directory. Atlanta: Atlanta City Directory Co., 1910.

Atlas of the City of Chattanooga, TN, and Vicinity. Philadelphia: G. M. Hopkins, 1889.

Chattanooga Business and Professional Directory. Chattanooga: Galligan and Crowley Publishing Co., 1919.

Chattanooga City Directory and Business Gazetteer, 1878–1879. Chattanooga: Ochs and Harris Publishing, 1878.

Chattanooga City Directory 1880. Chattanooga: Norwood, Kline and Co., Publishers, 1880.

Chattanooga City Directory 1881. Chattanooga: Norwood, Kline Bros., 1881.

Chattanooga Map. Chattanooga: Norris, Wellge, and Co., 1886.

Chattanooga Times. *Past, Present, and Future of Chattanooga, Tennessee: The Industrial Center of the South.* Chattanooga: Times Printing Company, Publishers, Printers, and Binders, 1885.

City Directory of Chattanooga and Suburbs, 1899. Chattanooga: G. M. Conelley and Co., 1899.

Connor, George C. *Historical Guide to Chattanooga and Lookout Mountain.* Chattanooga: T. H. Payne and Co., 1889.

Department of Commerce, Bureau of the Census. *Statistics of Women at Work.* Washington, D.C.: Government Printing Office, 1907.

———. *Thirteenth Census of the United States: 1910—Population.* Vol. 2. Washington, D.C.: Government Printing Office, 1913.

———. *Thirteenth Census of the United States: 1910—Population.* Vol. 3. Washington, D.C.: Government Printing Office, 1913.

———. *Thirteenth Census of the United States: 1910—Population.* (Manuscript census). Hamilton County, Chattanooga City, 1910.

———. *Twelfth Census of the United States, 1900—Population, pt. 1.* Washington, D.C.: Government Printing Office, 1901.

———. *Twelfth Census of the United States: 1900—Population.* (Manuscript census). Hamilton County, Chattanooga City, 1900.

———. *Occupations—The Twelfth Census.* Washington, D.C.: Government Printing Office, 1904.

Department of the Interior. *Eighth Census of the United States: Population.* Washington, D.C.: Government Printing Office, 1865.

———. *Eighth Census of the United States: 1860—Agriculture.* Washington, D.C.: Government Printing Office, 1864.

———. *Eighth Census of the United States: Manufacturers of the United States in 1860.* Washington, D.C.: Government Printing Office, 1865.

———. *The Seventh Census of the United States: Statistics of Tennessee.* Washington, D.C.: Government Printing Office, 1853.

Directory of Chattanooga, Tennessee, 1892. Chattanooga: Connelly and Fais Publishers, 1892.

Federal Writers Project. *Tennessee: A Guide to the State.* New York: Hastings House, 1939.

G. M. Connelley and Co.'s Alphabetical Directory of Chattanooga, Tennessee. Chattanooga: G. M. Connelly and Co., 1901–23.

Norwood's Directory of Chattanooga, Tennessee. Chattanooga: Norwood, Connelly, and Co., 1886.

Plat Book of Chattanooga, TN. Philadelphia: G. M. Hopkins Co., 1904.

Plat Book of the City of Chattanooga, TN, and Vicinity. Philadelphia: G. M. Hopkins, 1914.

Report on Population of the United States, Eleventh Census of the United States, 1890. Washington, D.C.: Government Printing Office, 1895.

Severance, Margaret A. E. *Descriptive and Historical Guide to Chattanooga, Lookout Mountain, and Walden's Ridge.* Chattanooga: Times Book and Job Office, 1892.

Tennessee Historical Records Survey. *Directory of Churches, Missions, and Religious Institutions of Tennessee.* No. 33. Hamilton County, 1940.

United States Census Reports, Negroes in the United States. Washington, D.C.: Government Printing Office, 1904.

U.S. Congress. *Report of the Joint Committee on Reconstruction at the First Session Thirty-ninth Congress.* Washington, D.C.: Government Printing Office, 1866.

Waring, George E., Jr. *Report on the Social Statistics of Cities, Part II: The Southern and Western States.* Washington, D.C.: Government Printing Office, 1886.

Reports

American Missionary Association. *Nineteenth Annual Report of the American Missionary Association, Brooklyn, N.Y., October 25–26, 1865.* New York: AMA Publishing, 1865.

———. *Seventeenth Annual Report of the American Missionary Association, Hopkinton, Massachusetts, October 21–22, 1863.* New York: AMA Publishing, 1863.

———. *Thirty-first Annual Report of the American Missionary Association, Syracuse, New York, October 23–25, 1877.* New York: AMA Publishing, 1877.

———. *Thirty-second Annual Report of the American Missionary Association, Taunton, MA, October 29–31, 1878.* New York: AMA Publishing, 1878.

———. *Twenty-first Annual Report of the American Missionary Association, Homer, New York, October 17–18, 1867.* New York: AMA Publishing, 1868.

———. *Twenty-second Annual Report of the American Missionary Association, Springfield, MA, October 28–29, 1868.* New York: AMA Publishing, 1868.

———. *Twenty-fourth Annual Report of the American Missionary Association, Lawrence, Massachusetts, November 9–10, 1870.* New York: AMA Publishing, 1870.

Bureau of Police. *Seventh Annual Report of the City of Chattanooga, Tenn.* Chattanooga: Police Bureau, 1899.

National Urban League. *A Study of the Economic and Cultural Activities of the Negro Population of Chattanooga, Tennessee.* National Urban League Papers, Manuscript Division, Library of Congress, 1947.

Tennessee Historical Records Survey. *Records and Histories of Certain Baptist Churches in Tennessee.* Nashville: U.S. Works Progress Administration, 1836–41.

Newspapers

Baltimore Afro-American
The Blade (Chattanooga)
Chattanooga Daily Times
Chattanooga Free Press
Justice (Chattanooga)
Chattanooga News
Chicago Defender
Indianapolis Freeman
Pittsburgh Courier
New York Amsterdam News
New York Clipper
New York Times

Interviews

Bailey, Gwendolyn Smith. Interviewed by George Ricks and Suzanne Marcus. March 3, 1987. Chattanooga African American Museum.

———. Interviewed by James Hardy. October 16, 1986. Chattanooga African American Museum.

Bryant, Ted. Interviewed by Paul Moss. June 9–10, 2000. Chattanooga African American Museum.

Goodwin, Jacola. Interviewed by Chattanooga African American Museum staff. August 1994. Chattanooga African American Museum.

Key, George A. Interviewed by Chattanooga African American Museum Staff. August 1994. Chattanooga African American Museum.

Suggs, Tena. Interviewed by Chattanooga African American Museum Staff. August 1994. Chattanooga African American Museum.

Recordings

Smith, Bessie. *The Complete Recordings.* Vols. 1–5. Columbia/Legacy compact discs.

Published Sources

Abbington, James, ed. *Readings in African American Church Music and Worship.* Chicago: Gia Publications, 2001.

Abrahams, Roger D. *Singing the Master: The Emergence of African American Culture in the Plantation South.* New York: Penguin Books, 1992.

Adero, Malaika, ed. *Up South: Stories, Studies, and Letters of This Century's Black Migrations.* New York: New Press, 1993.

Albertson, Chris. *Bessie.* Revised ed. New Haven, Conn.: Yale University Press, 2003.

———. Liner notes to *Bessie Smith: The Complete Recordings.* Vol. 1. Legacy/Columbia Records, 1991.

Albertson, Chris, and Gunther Schuller. *Bessie Smith: Empress of the Blues.* New York: Schirmer Books, 1975.

Allen, William Francis, Charles Pickard Ware, and Lucy McKim Garrison, eds. *Slave Songs of the United States: The Classic 1867 Anthology.* New York: A. Simpson and Co., 1867.

Aloisio, Gerard Salvatore. "A Historical Summary of Major Musical Developments in American Jazz from the End of World War I to the Beginning of World War II." Ph.D. dissertation, University of Cincinnati, 1995.

Anderson, James D. *The Education of Blacks in the South, 1860–1930.* Chapel Hill: University of North Carolina Press, 1988.

Armstrong, Louis. *Satchmo: My Life in New Orleans.* New York: DaCapo Press, 1954.

Armstrong, Zella. *The History of Hamilton County and Chattanooga, Tennessee.* Chattanooga, Tenn.: Lookout Publishing Co., 1931.

Atlanta University Press. *Atlanta University Publications,* nos. 1, 2, 4, 8, 9, 11, 13, 14, 15, 16, 17, and 18. New York: Arno Press and the New York Times, 1968.

Avakian, George. "Bessie Smith on Record." *Jazz Record* (September 1947): 5, 25–27.

Ayers, Edward L. *The Promise of the New South.* New York: Oxford University Press, 1992.

Bailey, Fred Arthur. "Tennessee's Antebellum Common Folk." In *Tennessee History: The Land, the People, and the Culture.* Ed. Carroll Van West. Knoxville: University of Tennessee Press, 1998. 80–100.

Barlow, William. *Looking Up and Down: The Emergence of Blues Culture.* Philadelphia: Temple University Press, 1989.

Bastin, Bruce. *Red River Blues: The Blues Tradition in the Southeast.* Urbana: University of Illinois Press, 1985.

Bechet, Sidney. *Treat It Gentle.* New York: Hill and Wang, 1960.

Berkeley, Kathleen. *Like a Plague of Locusts: From an Antebellum Town to New South City, Memphis, Tennessee, 1850–1880.* New York: Garland Publishing, Inc., 1991.

Berlin, Edward A. *Ragtime: A Musical and Cultural History.* Berkeley: University of California Press, 1980.

Berlin, Ira. "Time, Space, and the Evolution of Afro-American Society on British Mainland North America." *American Historical Review* 85.1 (February 1980): 44–78.

———, et al. *Freedom: A Documentary History of Emancipation, 1861–1867.* Series 1, vol. 1: *The Destruction of Slavery.* Cambridge: Cambridge University Press, 1985.

———, et al. *Freedom: A Documentary History of Emancipation, 1861–1867.* Series 1, vol. 2: *The Wartime Genesis of Free Labor: The Upper South.* Cambridge: Cambridge University Press, 1993.

Bernhardt, Clyde E. B., as told to Sheldon Harris. *I Remember: Eighty Years of Black Entertainment, Big Bands, and the Blues.* Philadelphia: University of Pennsylvania Press, 1986.

Best, Wallace D. *Passionately Human, No Less Divine: Religion and Culture in Black Chicago, 1915–1952.* Princeton, N.J.: Princeton University Press, 2005.

Biola, Heather. "The Black Washerwoman in Southern Tradition." *Tennessee Folklore Society Bulletin* 45.1 (March 1979): 17–27.

Blassingame, John W., ed. *Slave Testimony: Two Centuries of Letters, Speeches, Interviews, and Autobiographies.* Baton Rouge: Louisiana State University Press, 1977.

Bontemps, Arna, and Jack Conroy. *They Seek a City.* Garden City, N.Y.: Doubleday, Doran, and Co., 1945.

Botume, Elizabeth Hyde. *First Days amongst the Contrabands.* Boston: Lee and Shepard Publishers, 1893.

Bourgeois, Anna Stong. *Blueswomen: Profiles and Lyrics, 1920–1945.* Jefferson, N.C.: McFarland and Co., 1996.

Bradley, Jeff. *Tennessee Handbook.* Chico, Calif.: Moon Travel Handbooks, 1999.

Brooks, Edward. *The Bessie Smith Companion: A Critical and Detailed Appreciation of the Recordings.* New York: DaCapo Press, 1982.

Broome, P. J., and Clay Tucker. *The Other Music City: The Dance Bands and Jazz Musicians of Nashville, 1920 to 1970.* Nashville: American Press Printing Co., 1990.

Brown, Karen Fitzgerald. "The Black Press of Tennessee, 1865–1980." Ph.D. dissertation, University of Tennessee at Knoxville, 1982.

Brown, William Wells. "Black Religion in the Post Reconstruction South" (1880). In *African American Religious History: A Documentary Witness.* 2d ed. Ed. Milton C. Sernett. Durham, N.C.: Duke University Press, 1999. 256–60.

Bruno, Tony. "Dewey 'Pigmeat' Markham" (interview). In *Artist and Influence*. New York: Billtops Collection, Inc., 1994. 153–76.

Butcsch, Richard. *The Making of American Audiences: From Stage to Television, 1750–1990.* Cambridge: Cambridge University Press, 2000.

———, ed. *For Fun and Profit: The Transformation of Leisure into Consumption.* Philadelphia: Temple University Press, 1990.

Carby, Hazel V. "It Jus Be's Dat Way Sometime: The Sexual Politics of Women's Blues." In *Unequal Sisters: A Multicultural Reader in U.S. Women's History.* Ed. Vicki L. Ruiz and Ellen Carol Du Bois. New York: Routledge Press, 1994. 330–42.

———. "Policing the Black Woman's Body in an Urban Context." *Critical Inquiry* 18.4 (Summer 1992): 739–55.

Carter, E. R. *Biographical Sketches of Our Pulpit.* 1888; reprint, Chicago: Afro-American Press, 1969.

Cartwright, Joseph H. *The Triumph of Jim Crow: Tennessee Race Relations in the 1880s.* Knoxville: University of Tennessee Press, 1976.

Cash, Wilbur. *The Mind of the South.* New York: Alfred A. Knopf, 1941.

Centurion Committee. *Centurion: A History of the Chattanooga Police Department, 1852–1977.* Chattanooga, Tenn.: Intercollegiate Press, 1976.

Charles, Mario A. "The Age of a Jazzwoman: Valaida Snow, 1900–1956." *Journal of Negro History* 80.4 (Autumn 1995): 183–91.

Chattanooga Area Historical Association. *Walk with History.* Chattanooga, Tenn.: Chattanooga Area Historical Association Press, 1976.

Cimprich, John. *Slavery's End in Tennessee, 1861–1865.* Tuscaloosa: University of Alabama Press, 1985.

Cockrell, Dale. *Demons of Disorder: Early Blackface Minstrels and Their World.* Cambridge: Cambridge University Press, 1997.

Collier, James Lincoln. *The Making of Jazz: A Comprehensive History.* New York: Delta Books, 1978.

Collins, Patricia Hill. *Black Feminist Thought: Knowledge, Consciousness, and the Politics of Empowerment.* New York: Routledge Press, 1990.

Cone, James H. *The Spirituals and the Blues: An Interpretation.* Maryknoll, N.Y.: Orbis Books, 1972.

Coulter, Roy D. "The Negroes of Chattanooga, Tennessee." Master's thesis, Vanderbilt University, 1934.

Cowan, Ruth Schwartz. *More Work for Mother: The Ironies of Household Technology from the Open Hearth to the Microwave.* New York: Basic Books, 1983.

Crawford, R. J. "Business Negroes of Chattanooga." *Voice of the Negro* 1.11 (November 1904): 534–37.

Crockett, Norman. *The Black Towns.* Lawrence: Regents Press of Kansas, 1979.

Crowe, Charles. "Racial Massacres in Atlanta, September 1906." *Journal of Negro History* 54.2 (April 1969): 150–73.

Cuney-Hare, Maud. *Negro Musicians and Their Music.* Washington, D.C.: Associated Publishers, 1936.

Curriden, Mark, and Leroy Phillips Jr. *Contempt of Court: The Turn-of-the-Century Lynching that Launched 100 Years of Federalism.* New York: Faber and Faber, 1999.

Dall, Christine, prod. *Wild Women Don't Have the Blues.* California Newsreel, 1989.

Daughtry, Willa Estelle. "Sissieretta Jones: A Study of the Negro's Contribution to Nineteenth-Century American Concert and Theatrical Life." Ph.D. dissertation, Syracuse University, 1968.

Davin, Tom. "Conversations with James P. Johnson." In *Ragtime: Its History, Composers, and Music.* Ed. John Edward Hasse. New York: Schirmer Books, 1985. 166–77.

Davis, Angela. *Blues Legacies and Black Feminism: Gertrude 'Ma' Rainey, Bessie Smith, and Billie Holiday.* New York: Random House, 1998.

Deutsch, Sarah. *Women and the City: Gender, Space, and Power in Boston, 1870–1940.* New York: Oxford University Press, 2000.

Domosh, Mona. "Those 'Gorgeous Incongruities': Polite Politics and Public Space on the Streets of Nineteenth-Century New York City." *Annals of the Association of American Geographers* 88.2 (June 1998): 209–26.

Douglas, Ann. *Terrible Honesty: Mongrel Manhattan in the 1920s.* New York: Farrar, Straus, and Giroux, 1995.

Doyle, Don H. *New Men, New Cities, New South.* Chapel Hill: University of North Carolina Press, 1990.

DuBois, W. E. B. *Black Reconstruction in America: An Essay toward a History of the Part which Black Folk Played in the Attempt to Reconstruct Democracy in America, 1860–1880.* 1932; reprint, New York: Russell and Russell, 1962.

———. *The Gift of Black Folk: The Negroes in the Making of America.* Boston: Stratford Co., 1924.

———. "Of the Faith of Fathers" (1903). In *African American Religious History: A Documentary Witness.* 2d ed. Ed. Milton C. Sernett. Durham, N.C.: Duke University Press, 1999. 325–36.

———. "The Problem of Amusement." In *W. E. B. DuBois on Sociology.* Ed. Dan S. Green and Edwin D. Driver. Chicago: University of Chicago Press, 1995. 226–37.

———. *The Souls of Black Folk* (1903). In *Three Negro Classics.* New York: Avon Books, 1965.

———, ed. *The Negro Church: Report of the Eighth Conference for the Study of Negro Problems.* Atlanta: Atlanta University Press, 1903.

Eberhardt, Clifford. *Out of Chattanooga: The Bessie Smith Story.* Chattanooga, Tenn.: Ebco Inc., 1994.

Elam, Harry J., Jr. "The Black Performer and the Performance of Blackness." In *African American Performance and Theater History: A Critical Reader.* Ed. Harry J. Elam Jr. and David Krasner. New York: Oxford University Press, 2001. 288–306.

Elam, Harry J., Jr., and David Krasner, eds. *African American Performance and Theater History: A Critical Reader.* New York: Oxford University Press, 2001.

Ellison, Ralph. "Blues People." In *Shadow and Act*. New York: Quality Paperback Book Club, 1994. 247–58.

———. "Richard Wright's Blues." In *Shadow and Act*. New York: Quality Paperback Book Club, 1994. 77–94.

Epstein, Dena. *Sinful Tunes and Spirituals: Black Folk Music to the Civil War*. Urbana: University of Illinois Press, 1977.

Ezzell, Timothy Paul. "Yankees in Dixie: The Story of Chattanooga, 1870–1898." Ph.D. dissertation, University of Tennessee, 1996.

Faderman, Lillian. "Harlem Nights: Savvy Women of the '20s Knew Where to Find New York's Lesbian Life." *Advocate*, March 26, 1991, 54–55.

Feinstein, Elaine. *Bessie Smith*. Middlesex, U.K.: Viking Press, 1985.

Ferris, William. "Blue Roots and Development." *Black Perspectives in Music* 2.2 (Fall 1974): 122–27.

Fields, Vilma. *Precious Memories '88*. Chattanooga, Tenn.: Chattanooga Afro-American Heritage Museum, 1988.

———, dir. *Down by the Riverside: African-Americans in Chattanooga*. Cinebar Productions, 1994.

Finn, Julio. *The Bluesman: The Musical Heritage of Black Men and Women in the Americas*. London: Quartet Books, 1986.

Fleming, Walter L. *The Documentary History of Reconstruction: Political, Military, Social, Religious, Educational, and Industrial, 1865 to the Present Time*. Vol. 1. Cleveland: Arthur H. Clark Co., 1906.

———. *The Documentary History of Reconstruction: Political, Military, Social, Religious, Educational, and Industrial, 1865 to the Present Time*. Vol. 2. Cleveland: Arthur H. Clark Co., 1907.

Fletcher, Tom. *One Hundred Years of the Negro in Show Business!* New York: Burdge and Co., 1954.

Floyd, Samuel A. *The Power of Black Music: Interpreting Its History from Africa to the United States*. New York: Oxford University Press, 1995.

Flynt, Wayne. *Alabama Baptists: Southern Baptists in the Heart of Dixie*. Tuscaloosa: University of Alabama Press, 1998.

Foner, Eric. *Reconstruction: America's Unfinished Revolution, 1863–1877*. New York: Harper and Row, 1988.

Friedwald, Will. *Jazz Singing: America's Great Voices from Bessie Smith to Bebop and Beyond*. New York: Charles Scribner's Sons, 1990.

Fuller, Thomas Oscar. *The History of Negro Baptists of Tennessee*. Memphis: Haskins Print, 1936.

Furman, Jan, ed. *Slavery in Clover Bottoms: John Mcline's Narrative of His Life during Slavery and Civil War*. Knoxville: University of Tennessee Press, 1998.

Gaines, Kevin. *Uplifting the Race: Black Leadership, Politics, and Culture in the Twentieth Century*. Chapel Hill: University of North Carolina Press, 1996.

Gates, Henry Louis, Jr., and Nellie Y. McKay, eds. *The Norton Anthology of African American Literature*. New York: W. W. Norton and Co., 1997.

Gayle, Addison. *The Black Aesthetic.* New York: Doubleday and Co., 1971.

Giddings, Paula. *When and Where I Enter: The Impact of Black Women on Race and Sex in America.* New York: Quill, 1984.

Gilbert, Douglas. *American Vaudeville: Its Life and Times.* New York: Dover Publications, 1940.

Godspeed's General History of Tennessee. Nashville: Godspeed Publishing Co., 1887.

Goreau, Laurraine. *Just Mahalia, Baby.* Waco, Tex.: Word Books, 1975.

Gottlieb, Peter. *Making Their Own Way: Southern Blacks' Migration to Pittsburgh, 1916–1930.* Urbana: University of Illinois Press, 1987.

Gottlieb, Robert, ed. *Reading Jazz: A Gathering of Autobiography, Reportage, and Criticism from 1919 to Now.* New York: Vintage Press, 1999.

Govan, Gilbert E. "Some Sidelights on the History of Chattanooga." *Tennessee Historical Quarterly* 6 (March–December 1947): 148–60.

Govan, Gilbert E., and James W. Livingood. *The Chattanooga Country, 1540–1976: From Tomahawks to TVA.* Knoxville: University of Tennessee Press, 1977.

Graham, Sandra Lauderdale. *House and Street: The Domestic World of Servants and Masters in Nineteenth-Century Rio de Janeiro.* New York: Cambridge University Press, 1988.

Grant, Donald L. *The Way It Was in the South: The Black Experience in Georgia.* New York: Birch Lane Press, 1993.

Green, Dan S., and Edwin D. Driver, eds. *W. E. B. DuBois on Sociology and the Black Community.* Chicago: University of Chicago Press, 1978.

Green, Harvey. *The Uncertainty of Everyday Life, 1915–1945.* New York: Harper Collins, 1992.

Greene. Maud. "The Background of the Beale Street Blues." *Tennessee Folklore Society Bulletin* 7.1 (March 1941): 1–10.

Grimes Sara. *Backwater Blues: In Search of Bessie Smith.* Amherst, Mass.: Rose Island Publishing Co., 2001.

Grimes, Sally. "The True Death of Bessie Smith." *Esquire* 71.6 (June 1969): 112–13.

Grossman, James. *Land of Hope: Chicago, Black Southerners, and the Great Migration.* Chicago: University of Chicago Press, 1989.

Hampton, Lionel, and James Haskins. *Hamp: An Autobiography.* New York: Warner Books, 1989.

Handy, Antoinette D. *Black Women in American Bands and Orchestras.* Lanham, Md.: Scare Crow Press, 1998.

Handy, W. C. *Father of the Blues: An Autobiography.* New York: Macmillian Co., 1941.

Harris, Michael W. *The Rise of Gospel Blues: The Music of Thomas Andrew Dorsey in the Urban Church.* New York: Oxford University Press, 1992.

Harris, Paisley Jane. "'I'm as Good as Any Woman in Your Town': The Interconnections of Gender, Race, and Class in the Blues of Ma Rainey and Bessie Smith." Ph.D. dissertation, University of Minnesota, 1994.

Harrison, Daphne Duval. *Black Pearls: Blues Queens of the 1920s*. New Brunswick, N.J.: Rutgers University Press, 1988.

Harrison, Lowell H. "Recollections of Some Tennessee Slaves." *Tennessee Historical Quarterly* 33 (Summer 1974): 175–90.

Harrison-Pepper, Sally. *Drawing a Circle in the Square: Street Performing in New York's Washington Square Park*. Jackson: University of Mississippi Press, 1990.

Hartman, Saidya. *Scenes of Subjection: Terror, Slavery, and Self-Making in Nineteenth-Century America*. New York: Oxford University Press, 1997.

Hasse, John Edward. "The Creation and Dissemination of Indianapolis Ragtime, 1897–1930." Ph.D. dissertation, Indiana University, 1981.

———. "Ragtime: From the Top." In *Ragtime: Its History, Composers, and Music*. Ed. John Edward Hasse. New York: Schirmer Books, 1985. 5–20.

———, ed. *Ragtime: Its History, Composers, and Music*. New York: Schirmer Books, 1985.

Hazen, Margaret Hindle, and Robert M. Hazen. *The Music Men: An Illustrated History of Brass Bands in America, 1800–1920*. Washington, D.C.: Smithsonian Institution Press, 1987.

Hazzard-Gordon, Katrina. *Jookin': The Rise of Social Dance Formations in African American Culture*. Philadelphia: Temple University Press, 1990.

Helm, MacKinley. *Angel Mo' and Her Son, Roland Hayes*. Boston: Little, Brown, and Co., 1942.

Henderson, Donald H. "The Statistics of Migration." *Journal of Negro History* 6.4 (October 1921): 471–84.

Hennessey, Thomas J. *From Jazz to Swing: African American Jazz Musicians and Their Music, 1890–1935*. Detroit: Wayne State University Press, 1994.

Higginbotham, Evelyn Brooks. *Righteous Discontent: The Women's Movement in the Black Baptist Church, 1880–1920*. Cambridge, Mass.: Havard University Press, 1993.

Hill, Joseph A. "The Recent Northward Migration of the Negro." In *Up South: Stories, Studies, and Letters of This Century's Black Migrations*. Ed. Malaika Adero. New York: New Press, 1993. 19–32.

Hine, Darlene Clark. "Black Migration to the Urban Midwest." In *The Great Migration in Historical Perspective: New Dimensions in Race, Class, and Gender*. Ed. Joe Trotter. Bloomington: Indiana University Press, 1991. 127–46.

Hine, Darlene Clark, and Kathleen Thompson. *A Shining Thread of Hope: The History of Black Women in America*. New York: Broadway Books, 1998.

Hirshey, Gerri. "The Backstage History of Women Who Rocked the World." *Rolling Stone*, November 13, 1997.

Historical Statistics of the United States: Colonial Times to 1970. White Plains, N.Y.: Kraus International Publishers, 1989.

Hodes, Art. "Bessie Smith." *Jazz Record* (September 1947): 8–9.

Holiday, Billie. *Lady Sings the Blues*. Garden City, N.Y.: Doubleday, 1956.

Huggins, Nathan Irvin. *Harlem Renaissance*. New York: Oxford University Press, 1971.

Hughes, Langston. "The Negro Artist and the Racial Mountain." *The Nation*, June 23, 1926, 692–94.

———. "Songs Called the Blues." *Phylon* 2.2 (1941): 143–45.

Hughes, Langston, and Milton Meltzer. *Black Magic: A History of the African-American in the Performing Arts*. 1967; reprint, New York: DaCapo Press, 1990.

Hunter, Tera. *To 'Joy My Freedom*. Cambridge, Mass.: Harvard University Press, 1997.

Jackson, Mahalia, with Evan McLeod Wylie. *Movin' on Up*. New York: Hawthorn Books, 1966.

———. "Singing of Good Tidings and Freedom." In *Afro-American Religious History: A Documentary Witness*. Ed. Milton Sernett. Durham, N.C.: Duke University Press, 1985. 446–57.

Jansen, David A., and Gene Jones. *Spreadin' Rhythm Around: Black Popular Songwriters, 1880–1930*. New York: Schirmer Books, 1998.

Jenkins, Gary C. "An 1890s Tour of Chattanooga." *Tennessee Historical Quarterly* 52 (1993): 244–55.

Johnson, Daniel M., and Rex R. Campbell. *Black Migration in America: A Social Demographic History*. Durham, N.C.: Duke University Press, 1981.

Johnson, Gerald W. *An Honorable Titan: A Biographical Study of Adolph S. Ochs*. New York: Harper and Bros. Publishers, 1946.

Johnson, James Weldon. *Autobiography of an Ex-Colored Man*. In *Three Negro Classics*. New York: Avon Books, 1965. 393–511.

———. *Black Manhattan*. New York: Alfred. A. Knopf, 1930.

Jones, Jacqueline. *Labor of Love, Labor of Sorrow: Black Women, Work, and the Family from Slavery to the Present*. New York: Vintage Books, 1985.

Jones, LeRoi. *Blues People: Negro Music in White America*. New York: William Morrow and Co., 1963.

Jones, Marcus E. *Black Migration in the United States with Emphasis on Selected Central Cities*. Saratoga, Calif.: Century 21 Publishing, 1980.

Jones, William H. *Recreation and Amusement among Negroes in Washington, D.C.: A Sociological Analysis of the Negro in an Urban Environment*. Washington, D.C.: Howard University Press, 1927.

Katzman, David M. *Seven Days a Week: Women and Domestic Service in Industrializing America*. New York: Oxford University Press, 1978.

Kay, Jackie. *Bessie Smith*. Bath, U.K.: Absolute Press, 1997.

Kelley, Robin D. G. *Race Rebels: Culture, Politics, and the Black Working Class*. New York: Free Press, 1994.

Kellner, Bruce. *Carl Van Vechten and the Irreverent Decades*. Norman: University of Oklahoma Press, 1968.

———. *Keep a-Inchin' Along: Selected Writings of Carl Van Vechten about Black Art and Letters*. Westport, Conn.: Greenwood Press, 1979.

Kenzer, Robert C. "Black Businessmen in Post–Civil War Tennessee." *Journal of East Tennessee History* 66 (1994): 59–80.

King, Duane H. "The Cherokee Removal of 1838–1839." *Proceedings of the Trail of Tears Symposium*. North Little Rock, Ark. April 17–18, 1996. 11–24.

King, Wilma. "'Suffer with Them till Death': Slave Women and Their Children in Nineteenth-Century America." In *More than Chattel: Black Women and Slavery in the Americas*. Ed. David Barry Gaspar and Darlene Clark Hine. Bloomington: Indiana University Press, 1996. 147–69.

Klebenow, Anne. *Two Hundred Years through Two Hundred Stories: A Tennessee Bicentennial Collection*. Knoxville: University of Tennessee Press, 1996.

Kmen, Henry A. "Old Corn Meal: A Forgotten Urban Folksinger." *Journal of American Folklore* 75.295 (January–March 1962): 29–34.

Kolchin, Peter. *First Freedom: The Responses of Alabama's Blacks to Emancipation and Reconstruction*. Westport, Conn.: Greenwood Press, 1972.

Kubik, Gerhard. *Africa and the Blues*. Jackson: University of Mississippi Press, 1999.

Kyriakoudes, Louis M. *The Social Origins of the Urban South: Race, Gender, and Migration in Nashville and Middle Tennessee, 1890–1930*. Chapel Hill: University of North Carolina Press, 2003.

Larsen, Lawrence H. *The Urban South: A History*. Lexington: University Press of Kentucky, 1990.

Lamon, Lester C. *Black Tennesseans, 1900–1930*. Knoxville: University of Tennessee Press, 1977.

———. *Blacks in Tennessee, 1791–1970*. Knoxville: University of Tennessee Press, 1981.

Lemke-Santagelo, Gretchen. *Abiding Courage: African American Women and the East Bay Community*. Chapel Hill: University of North Carolina Press, 1996.

Lhamon, W. T., Jr. *Raising Cain: Blackface Performance from Jim Crow to Hip Hop*. Cambridge, Mass.: Harvard University Press, 1998.

Lee, George. *Beale Street, Where the Blues Began*. New York: Robert O. Ballou, 1934.

Lerner, Gerda, ed. *Black Women in White America: A Documentary History*. New York: Vintage Books, 1972.

Levine, Lawrence W. *Black Culture and Black Consciousness: Afro-American Folk Thought from Slavery to Freedom*. New York: Oxford University Press, 1977.

Lewis, David L. *When Harlem Was in Vogue*. New York: Alfred A. Knopf, 1981.

Lieb, Sandra R. *Mother of the Blues: A Study of Ma Rainey*. Amherst: University of Massachusetts Press, 1981.

Lincoln, C. Eric, and Lawrence H. Mamiya. "The Performed Word: Music and the Black Church." In *Readings in African American Church Music*. Ed. James Abbington. Chicago: Gia Publications, 2001. 39–75.

Lindenmeyer, Kriste. "Adolescence." In *The Family in the United States, Colonial Times to the Present: An Encyclopedia*. Ed. Joseph M. Hawes and Elizabeth F. Shores. Santa Barbara, Calif.: ABC-CLIO, 2001. 14–16.

Litwack, Leon. *Trouble in Mind: Black Southerners in the Age of Jim Crow.* New York: Alfred A. Knopf, 1998.

Livingood, James W. *Chattanooga, an Illustrated History.* Woodland Hills, Calif.: Windsor Publications, 1981.

———. *The Chattanooga Country: Gateway to History, the Nashville to Atlanta Rail Corridor of 1860s.* Chattanooga, Tenn.: Chattanooga Area Historical Association, 1995.

———. *Hamilton County.* Memphis: Memphis State University Press, 1981.

Locke, Alain Leroy. *The Negro and His Music.* 1936; reprint, New York: Arno Press, 1969.

———. *The New Negro.* New York: Albert and Charles Boni, 1925.

Lomax, Alan. *The Land Where the Blues Began.* New York: Pantheon Books, 1996.

Lott, Eric. *Love and Theft: Blackface Minstrelsy and the American Working Class.* New York: Oxford University Press, 1995.

Lovett, Bobby, and Linda T. Wynn, eds. *Profiles of African-Americans in Tennessee.* Nashville: Annual Local Conference on Afro-American Culture and History, 1996.

Lovell, John, Jr.. *Black Song: The Forge and the Flame; The Story of How the Afro-American Spiritual Was Hammered Out.* New York: Macmillian Co., 1972.

Lueders, Edward. *Carl Van Vechten and the Twenties.* Albuquerque: University of New Mexico Press, 1955.

Lyttleton, Humphrey. "Bessie Smith." In *Reading Jazz: A Gathering of Autobiography, Reportage, and Criticism from 1919 to Now.* Ed. Robert Gottlieb. New York: Vintage Press, 1999. 925–32.

Malone, Jacqui. *Steppin' on the Blues: The Visible Rhythms of African American Dance.* Urbana: University of Illinois Press, 1996.

Marks, Carole. *Farewell, We're Good and Gone: The Great Black Migration.* Bloomington: Indiana University Press, 1989.

Martin, Florence. *Bessie Smith.* Paris: Editions du Limon, 1994.

Marvin, Thomas Fletcher. "Children of Legba: African American Musicians of the Jazz Age in Literature and Popular Culture." Ph.D. dissertation, University of Massachusetts, 1993.

———. "'Preachin' the Blues': Bessie Smith's Secular Religion and Alice Walker's *The Color Purple.*" *African American Review* 28.3 (Fall 1994): 411–21.

Mason, Bim. *Street Theater and Other Outdoor Performance.* New York: Routledge, 1992.

Matthews, Jean V. *The Rise of the New Woman: The Women's Movement in America, 1875–1930.* Chicago: Ivan R. Dee, 2003.

Maultsby, Portia. "The Use and Performance of Hymnody, Spirituals, and Gospels in the Black Church." In *Readings in African American Church Music.* Ed. James Abbington. Chicago: Gia Publications, 2001. 71–98.

McCorkle, Susannah. "Back to Bessie." *American Heritage* (November 1997): 54–68.

McGehee, C. Stuart. "E. O. Tade, Freedmen's Education and the Failure of Reconstruction in Tennessee." *Tennessee Historical Quarterly* 43 (Winter 1984): 376–89.

McKee, Margaret, and Fred Chisenhall. *Beale Street Black and Blue: Life and Music on Black America's Main Street.* Baton Rouge: Louisiana State Press University, 1981.

McKenzie, Robert Tracy. *One South or Many? Plantation Belt and Upcountry in Civil War–Era Tennessee.* Cambridge: Cambridge University Press, 1994.

McMillan, Terry. *A Day Late and a Dollar Short.* New York: Signet, 2002.

Mezzrow, Milton. "Really the Blues." *Jazz Record* (September 1947): 9–10.

Montgomery, William E. *Under Their Own Vine and Fig Tree: The African-American Church in the South, 1865–1900.* Baton Rouge: Louisiana State University Press, 1993.

Mooney, Chase C. *Slavery in Tennessee.* Westport, Conn.: Negro Universities Press, 1957.

Moore, Carman. *Somebody's Angel Child: The Story of Bessie Smith.* New York: Thomas Y. Crowell Co., 1969.

Morgan, Thomas L., and William Barlow. *From Cakewalks to Concert Halls: An Illustrated History of African American Popular Music from 1895–1930.* Washington, D.C.: Elliott and Clark Publishing, 1992.

Morris, Ronald L. *Wait until Dark: Jazz and the Underworld, 1880–1940.* Bowling Green, Ohio: Bowling Green University Popular Press, 1980.

Murphy, Michael, dir. *Make It Funky.* Sony Pictures, 2005.

Murray, Albert. *Stomping the Blues.* New York: McGraw Hill, 1976.

Myers, Robert Manson, ed. *Children of Pride: A True Story of Georgia and the Civil War.* New Haven, Conn.: Yale University Press, 1971.

Nager, Larry. *Memphis Beat: The Lives and Times of America's Musical Crossroads.* New York: St. Martin's Press, 1998.

Nathan, Hans. *Dan Emmet and the Rise of Early Negro Minstrelsy.* Norman: University of Oklahoma Press, 1962.

Neal, James H. *Music Research in Tennessee: A Guide to Special Collections.* Mursfreeboro, Tenn.: Center for Popular Music, 1989.

Nelson, Stanley, and Elizabeth Clark-Lewis, prod. *Freedom Bags.* 1991.

Newsom, Jon. "The American Brass Band Movement: A Historical Overview." *Band Music from the Civil War Era.* July 20, 2000. Accessed October 19, 2005. <www.memory.loc.gov/ammen/cwmhtml/crmpres01.html>.

Norton, Herman A. *Religion in Tennessee, 1777–1945.* Knoxville: University of Tennessee Press, 1981.

Oakley, Giles. *The Devil's Music: A History of the Blues.* New York: DaCapo Press, 1997.

O'Connor, Patrick J. "Discovering the Rich Differences in the Blues: The Rural and Urban Genres." *Midwest Quarterly* 33.1 (Fall 1991): 28–42.

Oliver, Paul. *Bessie Smith.* London: Cassell and Co., 1959.

Olmstead, Marty. *Hidden Tennessee.* Berkeley, Calif.: Ulysses Press, 2005.

Olsson, Bengt. *Memphis Blues and Jug Bands.* London: November Books, 1970.

O'Meally, Robert G. Liner notes to *The Norton Anthology of African American Literature, Audio Companion.* Ed. Robert G. O'Meally. New York: W. W. Norton and Co., 1997.

Patterson, Caleb Perry. *The Negro in Tennessee, 1790–1885.* Austin: University of Texas Press, 1922.

Payne, Daniel Alexander, and C. S. Smith. *Recollections of Seventy Years.* Nashville: Publishing House of the A. M. E. Sunday School Union, 1888.

Perata, David D. *Those Pullman Blues: An Oral History of the African American Railroad Attendant.* New York: Twayne Publishers, 1996.

Phillips, Paul David. "Education of Blacks in Tennessee during Reconstruction, 1865–1870." *Tennessee Historical Quarterly* 46 (Summer 1987): 98–109.

Pleck, Elizabeth. "A Mother's Wages: Income Earning among Married Italian and Black Women, 1896–1911." In *The American Family in Social-Historical Perspective.* Ed. Michael Gordon. New York: St. Martin's Press, 1978. 490–509.

Points of Interest and How to Reach Them in and around Chattanooga, the Most Beautiful Scenic City in the United States. Chattanooga, Tenn.: Chattanooga Railway and Light Company, 1910.

Pomerantz, Gary M. *Where Peachtree Meets Sweet Auburn: A Saga of Race and Family.* New York: Penguin Books, 1997.

Powell, Herbert Preston. *The World's Best Book of Minstrelsy.* Philadelphia: Penn Publishing Co., 1926.

Pride, Armistead Scott. "A Register and History of Negro Newspapers in the United States: 1827–1950." Ph.D. dissertation, Northwestern University, 1950.

Prince, Richard. *The Nashville, Chattanooga, and St. Louis Railroad: History and Steam Locomotives.* Green River, Wyo.: Richard Prince, 1967.

Rabinowitz, Howard N. *The First New South, 1865–1920.* Arlington Heights, Ill.: Harlan Davidson, 1992.

———. *Race Relations in the Urban South, 1865–1890.* Urbana: University of Illinois Press, 1978.

Raboteau, Albert. *Slave Religion: The Invisible Institution in the Antebellum South.* New York: Oxford University Press, 1978.

Rawick, George P., ed. *The American Slave: A Composite Autobiography.* Westport, Conn.: Greenwood Press, 1978.

Reconstruction and Industrialization. Vol. 10 of *Annals of America.* Chicago: Encyclopedia Britannica, Inc., 1976.

Richardson, Joe M. *Christian Reconstruction: The American Missionary Association and Southern Blacks, 1861–1890.* Athens: University of Georgia Press, 1986.

Riis, Thomas Lawrence. "Pink Morton's Theater, Black Vaudeville, and the TOBA: Recovering the History, 1910–1930." In *New Perspectives on Music: Essays in Honor of Eileen Southern.* Ed. Josephine Wright. Warren, Mich.: Harmonie Park Press, 1992. 229–43.

Roberts, J. R. *Black Lesbians: An Annotated Bibliography.* Tallahassee, Fla.: Naiad Press, 1981.

Rosengarten, Theodore. *All God's Dangers: The Life of Nate Shaw.* New York: Alfred A. Knopf, 1974.

Runyan, Donald Clyde. "The Influence of Joseph O. Cadek and His Family on the Musical Life of Chattanooga, Tenn. (1893–1973)." Ph.D. dissertation, Vanderbilt University, 1980.

Russell, Michele. "Slave Codes and Liner Notes." In *All the Women Are White, All the Blacks Are Men, Bbut Some of Us Are Brave: Black Women's Studies.* Ed. Gloria T. Hull, Patricia Bell Scott, and Barbara Smith. New York: Feminist Press, 1982. 129–40.

Ryder, Georgia. "Black Women in Song: Some Socio-Cultural Images." *Negro History Bulletin* 39.5 (Fall 1976): 601–3.

Sacks, Howard L., and Judith Rose Sacks. *Way Up North in Dixie: A Black Family's Claim to the Confederate Anthem.* Urbana: University of Illinois Press, 2003.

Sales, Grover. *Jazz: America's Classical Music.* New York: DaCapo Press, 1992.

Sampson, Henry T. *Blacks in Blackface: A Source on Early Black Musical Shows.* Metuchen, N.J.: Scarecrow Press, 1980.

Santelli, Robert. *The Big Book of Blues: A Biographical Encyclopedia.* New York: Penguin, 1993.

Savitt, Todd L., and James Harvey Young, eds. *Disease and Distinctiveness in the American South.* Knoxville: University of Tennessee Press, 1988.

Schuller, Gunther. "Bessie Smith." In *Early Jazz: Its Roots and Musical Development.* Ed. Gunther Schuller. New York: Oxford University Press, 1968. 226–41.

Schneider, Richard C. *African American History in the Press, 1851–1899.* New York: Gale, 1996.

Schweninger, Loren. *Black Property Owners in the South, 1790–1915.* Urbana: University of Illinois Press, 1990.

Seroff, Doug, and Lynn Abbott. "'They Cert'ly Sound Good to Me': Sheet Music, Southern Vaudeville, and the Commercial Ascendancy of the Blues." *American Music* 14 (Winter 1996): 401–54.

Shapiro, Nat, and Nat Hentoff, eds. *Hear Me Talkin' to Ya: The Story of Jazz by the Men Who Made It.* New York: Penguin Books, 1962.

Shaw, Arnold. *The Jazz Age: Popular Music in the 1920s.* Oxford: Oxford University Press, 1987.

Singleton, Zutty. "I Remember the Queen." *Jazz Record* (September 1947): 10–11.

Slide, Anthony. *The Encyclopedia of Vaudeville.* Westport, Conn.: Greenwood Press, 1994.

Southern, Eileen. "Hymnals of the Black Church." In *Readings in African American Church Music.* Ed. James Abbington. Chicago: Gia Publications, 2001. 137–51.

———. *The Music of Black Americans: A History.* 3d ed. New York: W. W. Norton and Co., 1997.

Spencer, Jon Michael. *The New Negroes and Their Music.* Knoxville: University of Tennessee Press, 1997.

Starkey, Marion L. *The Cherokeee Nation.* New York: Alfred A. Knopf, 1946.

Steckel, Richard H. "Women, Work, and Health under Plantation Slavery in the United States." In *More than Chattel: Black Women and Slavery in the Americas.* Ed. David Barry Gaspar and Darlene Clark Hine. Bloomington: Indiana University Press, 1996. 43–60.

Stewart, Jack, Michael White, John Hasse, Bruce Raeburn, Ellis Marsalis, and Joan Brown. "The Origins of Jazz—Pre-1895." *Jazz History.* Accessed November 8, 2005. <www.nps.gov/jazz/Jazz%20History_origins_pre1895.htm>.

Stewart-Baxter, Derrick. *Ma Rainey and the Classic Blues Singers.* New York: Stein and Day, 1970.

Streaty, Donna. "Empress of the Blues: Bessie Smith." *Negro History Bulletin* 44.1 (January–March 1981): 22.

Stuckey, Sterling. "Through the Prism of Folklore: The Black Ethos in Slavery." *Massachusetts Review* 9 (Summer 1968): 417–37.

Sweeley, Charles C. *The Minstrel King March Two Step.* Sheet music. Williamsport, Penn.: Vandersloot Music Publishing Co., n.d.

Taylor, Altrutheus Ambush. *The Negro in Tennessee, 1865–1880.* 1941; reprint, Spartanburg, S.C.: The Reprint Co., 1974.

Temple, Oliver P. *East Tennessee and the Civil War.* Cincinnati: Robert Clarke Co., 1899.

Terrell, Mary Church. "The Progress of Colored Women." *Voice of the Negro* 1.5 (July 1904): 291–94.

Tifft, Susan, and Alex S. Jones. *The Trust: The Private and Powerful Family behind the* Neww York Times. New York: Little, Brown, and Co., 1999.

Tindall, George Brown. *America: A Narrative History.* New York: W. W. Norton Co., 1984.

Titon, Jeff Todd. *Early Downhome Blues: A Musical and Cultural Analysis.* Urbana: University of Illinois Press, 1977.

Toll, Robert C. *Blacking Up: The Minstrel Show in Nineteenth-Century America.* New York: Oxford University Press, 1974.

Townsend, Charles. *Negro Minstrels.* Chicago: T. S. Denison, 1891.

Trotter, Joe William, ed. *The Great Migration in Historical Perspective: New Dimensions in Race, Class, and Gender.* Bloomington: Indiana University Press, 1991.

Tucker, Susan, ed. *Telling Memories among Southern Women: Domestic Workers and Their Employers in the Segregated South.* Baton Rouge: Louisiana State University Press, 1988.

Van Vechten, Carl. "The Black Blues." *Vanity Fair* (August 1925): 57.

———. "Memories of Bessie Smith." *Jazz Record* (September 1947): 6–7, 29.

———. "Negro Blues Singers." *Vanity Fair* (March 1926): 67, 106–8.

Walton, Lester A. "The Future of the Negro on the Stage." *Colored American Magazine* (May–June 1903): 439–42.

Ward, Andrew. *Dark Midnight When I Rise: The Story of the Jubilee Singers Who Introduced the World to the Music of Black America.* New York: Farrar, Straus, and Giroux, 2000.

Washington, Booker T. *Up from Slavery* (1901). In *Three Negro Classics*. New York: Avon Books, 1965. 23–205.

Waters, Ethel, and Charles Samuels. *His Eye Is on the Sparrow*. Garden City, N.Y.: Doubleday and Co., 1951.

Waters, Ethel, Eugenia Price, and Joyce Blackburn. *To Me It's Wonderful*. New York: Harper and Row, 1972.

West, Carroll Van, ed. *Tennessee History: The Land, the People, and the Culture*. Knoxville: University of Tennessee Press, 1998.

White, J. Bliss, comp. *Biography and Achievements of the Colored Citizens of Chattanooga*. Chattanooga: N.p., 1904.

White, John. *Billie Holiday: Her Life and Times*. New York: Universe Books, 1987.

Williams, Fannie Barrier. "The Club Movement among the Colored Women." *Voice of the Negro* 1.3 (March 1904): 102.

Williams, Sylvanie Francaz. "The Social Status of the Negro Women." *Voice of the Negro* 1.5 (July 1904): 298–300.

Williamson, Joel. *A Rage for Order: Black/White Relations in the American South since Emancipation*. New York: Oxford University Press, 1986.

Wilson, John. *Chattanooga's Story*. Chattanooga, Tenn.: Chattanooga Free Press, 1980.

Wolfe, Charles. Liner Notes to *Black Stringband Music from the Library of Congress*. CD. Rounder Records, 0238.

Woll, Allen. *Black Musical Theater: From Coontown to Dreamgirls*. Baton Rouge: Louisiana State University Press, 1989.

Work, John W., III. "The Negro Spiritual." In *Readings in African American Church Music*. Ed. James Abbington. Chicago: Gia Publications, 2001. 15–24.

Woods, Clyde. *Development Arrested: Race, Power, and the Blues in the Mississippi Delta*. London: Verso, 1998.

Woodson, Carter G. "The Negro Washerwoman, a Vanishing Figure." *Journal of Negro History* 15.3 (July 1930): 269–77.

Woodward, C. Vann. *Origins of the New South, 1877–1913*. Baton Rouge: Louisiana State University Press, 1951.

Wright, Josephine, and Samuel Floyd Jr., eds. *New Perspectives on Music: Essays in Honor of Eileen Southern*. Warren, Mich.: Harmonie Park Press, 1992.

Wright, Kai, ed. *The African American Archive: The History of the Black Experience through Documents*. New York: Black Dog and Leventhal Publishers, 2001.

INDEX

Note: page numbers in *italics* denote illustrations.

Abernathy, Hustin, 25
African Methodist Episcopal (AME) church, 66
A. H. Johnston and Company, 16, 142n25
Albertson, Chris, 138
Alexander, Hinton D., 33, 100
alternative resistance, 108–11
American Missionary Association (AMA), 26–27, 30, 144n80, 145–46n104
antebellum era: agricultural work, 14–15; black music, 14–16, 18–19; black recreation, 14–16, 18; black women's work, 17; self-emancipated slaves, 18; slave literacy access, 14; slavery, 16–17, 141n11, 142n34, 142n37, 142n25; urban work, 17–18
Argus, 51
Armstrong, Louis, 85
Atlanta, 115–17, 166nn9–12
Austin, Lovie, 100
Ayers, Edward, 70

Bailey, Buster, 8
Bailey, Charles P., 128
Bailey, Gwendolyn Smith, 57, 91
Barge, Nancy, 43
Barker, Danny, 125
Beale Street, 82, 159n5

Bernhardt, Clyde, 94, 117, 122
Bessie Smith Hall, 136–38
Bessie Smith Strut, 138
"Big Nine." *See* Ninth Street
"Bill Bailey," 99
Black, Nat, 22, 23
black community development, 52, 53; churches, 31–32, 146n108; class dynamics, 7, 42; commercial district, 142n25; lodge meetings, 33, 34; manufacturing plants, 51; newspapers, 50, 51; origins, 12; overviews, 5, 6; political protests and boycotts, 50; population increase impact, 47–48; religious celebration, 19–20; self-definition, 5–6; self-emancipated slave element, 18; self-sufficiency, 50–51
black migration to cities. *See* urbanization
black musical culture: amateur music, 90–92; brass bands, 84–85; Chattanooga importance, 100; coon songs, 89; minstrel shows, 85–88; parades, 94; professional entertainment, 92–96; ragtime, 87–88; theater, 88–89; worksongs, 84, 90–91
Black Patti Musical Comedy Company, 93–94, 95
black periodicals, 110
black recreational spaces: as alternative resistance areas, 108–11; blues culture formation, 51, 53–54; church disapproval, 8, 105–8; as economic resistance settings,

MICHELLE R. SCOTT is an assistant professor of history at the University of Maryland, Baltimore County.

The University of Illinois Press
is a founding member of the
Association of American University Presses.

Composed in 10.5/13 Adobe Minion Pro
with FF Meta display
by Jim Proefrock
at the University of Illinois Press
Designed by Kelly Gray
Manufactured by Sheridan Books, Inc.

University of Illinois Press
1325 South Oak Street
Champaign, IL 61820-6903
www.press.uillinois.edu